Kildare Barracks

Dedicated to

Colonel James McLoughlin
1895 – 1966

Lieutenant-Colonel Dermot McLoughlin
1927 – 1999

Kildare Barracks

From the Royal Field Artillery
to the Irish Artillery Corps

MARK McLOUGHLIN

MERRION

First published in 2014 by Merrion
an imprint of Irish Academic Press

8 Chapel Lane
Sallins
Co. Kildare
Ireland

British Library Cataloguing in Publication Data
An entry can be found on request

978-1-908928-46-7 (paper)
978-1-908928-47-4 (cloth)
978-1-908928-48-1 (PDF)

Library of Congress Cataloging in Publication Data
An entry can be found on request

Designed and typeset by www.sinedesign.net

Printed in Ireland by SPRINT-print Ltd

Contents

List of Plates

15: Sergeants of VIII Brigade who were posted to Kildare in 1913. (Author's collection)

16: 4.5-inch Howitzer Battery, Royal Field Artillery at Kildare 1916. (Courtesy of Reggie Darling)

17: Lieutenant John Hubert Wogan-Browne. (Cheltenham College)

18: Civic Guards at Kildare town wearing the first ever issue of uniforms, 1922. (Garda Museum)

19: Civic Guards undergoing physical training at Kildare in 1922. (Garda Museum)

PLATE SECTION 2

20: Officers of the Artillery Corps, Kildare 1931. (Courtesy of Artillery School, Curragh)

21: Gunners at Kildare enjoying a lighter moment. (Courtesy of Mary D'Arcy)

22: D Sub-section No. 1 Battery 1929. (Courtesy of Mary D'Arcy)

23: A drawing by Captain Bertie Stuart Campbell Thomson. (Courtesy of Reggie Darling)

24: No. 1 Battery, Artillery Corps, 1931. (Courtesy of Brendan Culleton)

25: Sergeant Patrick McGough overseeing the instruction of members of the Volunteer Reserve on a 3.7-inch howitzer. The gunner on the left is David Wilson of Hospital Street, Kildare suggesting that these are members of the Kildare-based 2 Light Battery circa 1935. (Courtesy of Paddy Newman)

26: The Mounted Escort, more commonly known as the Blue Hussars, was formed from Kildare gunners and made their first appearance in 1932. (Courtesy of Military Archives, Dublin)

27: The first Anti-Aircraft Battery, 1932. (Courtesy of Conor Copley)

28: Colonel James McLoughlin, Director of Artillery demonstrates a 25-pounder High Explosive shell. (Courtesy of Colonel Michael Moriarty (Retd))

29: Major Charles Trodden (1904–47) who participated in the Military Mission to the USA in 1926 and attended Fort Sill, Oklahoma. Trodden Hall at Kildare was named in his memory. (Courtesy of Eibhir Mulqueen)

30: Commandant Thomas Wickham was killed in Syria on 5 June 1967 while serving with the United Nations Truce Supervision Organisation. Wickham Hall at Kildare was named in his memory. (Courtesy of Colonel Ray Quinn (Retd))

31: Standing: Lieutenants Kevin Duffy and William Phillips, Seated: Lieutenants Padraic O'Farrell, Noel Bergin, Michael McMahon training on an L70 Bofor anti-aircraft gun at Gormanston Camp, 1955. (Courtesy of Lieutenant-General Noel Bergin (Retd))

32: Heavy Mortar Troop, 19 Infantry Group, Cyprus 1970–71. (Courtesy of Lieutenant-Colonel J.H. Murphy (Retd))

33: A combined shoot by members of the 5 and 6 Field Batteries of the VI Field Artillery Regiment in 1984 on the occasion of the twentieth-fifth anniversary of the foundation of the unit in 1959. (Courtesy of Commandant Paddy Walshe (Retd))

34: Gunners of the 3 Field Battery shortly after the arrival of the 105 mm light gun in 1981 which they fired for the first time on 12 March 1981 in the Glen of Imaal. (Courtesy of RSM Donnie Finn (Retd))

35: Brigadier-General P.D. Hogan plants a tree with senior officers, 1985. (Courtesy of Commandant Paddy Walshe (Retd))

36: Captain Pat Graham and Sergeant Joe Foley perform the ceremonial lowering of the tricolour for the lst time on 24 September 1998 saluted by the Commanding Officer Lieutenant-Colonel Gerry Swan. (Courtesy of Commandant Paddy Walshe (Retd))

Acknowledgements

This book would not have been possible without the assistance of countless individuals and organisations who gave their invaluable time, advice, technical assistance and photographs. I would like to especially acknowledge the permission of the military journal *An Cosantóir* to quote from their journal and Captain Tom Clonan for the Artillery Corps 1923–1998; to the Imperial War Museum for permission to quote from the papers of Gunner Percy Whitehouse, to Captain Claire Mortimer and her predecessor Commandant Victor Laing, Lisa Dolan and Hugh Beckett at Military Archives, Dublin; to Lieutenant-Colonel Arthur Armstrong and his predecessor Lieutenant-Colonel Eamonn Fogarty of the Artillery School, Curragh; Sergeant Thomas McCormack at the Military College Library, Curragh; Mercier Press and Colonel Michael Moriarty for permission to quote from 'An Irish Soldier's Diary'; the National Army Museum, London for the photograph of Roderick MacLeod and Commandant Paddy Walshe (Retd) for access to his photographs of the Artillery Corps. Joe Connelly, Cill Dara Historical Society; Mario Corrigan, Local Studies Department, Kildare County Library; Lieutenant-General Noel Bergin (retd), Robbie Doyle, James Durney, Niall Brannigan; Hugh Crawford, Naas; Brendan Culleton, Laois; Conor Dalton, Mary D'Arcy, Kildare; Stephen Fayers, RSM Donnie Finn (Retd), Kildare; Billy Graham, Kildare; Frank Goodwin, Paula Lalor; Colin McKay, Colonel Cyril Mattimoe (RIP), Eibhir Mulqueen, Seamus Moore; Lieutenant-Colonel James H. Murphy (Retd), Kildare; Lieutenant-Colonel George Murphy (Retd), Naas; Alastair Allan; Reggie Darling; Sergeant Martin Drew, Garda Museum; Mary Fenton for permission to use the photographs of Martin P. Fleming; Sergeant John Gibson (retd); Karen Golden; Ian Jones; Paul McLoughlin; Captain Ian Stewart; the Irish Architectural Archive, Dublin; Sergeant Wayne Fitzgerald, *An Cosantóir* magazine, Oliver Murphy, Paddy Newman, Kildare; Major-

General P.F. Nowlan (Retd), Lieutenant-Colonel Ciaran O'Halloran (RIP), Liam O'Keeffe, Paul O'Rorke, Mary Quinn, Colonel Ray Quinn (Retd), Ralph Riccio; Regimental Sergeant-Major John Ryan (Retd), Kildare; Paul Skingsley, David Scott, Kildare; Margie Sheridan; Lieutenant-Colonel Gerry Swan (Retd) and Charlie Talbot for assistance and advice with proofing the text. Finally, I would like to acknowledge the perseverance of my wife Natasha and children Orlaith and Diarmaid during my many hours of research.

Mark McLoughlin
Kildare

Foreword

The Kildare Barracks – named Magee Barracks in 1952 – was closed on 24 September 1998. The Artillery personnel in it had to evacuate as quickly as possible to permit the imminent sale of the barracks, as intended by the Department of Defence. Since the evacuation the sale has not occurred. Instead it became a temporary residence for a limited number of refugees from Kosovo. They departed in 2007. The barracks remains empty, officially, but there are rumours about other occupants and an intention to locate a Gaelscoil there in 2014.

Mark McLoughlin, the author of this book, has produced a comprehensive and very interesting record of its existence from the British Army occupation in 1902 and the new civic guards in 1922 until September of that year. The Irish Artillery Corps moved into Kildare Barracks in February 1925. It was named Magee Barracks in 1952.

Magee was one of the many militia soldiers in Ireland who were selected and trained in their company by the Royal Irish Artillery that was following the practice in Britain, i.e. Royal Artillery training members of the British militia in gunnery. That system increased the guns and gunners in the British Army, including those based in Ireland in the eighteenth century.

The Longford Militia was part of the British forces fighting the French under General Humbert in 1798 and included their own artillery company. Many of the Longford Militia, including Gunner Magee, deserted the British forces and joined Humbert's forces at Castlebar where the British reported the loss of six field pieces. The French were victorious there on 3 September and headed towards Sligo. Eventually they were not successful and surrendered with their cannon – 2 and 4 pounders. Magee, with four gunners to help, made a last stand at Ballinamuck, with a 6-pounder of the Longford Militia. The gun was broken when it fired its last shot, his comrades were killed and Magee – a British soldier – was arrested and hung for desertion.

Gunner Magee was honoured in 1952 when the Irish Artillery Corps named the Kildare Barracks the Magee Barracks. Furthermore he is remembered for his loyalty to Ireland and bearing death for Ireland's cause. It is remembered in the 'Magee Gun Trophy' also, a model of the 6-pounder gun he fired for the last time at Ballinamuck.

Mark McLoughlin has recorded the history of the Artillery Corps. He is recording actions and personnel of the various regiments, schools and other artillery units and gives special attention to various special times such as the Emergency 1939–46.

This history of Kildare Barracks is a welcome and readable record of the barracks, its many occupants through the years and their performance, in various periods, for service to Ireland.

Major-General
P.F. Nowlan (Retd).

Introduction

A young gunner, working in the barrack stables, decided to take a short nap while leaning on a pitchfork. He never noticed the figure come into the stables who took the opportunity to sketch the peaceful scene before him and before the gunner had awoken, the drawing was pinned onto a barrack notice-board. Bertie Thomson never missed an opportunity to sketch a scene. Born in England, he served in the Artillery Corps at Kildare during its formative years. Thomson saw service with Canadian gunners during the First World War and with British gunners during the Boer War and would serve as an Irish gunner during the Emergency when the new Irish State faced its most serious threat. The gunners share a common bond across nations and Thomson with his own contribution perhaps sums up what Kildare Barracks meant to those who served with the guns.

History, it is often said, is written by the victors. In many more cases, however, history is never recorded and the memories are lost with the passage of time. There are no great memoirs written about Kildare Barracks, nor are there unit records of any substance. Instead there are fleeting references to the barracks in a number of sources of the careers of those who passed through Kildare. The Royal Field Artillery of the British Army was stationed at Kildare from April 1902 to April 1922 and the Artillery Corps of the Irish Army was there from February 1925 to September 1998 with the Civic Guards in occupation for some of the intervening period. It was known as Kildare Barracks during its first fifty years of occupation and Magee Barracks for the remaining forty-six years but to most, Kildare, in the twentieth century was the home of artillery in Ireland.

Thousands of gunners passed through Kildare Barracks, and for many people, as a consequence, it is the reason that they have a connection with Kildare town as gunners moved in, and more often than not moved on. My grandfather, James McLoughlin, was transferred to Kildare as a young Captain with the Artillery Corps in February 1925 in command of No. 1 Battery, starting our family link to Kildare. This is the same story for many who came to Kildare over the years.

All who served in artillery are referred to as gunners irrespective of their rank. Most people in Kildare will not know that a howitzer and a gun are very different pieces of equipment or that all officers and men who served in artillery are known as gunners, or that Artillery were always the most prestigious element of the army with the brightest and best army men.

This volume is not the definitive history of the barracks but rather a glimpse into the units and men that served there over almost 100 years and its impact on Kildare town. For the gunners who passed through Kildare, the ranges in the Glen of Imaal, County Wicklow are an intrinsic part of the history of Kildare and places such as Coolmoney Camp, Seskin, Camara and Leitrim gun positions are imbedded in the memory of all those who served. This book is divided into two parts, the British occupation and Irish occupation, and the reader, I hope, will gain some understanding about military life in Kildare, the continuity from one army to the next and the importance of the Barracks to the development of our town. I hope, with the publication of this book to raise an awareness of an intrinsic part of Kildare life for almost a century and to record, for posterity the memories of many of those who passed through the town. The chapter on the killing of Lieutenant John Hubert Wogan-Browne is also the subject of a piece that appeared in the Journal of the County Kildare Archaeological Society, Volume XX which was awarded the Lord Walter Fitzgerald Prize 2013 for historical research on subjects relating to the history of County Kildare.

Part I

The British 1902–1922

CHAPTER 1

CONSTRUCTION OF THE BARRACKS

Kildare town is going ahead. It was ever a quiet and plod-along town, but now it is awakening to its importance, and bids fair to outrival the best town in the county in energy and progress.

KILDARE OBSERVER, 13 OCTOBER 1900

Construction works at Kildare Barracks, 1901. (Courtesy of Rory Hopkins)

The first decade of the twentieth century has arguably had more of an influence in shaping the modern town of Kildare than any other decade in recent centuries. It was the decade that saw the arrival of electricity to the town, improved access to water and proper sewage treatment, the paving of proper footpaths and the reopening of the Kildare Infirmary. Colonel William Hall-Walker established his stud farm at Tully on the edge of the town and set out his famous Japanese Gardens with his gardener Tassa Eida. A few years earlier, the Cathedral, the original of which was established by St Brigid in the fifth century, which had lain in ruins since the 1600s, was rebuilt in the 1890s and restored to its former glory under the direction of the eminent architect George Edmund Street.

Kildare's status and military tradition extends back centuries. The town was originally the site of a significant and wealthy ecclesiastical foundation, its name having derived from the Irish Cell Dara or 'church of the oak'. In the year 909, the king of Leinster, Cerball MacMuirecan was killed off his horse as a result of an accident outside the house of a combmaker along 'the street of the stone step'.[1] The town's defensive walls and twelfth-century round tower were a necessary measure, as the Irish annals record thirty-eight occasions on which Kildare was burnt or plundered between 710 AD and 1155 AD. The Anglo-Norman conquest saw Richard de Clare (Strongbow) use the town as a base as did his successor William Marshall the lord of Leinster, and a castle was built in the town in the early 1200s. The castle was unsuccessfully besieged for three days by the Bruce army in 1316 and acted as a place of imprisonment. Following the Bruce invasion, Kildare came under the control of the FitzGerald family with the new title of Earl of Kildare and subsequently the county was shired with the town's name. There was one other significant upheaval in the town's history when the town was destroyed during the Elizabethan Wars of the 1590s and was described as altogether uninhabited in 1600.

The first military barracks in the town was at the Kildare Infirmary, which was occupied in 1797 and the circumstances of it becoming a barracks were described in Fr Delaney's history of the Kildare Infirmary:

> It appears that in 1797 the Cork Militia occupied the town of Kildare, and were billeted on the people, but for reasons made known at headquarters an order was issued by the Quartermaster-General residing in Dublin to seize the County Kildare Infirmary and hold it as a military barracks. This order was quickly carried into effect by Captain Frayne, commanding the Cork Militia. He came on the infirmary 'by surprise', captured the doctor inside, and landed him out on the road with such of his effects as probably were devoid of utility to military maneuvering men.[2]

The North Cork Militia had been stationed in Kilkenny in 1796 and transferred its headquarters to Naas with detachments throughout the county, including that at the Kildare Infirmary. This was a time of great uncertainty in Ireland with threats of French invasion. The rebellion of 1798 saw Kildare occupied by 2,000 rebels on 24 May 1798 as part of a coordinated action throughout the county forcing British troops under the command of General Wilford out of the town. During the course of the same day George Crawford of Taylor's Yeomanry and his 14-year-old granddaughter were murdered in the town and a 17-year-old, Lieutenant William Gifford of 82 Regiment, who had the misfortune to be a passenger on the Limerick mail coach, was piked to death when the coach drove into the town, unaware of its occupation. On 29 May, the rebels were forced to abandon the town. This was followed by the massacre of up to 300 men which occurred at Gibbet Rath, a short distance from Kildare on the Curragh. General Duff, commander of the British troops reported:

> We found the rebels retiring from the town on our arrival, armed, we followed them with the dragoons. I sent some of the Yeomen to tell them, on laying down their arms, they should not be hurt. Unfortunately some of them fired on the troops; but from that moment they were attacked on all sides – nothing could stop the rage of the troops. I believe from two to three hundred of the

rebels were killed. We have three men killed and several wounded. I am too fatigued to enlarge.[3]

The women of Kildare town spent the evening turning the bodies over and it was reported that there were eighty-five widows on one street in the town. There is no record as to when the Kildare Infirmary was abandoned as a military barracks but its military use had most likely ended by the time of Act of Union in 1801. The Duke of Leinster had sent a petition to the lord lieutenant in December 1799 'protesting against the seizure of the building and the injury done to the building by the quartering of the troops'.[4] The nearby barracks at Newbridge was opened in 1819 for horse and field artillery and the permanent military base at the Curragh was built in the 1850s as a response to the Crimean War. Despite having no barracks in Kildare town, many local men served in the British army. One of the earliest military records relating to a Kildareman records a Peter Kelly who served in the Peninsular Wars with the 11 Regiment of Foot. When he left the British army in 1800 he was issued with the following letter:

> These are to certify that the bearer hereof Peter Kelly Private in the General Company of the aforesaid regiment, born in the Parish of Kildare, in or near the market town of Kildare in the County of Kildare, Ireland, Aged 29 years and by trade a carpenter has served honestly and faithfully in the said Regiment seven years but having suffered his health so as to be unfit for active service is hereby discharged to serve in one of his majesty's garrisons.
>
> 22 Jan 1800, 11th Regiment of Foot, Colonel James Grant.[5]

The Charge of the Light Brigade – Private Henry Keegan
The story of one Kildareman stands out and is worth recording because he was involved in the most celebrated British military action of the nineteenth century, the Charge of the Light Brigade at Balaclava in 1864. Henry Keegan who was born in Kildare town in 1823 joined the 4 Light Dragoons at Athlone Barracks on 17 January 1850 with his age recorded as 21 years old. He was formerly employed as a cooper. His obituary in 1892 gave the following information:

He was born at Kildare in 1823 and early in life enlisted in the 4th Light Dragoons. In 1854 he went with his regiment to the Crimea and was at Alma and Balaclava. In the Balaclava charge he received a sabre wound in the leg. In 1861 he was invalided on account of varicose veins in the legs, and after eleven years and eleven months' service left the army on the small pension of 6d. per day for two and a half years. Through old age and ill-health he has recently been in very poor circumstances, and but for the assistance of some kind friends would probably have had to apply for parish relief.[6]

The Charge of the Light Brigade at Balaclava occurred on 25 October 1854 when four cavalry regiments of the Light Brigade commanded by the Earl of Cardigan attacked the heavily-defended Russian positions apparently as a result of confusing orders issued by Lord Raglan. A total of 247 men out of the 647 who attacked the Russian positions were killed or wounded. Keegan's regiment, the 4 Light Dragoons, suffered four officers and fifty-five men killed.

Keegan's service records shows that he served eleven years and 220 days in the army being discharged at Cahir, County Tipperary on 5 October 1861 when he was described as being 32 years and 10 months old. He had served one year and ten months abroad with the army in East Turkey and the Crimea. After returning from the Crimea with his regiment, Keegan found himself in trouble for some unspecified military transgression and served a short sentence in military custody. He completed his military service at Cahir, County Tipperary before moving to Birmingham, and after his wife died, he lived with another veteran of the campaign, John Howes. He suffered from ill-health and gained employment in a gun factory and later as a labourer at a firewood shop. The comment in the newspaper article about his pension lasting two-and-a-half years demonstrates how injured war veterans must have suffered during the Victorian period. In 1879 Keegan was one of many who made a claim from the Light Brigade Relief Fund. He spent his last years living with his son John and when he died in 1892 he was interred in an unmarked public plot. A firing party of the 14 Hussars accompanied the hearse and a Union Jack, his sword and busby were placed on the coffin. The *Bermingham Daily Post* reported that an unfortunate incident occurred when 'the coffin slipped from its position on the gun carriage' and a horse suffered a serious leg wound.

A newspaper noted that 'Poor old Keegan – that there should have been any need to send the hat around for one of our Light Brigade is a reflection on our whole military system.' Another report stated that 'A grateful country and an appreciative War Office left him to the cold mercy of occasional charity – he asked for bread and they gave him a stone.' A list of survivors and their desperate circumstances was published in the *Pall Mall Gazette* on 15 April 1890 and noted that along with Keegan, Patrick Doyle (8 Light Dragoons) was starving in Dublin. The Balaclava Committee recalled that Lord Cardigan told the survivors of the Charge on the day after the attack that they would always be provided for and never be forgotten.

Of the 673 men who participated in the charge, over twenty per cent were Irish. At least one other Kildareman served with Keegan in the 4th Light Dragoons – Private Dennis James Heron – who was born in Maynooth, County Kildare. He was born on 27 June 1829, enlisted in June 1847, and was sent to Scutari Hospital the day after the charge and repatriated to England in March 1855. He died at Bridgewater, Somerset on 9 January 1895. Two other Kildaremen who participated in the Charge were Private Patrick Dowling (17 Lancers) of Athy and Private William Sheppard (11 Hussars) of Newbridge. In many respects Henry Keegan was fortunate in receiving some charitable benefit and recognition for participation in one of the most daring and well-remembered nineteenth-century military episodes, but the vast majority of other Irishmen who served in the Crimean campaign would have lived out the remainder of their lives in poverty. Alfred Tennyson's poem on the Charge of the Light Brigade is well known but there is a lesser remembered poem about the survivors penned by Rudyard Kipling in 1890:

> There were thirty million English who talked of England's might,
> There were twenty broken troopers who lacked a bed for the night.
> They had neither food nor money, they had neither service nor trade;
> They were only shiftless soldiers, the last of the Light Brigade.

Military Improvement Works
Despite the availability of military accommodation at the Curragh, Newbridge and Naas, it was the Boer War in South Africa and the need for increased artillery

capacity which necessitated the construction of another barracks close to the Curragh with accommodation for two brigades of artillery. In 1897 the British government took out a loan of £4 million for military improvement works. The British parliament sanctioned a large increase in the size of the army in 1898 and in 1899 identified the specific military deficiencies that required attention.

> In regard to barracks at home we find, upon a review of our requirements, of the number of barracks available, of the number under construction, and of the number which we have been obliged to condemn, that we are deficient in barrack accommodation for three regiments of Cavalry, eighteen batteries of Horse and Field Artillery, four companies of Garrison Artillery, and seven battalions of Infantry.[7]

The new barracks at Kildare was built on Broadhook Farm, on the eastern side of the town, on a site bought from the Duke of Leinster, to accommodate 1,200 men and six batteries of the Royal Field Artillery (two brigades) with their considerable number of horses. Part of the site was already owned by the War Office where a lock hospital for the treatment of destitute women was in operation in the 1870s and 1880s. The abandoned hospital buildings were included in the plans, to be converted into the commanding officers' offices and recreational rooms, with the rest of the barracks to be built with wooden hutments on concrete bases and corrugated iron shelling. Construction commenced in August 1900 and was greeted enthusiastically in the town with the expected increase in business for local traders. Sixty-five carpenters and joiners and twenty-six plasterers and painters set about the task of erecting the wooden hutments to accommodate the men and stabling for the horses.

The wooden hutments were intended for twenty-four non-commissioned officers (NCOs) and men in each hut – the equivalent of a section of an artillery battery. Each hut included two stoves for heating, an ablutions room and separate quarters for an NCO. Warrant officers received better accommodation in purpose-built married quarters with a similar-sized hutment divided into two separate living spaces each containing a kitchen, living space, two bedrooms and a veranda. The horses were accommodated in corrugated iron roof stables on steel frames, 143 feet long, twenty-one feet wide and ten feet high with accommodation for fifty horses per stable. The barracks were divided into an east brigade and a west brigade with a separate parade grounds and facilities for each which, in effect, meant that Kildare operated as two separate barracks. The plans for the barracks were prepared by the Royal Engineers. At the time, standard plans prepared for typical huts for accommodating infantry and artillery brigades were used throughout the United Kingdom. Each brigade contained eighteen men's huts, three latrine huts, a cookhouse and baths. There was a sergeant's mess, shops, a forge, a shoeing hut and a gymnasium. Gunner Percy Whitehouse who was stationed at Kildare in 1913 gave a brief description of the barracks: 'The barracks were of one story buildings, each accommodating about 24 men and NCOs, the number needed to drive the gun and drive it into action (i.e. in peacetime).'[8]

In respect of the horses there were twenty-seven stable blocks for each brigade known as 'T stables' or troop stables and three officers' stables for each brigade. There were also forage sheds, an infirmary stall, a riding school and six separate maneges to cater for training horses. In respect of the married establishment of the barracks, there were five married quarters hutments for each brigade. Despite the fact that the barracks was being built beside a town, there was one infant school and two other schools, together with an accommodation block for teachers. This would be far more understandable as in the case of the barracks at Larkhill in England or other relatively isolated locations but the military preferred that their barracks be models of self sufficiency.

The officers' quarters were grouped together at the front of the barracks with no great distinction between the two brigades – a concession to practicality. The officers' servant quarters were situated close by, as was the kitchen, mess-room, ante and billiards room. The gun and wagon sheds were also divided between the brigades – eighteen sheds to each brigade divided into six per battery with an additional mobile shed assigned per battery – and the battery stores were located nearby. These gun sheds were still standing when the barracks closed in 1998. Twelve marker stones, each individually numbered, were erected at points on the boundary of the military property with the War Department markings on each to signify that they were on military property.

The estimated cost of the building project was £90,000 and the contractors were expected to complete the project in five months, with substantial penalties for delays.[9] The works were carried out at the same time as extensive works at the Curragh. The Barrack Act of 1890 improved the conditions of many military barracks in the United Kingdom with wooden buildings replaced by stone structures at Aldershot, the Curragh and Colchester. There was a recognition in the years after the Crimean War that improved sanitation for soldiers was necessary to reduce mortality and illness rates in the military and make a more efficient army. Kildare Barracks was built with funds provided by under the Military Works Acts of 1897, 1899 and 1901 yet, against the wisdom of the time and probably because of the urgency of the Boer War, Kildare and a number of other barracks were constructed primarily as wooden hutments. Complaints about the various wooden barracks made it to the British parliament where Courtenay Warner MP, voiced his concerns:

> Wooden huts were being put up at Aldershot, Kildare, Lichfield, Salisbury, and Shorncliffe, and he [Mr. Courtenay Warner] submitted that that was not a convenient method of housing the troops. The huts put up in the days of the Crimean War had proved productive of the greatest possible discomfort to the troops, and he believed that we had already far more of them than could be occupied. He remembered in connection with some erected at Shorncliffe Camp that the men occupying them last winter were up to their knees in mud and water because the site was not properly drained, and he trusted that the authorities would at least take care that a similar state of things should not recur.[10]

Shortly after the construction of wooden huts at Kildare, the Curragh underwent a massive transformation as its huts were replaced by redbrick barracks. The programme of military expenditure on capital works at this time was extensive:

	1900	1901
Barracks Act 1890	£186,000	£76,500
Military Works Act	£866,000	£1,085,000

The contract for Kildare was awarded to W. Harbrow Ltd., Iron Building Contractor of London who tendered a price of £71,482 which was much lower than the other tenders. Patrick Sheridan, Newbridge was awarded the contract for the formation of the roads, drainage and sites.[11] William Harbrow ran an extensive iron building company situated at South Bermondsey railway station. An advertisement for the company from 1902 declared: 'Iron building and roofing and every description of joiners' work. Buildings shipped and erected in any part of the world.' They built the most modern iron structures of the time dealing primarily with iron churches and chapels and in later years, aviation buildings. The company also attended the Cork International Exhibition in 1903. The main works in Kildare were supervised by a Lancashire man named Richard Rodley who came to Ireland with his wife Lilian for the duration of the project. Despite an original estimate of five months to complete the works, it was reported that 'the work is to be hastily executed in three months'. Patrick Sheridan was a builder and contractor of Eyre Street, Newbridge and he did not live to see the works completed as he died on 26 June 1901. His two sons Patrick and Edward were also in the building industry.[12] Sheridan was also the contractor on building an extension to Newbridge College in 1900. The *Leinster Leader* newspaper reported:

> The work in connection with the proposed erection of a military barracks at Kildare has commenced. Already eighty men are employed, but this is only a small number in comparison with what will be engaged later on when the undertaking assumes more definite shape. It is stated that the building when finished will accommodate seventeen hundred men. The townsfolk of Kildare are naturally jubilant at the prospect of the increased commercial activity which will arise from the presence of a big military station in their midst.

The plans for the barracks underwent a number of revisions and in early 1901 there were proposals for a larger barracks to make room for a battery of the Royal Horse Artillery. Before the works were completed, plans were already prepared to expand the barracks with additional space for a hospital and further block-built buildings as opposed to the wooden structures. Work continued throughout 1900 and in January 1901 the workers held a party in the barracks:

On Saturday night last the Irish foremen and timekeepers employed at the military barracks in course of erection in Kildare, entertained their English friends in the same employment. A number of guests were invited, and when supper was served at twelve o'clock about fifty sat to table. The health of the strangers was proposed and Mr. Oram foreman, responded in suitable terms. Dancing commenced after supper, the music being supplied by the employers. Songs were also rendered by Mr. Oram, Mr. White, Mrs. O'Brien, Mrs. Studley, Miss Dollard, Miss Farrelly, and Mr. McLoughlin. Proceedings were kept up until the small hours, when the party separated well pleased with their night's pleasure. Messrs. Behan, Hickey, and Murphy, who organised the entertainment, are to be congratulated on the success of their efforts.[13]

A local man employed on the project, Thomas Melia of Lackagh, was killed on 20 January 1901 outside Kildare after apparently falling asleep on the railway line following a few drinks in Monasterevin with Edward Nolan. Nolan was found asleep beside the railway line and was advised at the Coroner's Court that any evidence he gave could not be used in any other court.[14] Melia's gravestone at Lackagh cemetery between Kildare and Monasterevin carries the inscription:

IN MEMORY OF THOMAS MELIA WHO WAS
ACCIDENTALLY KILLED 20TH JANUARY 1901
AGED 21 YEARS.
ERECTED BY HIS FELLOW WORKMEN EMPLOYED AT
THE NEW BARRACKS KILDARE

The construction of the barracks coincided with the census of April 1901. The enumerator recorded all who were residing at the 'camp hutments' including the Lock Hospital where the engineer on the project, John A. Guerrini, and his family resided. Guerrini (1872–1939) was from Dublin and his father, Vincent Guerrini, was an engineer with the Great Southern and Western Railway. Guerrini would later become an engineer with Kilkenny Corporation. The senior construction staff were listed as follows:

John A. Guerrini	Engineer
Frank Barber	Foreman
Thomas White	Foreman
John Oram	Foreman
Henry White	Foreman
Thomas Ryan	Foreman
Robert Johnson	Clerk of Works

The nature of the project becomes apparent from the list of men on site. The primary occupations were carpenters/joiners, painters, plasterers, iron workers, bricklayers and general labourers. According to the 1901 census, there were thirty-seven Englishmen and thirteen Scots living on the building site, although there were also many local men employed. One local worker was Stephen Byrne of Mayfair, Monasterevin who was charged, in August 1901 with the crime of 'maliciously injuring one of the new huts at the Kildare Camp'.[15] Head-Constable Roche testified that Byrne went into one of the huts and painted it over with a brush and black paint. A man named Browning who was employed at the new works estimated the damage at thirty shillings. Byrne admitted that he was drunk at the time and agreed to pay thirty shillings compensation and a fine of twenty-one shillings.

Thomas McLoughlin ran a public house in Rathangan and illegally supplied alcohol to the workers at the site. At Kildare Petty Sessions in August 1901 he was prosecuted for operating a 'shebeen' in the new hutments. Head Constable Roche, Sergeant Philips and Sergeant McGrath of the Kildare Royal Irish Constabulary raided the site on 6 April 1901 and found sixty-five bottles of stout in a case marked mineral water and six empty bottles with traces of porter. On forcing opening a locked press, the policemen seized a further sixteen bottles of stout, 228 empty bottles, an empty whiskey bottle and an empty rum bottle. McLoughlin was fined forty shillings plus costs or two months imprisonment, and the stout was forfeited. Nevertheless, this did not dampen spirits on the project:

> At the New Barracks, Kildare, on Saturday evening, the members of the Scotia Villa held an 'At Home'. The company present included Mr. and Mrs. Rodley [the manager of the works], Mr. and Mrs.

Barber, Mr. and Mrs. Lewis, Mr. and Mrs. Stoodley [Studley], the Misses Kirby, Plant, Thompson, Forde and Costelloe, and Messrs. Oram, White and Culver. About forty ladies, and gentlemen sat down to collation, which was served at 7.30 p.m. Subsequently Scotch selections were played by Messrs. Culver and Duffus, and songs were given by Messrs. Knight, Williams and Mackintosh, the latter being much appreciated. Mr. Stephenson's recitation in Scotch was also much admired. Dancing and games completed the evening's programme. The manner in which the 'At Home' was carried out reflects great credit upon Mr. W. Duffus (the secretary) and the other gentlemen forming the committee. Everyone present thoroughly enjoyed the evening's entertainment.[16]

In January 1901 the *Kildare Observer* was able to report that:

It must be said that the work of the erection of the new military barracks at Kildare has gone on apace within the last few months. The huts are almost finished, and with the exception of the making of the squares – which will not be an easy task – there is little to be done. It is expected that the place will be inhabited by May, although the work will not then be completed.[17]

The dramatic improvement in the fortunes of Kildare town was noted by the *Kildare Observer* newspaper.

Kildare town is going ahead. It was ever a quiet and plod-along town, but now it is awakening to its importance, and bids fair to outrival the best town in the county in energy and progress. The building of the military hutments there has given the residents the fillip. The water supply in the town is being extended to the military, so is the existing sewerage system, and now comes the proposal to light the place. Electricity has been decided on, and this it is expected will also be extended for military use. All these will mean a big source of revenue for the benefit of the town and rates, so that Kildare is likely to prove by this lucky stroke of progression an important factor in the rate-reducing element in the union. They say everything comes to those who wait. Naas, Newbridge and Athy had now better look to their laurels. Certainly Kildare deserves every encouragement, and so do Mr. P. Talbot and Mr. J. T. Heffernan who have each displayed a considerable amount of energy in the past in bringing their town to the front.[18]

The impression of Kildare town before the arrival of the barracks was quite poor. The following comments were recorded by a soldier stationed at the Curragh in 1888 who had a poor view of both Kildare and Newbridge:

> The town of Kildare – another street or so with a few back lanes – is three miles in another direction [from Newbridge]. There are no public places of entertainment, at either place, but those who wish to study Irish life in the squalid forms can do so to any extent. They can watch the family pig engaged in frolicsome enjoyment with little balls of infant humanity, whose almost only clothing is a succession of layers of native dirt that nothing short of boiling would remove – children pretty in their filth even, with fine brown eyes and shapely limbs. Beggars abound. Their hands are ever stretched out for charity, which, when obtained is most frequently spent in 'John Jamieson'.[19]

Mrs Mary Goode of Hospital Street, sought a licence for a public house in October 1900 to cater for almost 200 men employed in the construction of the barracks and the 1,400 who would be stationed there when it eventually opened. Head Constable Roche opposed the granting of the application as there were fourteen licensed premises in the town and five in the surrounding countryside and the application was refused.[20] There was already a licensed premises on Hospital Street run by Mrs Donohoe, and the constable appeared before the local magistrate in December 1900 when Thomas Leech and Henry Chank were charged with being on the premises on 9 December 1900 in breach of the licensing laws.[21]

The barracks was ready for occupation by the middle of 1901 and the contractor, William Harbrow, sold off all of his building equipment in June

1901.[22] However, the urgent necessity for occupation was no longer an issue with the bulk of the British army on active service in South Africa. The new barracks lay vacant for close to one year before the accommodation was required for troops returning home from the Boer War in the early months of 1902.

The barracks received a visit by some distinguished guests in January 1902 in preparation for its opening. On 7 January 1902, Mr Broderick, Secretary of State for War accompanied by His Royal Highness, the Duke of Connaught, Commander-in-Chief of the Forces, visited Newbridge Barracks, the newly-constructed G and H Lines infantry barracks and water tower at the Curragh, followed by a visit to the barracks at Kildare.[23]

With the redevelopment of the Curragh and the opening of Kildare Barracks, the county now had a sizeable military accommodation. A comparison of the available military accommodation in County Kildare in 1904 shows the scale of this presence, with the larger proportion of stabling for horse at Kildare and Newbridge illustrating the reliance of artillery units on the horse.[24]

	Accommodation	Stabling
Curragh	4,250	1,686
Kildare	892	614
Newbridge	777	524
Naas	260	6
Total:	6,179	2,830

Before the barracks opened in 1902 plans were prepared for the addition of a brigade of the Royal Horse Artillery. The plans, prepared in July 1902, would have doubled the size of the barracks with a hospital, a military prison, and an isolation hospital for horses in addition to the accommodation for officers, NCOs, men, a gymnasium, recreational grounds and the additional extra guns parks and stabling required. The new barracks was to be built of permanent material – i.e. brick – and much of the existing wooden barracks was to be replaced by permanent structures. The architectural plans were not drawn up by the Royal Engineers but instead were prepared by J. J. McAuley of Trinity College Dublin.[25] There were some suggestions that the enlarged barracks might accommodate up to 8,000 men, which would have been twice the accommodation available at the Curragh. The plans never came to fruition, probably as a consequence of a change in requirements as a result of the improved situation in South Africa.

CHAPTER 2

ROYAL FIELD ARTILLERY: 1902

The 133rd Battery of the Royal Field Artillery, which has been stationed at Horfield since November 1900, left on Tuesday evening for Kildare, Ireland.

WESTERN DAILY PRESS, 10 APRIL 1902

138 Battery, Royal Field Artillery in action at practice camp in the Glen of Imaal, County Wicklow, August 1902. (Author's collection)

Kildare Barracks was occupied in the first week of April 1902 when almost 1,000 men from the XXXI Brigade and XXXIII Brigade, Royal Field Artillery arrived from Aldershot in England. It took two weeks before the barracks was fully occupied by the batteries and their equipment. The departure of one battery from Horfield, England was recorded in an English newspaper:

> The 133rd Battery of the Royal Field Artillery, which has been stationed at Horfield since November 1900, left on Tuesday evening for Kildare, Ireland. The heavy baggage and guns were dispatched on the previous day, and the men of the battery, which is under the command of Major Ellice, left Horfield at a quarter past six on Tuesday evening, and were played down to the railway arches in Cheltenham Road by the depot fife and drum band. There were about a hundred horses which had to be entrained, and Montpelier Station was left at ten minutes past eight. The 144th Battery will probably succeed 133rd at Horfield.[1]

The first units to occupy the barracks at Kildare were as follows:

XXXI Brigade
Brigade Headquarters
Brigade Commander: Lieutenant-Colonel C.V.B. Kuper
Divisional Adjutant: Captain W.R. Eden
131 Battery, Royal Field Artillery (4 x 15 pounder guns)
Major C.C. Owens
Captain H.G. Pringle
Lieutenant L.M. Bucknill
Second-Lieutenant W.A. Nicholls
Second-Lieutenant J.A. Don

132 Battery, Royal Field Artillery (4 x 15 pounder guns)
Major H.D. White-Thompson
Captain J.G. Ratten
Lieutenant R.C. Reeves
Second-Lieutenant H.G.O. Bridgeman
Second-Lieutenant J.A. Bowles
133 Battery, Royal Field Artillery (4 x 15 pounder guns)
Major R. F. Ellice

In May 1902, due to a shortage of space, after less than a month in Kildare, this battery was moved to Belturbet Barracks in County Cavan.

XXXIII Brigade

Brigade Headquarters

Brigade Commander: Lieutenant-Colonel A.C. Bailward
Divisional Adjutant: Captain H.E.T. Kelly
137 Battery, Royal Field Artillery (4 x 15 pounder guns)
Major A.R. Knox
Captain H.M. Thomas
Second-Lieutenant L.E.O. Davidson
Second-Lieutenant A.J.R. Kennedy
Second-Lieutenant R.B. Macan
138 Battery, Royal Field Artillery (4 x 15 pounder guns)
Major H.S. White
Captain A.E.M. Head
Second-Lieutenant R.C. Dodgson
Second-Lieutenant H.G. Lee Warner
Second-Lieutenant C.J.H. Clibborn
139 Battery, Royal Field Artillery (4 x 15 pounder guns)
Major G.S. Duffus
Captain F.W. MacKenzie
Second-Lieutenant R.F. Parker
Second-Lieutenant C.E. Boyce
Second-Lieutenant H.G. Hitchcock

British Army Organisation and Artillery Terminology

After the Boer War, the British Army was reorganised with the Third Army Corps comprising the Seventh, Eighth and Ninth Divisions stationed in Ireland. The Seventh Division consisted of the following units:[2]

7 Division (Headquarters – Curragh)
XIII Brigade: Dublin
XIV Brigade: Curragh and Dublin
Divisional Cavalry: Ballincollig
Divisional Artillery: Kildare

An army division included a number of regiments of infantry together with the engineering, artillery and other support necessary to maintain the unit in the field. The divisional artillery was organised into brigades. A brigade of artillery was the basic tactical unit used at this time. Each brigade consisted of a brigade headquarters and a number of batteries of guns or howitzers. At full establishment, a brigade of 15-pounder field guns such as the XXXI Brigade or XXXIII Brigade at Kildare consisted of twenty-three officers and 772 other ranks. A 4.5-inch howitzer brigade consisted of twenty-two officers and 755 other ranks.

In British military terminology Roman numerals were used to designate higher artillery formations such as brigades, for example XXXI Brigade, the sub-division of a brigade i.e. a battery was described in Arabic numerals such as 131 Battery. This practice also continued into the Irish army.

The British army used guns and howitzers. Howitzers differ from guns in that the barrel of a gun is elevated to gain distance when firing, while the barrel of a howitzer is depressed to gain distance. The artillery at Kildare were armed with 15-pounder field guns which were replaced in many batteries in 1904 with the larger 18-pounder field gun which remained the preferred gun until the Second World War.

A brigade of artillery was usually commanded by an officer with the rank of lieutenant-colonel. The brigade headquarters had two other officers: a captain or lieutenant filled the role of adjutant (in charge of administration); while a captain or lieutenant was the orderly officer (responsible for stores and transport). In addition, an officer of the Royal Army Medical Corps and an officer of the Royal Veterinary Corps was attached to each brigade.

Brigade headquarters also included a sergeant-major, two corporals, two bombardiers, nine drivers, seven gunners, a clerk, and a trumpeter. These filled roles as signallers, and telephonists and assisted with range-taking duties. A corporal and three privates of the Royal Army Medical Corps were attached for water duties; eight gunners acted as officers' batmen (personal servants), and two as orderlies for the medical officer. Each brigade headquarters was in command of three batteries and an ammunition column.

Each battery consisted of 198 soldiers at full establishment. Each was commanded by a major or captain, with a captain as second-in-command, and three lieutenants or second-lieutenants in charge of two-gun sections. Battery establishment also included a battery sergeant-major, a battery quartermaster sergeant, a farrier-sergeant, four shoeing-smiths (of which whom one would be a corporal), two saddlers, two wheelers, two trumpeters, seven sergeants, seven corporals, eleven bombardiers, seventy-five gunners, seventy drivers and ten gunners acting as batmen. While these figures indicate the establishment of the barracks, the actual strength of the batteries stationed at Kildare was well below what it should have been.

Many of the officers and man who were posted to Kildare in April 1902 were recently returned from the Boer War in South Africa where twenty-five batteries of the Royal Field Artillery had served. Lieutenant-Colonel Arthur Charles Bailward (1855–1923), the XXXIII Brigade commander and most senior officer in Kildare Barracks was an amateur bird and mammal collector. He travelled to Iran and Armenia in 1905 while stationed at Kildare collecting specimens of small mammals which were presented to the Natural History Museum in London. He also gave his name to an Iranian mouse-like hamster now referred to as the Bailward hamster. He was attached to the Turkish army in 1897 and was made a prisoner of war during the Boer War in 1899.

The other brigade commander, Lieutenant-Colonel Charles Kuper had just returned from South Africa in March 1902 before taking command of the XXXI Brigade. It was his last posting as he retired from the army in June 1903 and was replaced by Lieutenant Colonel Edward A. Fanshawe. Major Arthur Rice Knox (1863–1917), Battery Commander of 137 Battery, served in South Africa in 1899–1900 at the Relief of Ladysmith, Colenso and Spion Kop amongst other actions. He was mentioned in dispatches and was created a Companion of the

Distinguished Service Order. The adjutant of XXXI Brigade, Captain William Rushbrooke Eden, served in South Africa in 1900 and would subsequently see action during the First World War as a Brigadier General.

George Edward Nurse – Victoria Cross winner

A gunner of 131 Battery who arrived at Kildare in April 1902 was a recipient of the highest British military award – the Victoria Cross. Corporal 88351 George Edward Nurse was born in Enniskillen, County Fermanagh in 1873 and enlisted in the Royal Artillery in 1892. He served in the Boer War with 67 Battery and won the Victoria Cross for the following action:

> At the Battle of Colenso, South Africa, on 15th December, 1899, when the detachments who had been serving the guns had either been killed, wounded or had been driven away from their guns by enemy infantry fire, Corporal Nurse and several others tried to save the guns of the 14th and 66th Batteries. The intervening space between the guns and where some of the horses and drivers, who were still alive, were sheltering, a distance of 500 yards, was swept by rifle and shell fire. Corporal Nurse, along with three officers, Captain W.N. Congreve of the Rifle Brigade, Lieutenant F.H.S. Roberts, who fell wounded, and Captain H.N. Schofield helped to harness a team to a limber and then line up a gun. Corporal Nurse, alone, managed to limber up a second gun.[3]

He was promoted to the rank of sergeant in 1902 with 131 Battery and transferred with his unit to Kildare in April 1902. In December 1903, he re-enlisted to complete twenty-one-years service at Kildare. He would subsequently serve during the First World War. Nurse's first marriage prior to the Boer War was deemed null and void when it was discovered that his wife was legally married to another man. Nurse married a second time at Waterford in 1908.[4]

The first barrack warden appointed to Kildare Barracks was J.B. Bassett of Athlone. The warden was responsible for the general maintenance and upkeep of the barracks, in addition to the provision of fuel and bedding. Barrack wardens were employed by the Army Service Corps. This role was almost always given to army pensioners, and the warden at Kildare was allocated his own quarters in addition to accommodation being made available for two barrack labourers. Bassett was no exception and had served in the Royal Horse Artillery for over twenty-one years, thirteen of these spent in India. He served until his death on 30 April 1906.[5] His replacement at Kildare was Barrack Warden Edward Duggan, originally from Cork city.

The surviving service records of many gunners give an indication of how soldiers ended up serving in Kildare. James Coburn enlisted at No. 2 Depot in Glasgow on 19 May 1903. He was issued with the regimental service number 31607. Following initial assessment, he was posted to 133 Battery at Kildare on 9 June 1903 for basic training.

The rural nature of Kildare was a shock for many soldiers reared in English cities and larger towns and was reflected in their correspondence. One gunner, Reggie Goverd, who sent a photograph of Kildare home in May 1905 wrote to his family in Shepton Mallet, Somerset, a small town of about 5,000 people: 'This is the camp were [sic] we are stopping so you can see what sort of place it is. Shepton is fifty times bigger than this so I hope you wont like coming to this part of the world.'[6]

At this time soldiers generally enlisted for three years with the colours and were transferred to the reserves for a further nine years meaning that even those men who served at Kildare in the early 1900s, even if they left the military, were still liable for military service during the First World War. Many did not like military life and left on the expiration of their service. Others extended their service and signed up for a further period as in the case of Driver William Hall who enlisted in December 1902 and after three years with 138 Battery at Kildare agreed to enlist for a further five years to complete eight years' service.

CHAPTER 3

THE EARLY YEARS

With reference to the agreement for the supply of water to the War Department for the Kildare hutments, I am directed to enquire whether you are prepared to supply water at the rate of 9d per 1,000 gallons for actual consumption in lieu of, as at present, the fixed minimum of 40,000 gallons a day. Such alterations would of course, only take effect after 12 months' notice.

COLONEL A. H. THOMAS, ROYAL ENGINEERS, CURRAGH[1]

Postcard view of the new barracks circa 1901. (Author's collection)

The construction of the barracks, which virtually doubled the population of the town between soldiers, their families and the additional business opportunities in the town, had an enormously positive impact on the development of Kildare. Once it was opened, concerned local representatives were keen to ensure that the barracks remained open. An immediate consequence of the arrival of the barracks was the decision by the National Bank Limited to open a sub-office in the barracks in 1902 on Fridays, operated by the Newbridge Branch Manager, Mr C.A. Townley.[2]

Water and sanitation were always problems in the town with no river nearby and the town situated on a ridge. Naas No. 1 District Council of Kildare County Council was responsible for providing sanitation and commenced the laying of a new sewerage scheme through the town in conjunction with the construction of the barracks. The military contributed £300 towards the development of the scheme as the outfall sewer had to be diverted to the barracks at a late stage in the planning of the project. The laying of a public sewer through the town during this period caused considerable disruption and arbitration hearings were held in the courthouse in March 1902 to deal with issues of compensation. A new sewer was added to Bride Street in June 1905 and a motion to build a concrete footpath from Bride Street to the Post Office was agreed in late 1907 after initially being rejected in February 1907 at a meeting of the District Council. Work was also carried out in 1906 in steamrolling the streets of the town with the County Surveyor Mr E. Glover reporting that the works cost £85. The mud on the streets caused considerable problems and cyclists often took to the footpaths for safety. The Royal Irish Constabulary took a poor view of cyclists on footpaths, irrespective of the weather. Richard Moody and Thomas Cunningham were fined one penny for cycling on the footpath at Kildare having been charged by Constable Stephenson in March 1907 and being brought before the resident magistrate at the Kildare petty sessions which were held in the courthouse every Thursday.

Electricity

The War Office was also anxious to have electric lighting in the town and barracks. A committee was established in 1900 under the auspices of Naas No. 1 District Council to bring electricity to the town with a proposal for thirty-five public lights and a generating station on Pound Green with electricity supplies also made available to private consumers. The district council intended to pay for the scheme through the rates from the area and a subsidy from the military. In 1902, there were serious doubts about the viability of the scheme.

> The Council are in this position. They counted on a large supply of illuminant being taken for the military hutments, and no reply from the War Office was received which would lead them to count upon a substantial yearly payment which would go far to decrease the burden of the loan. Now it is rumoured that the military authorities contemplate putting in an installation at the Curragh which would supply the Camp, the barracks at Newbridge and the Kildare hutments with electric light. If this scheme be carried out, those who want to rescue Kildare from its present darkness will lose a very considerable source of help towards paying off the expense.[3]

The chairman of the district council, J.S. O'Grady felt that the scheme was very much needed as the town was increasing in size, and with such a large military population he did not think darkness was good for the morality of the town.[4] In April 1903, tenders were requested from electrical experts to provide detailed specifications at a cost not exceeding £3,000.[5] One Dublin contractor, E.A. Aston, took a poor view of the process when writing in *The Irish Builder*: 'I think that a protest cannot too soon be raised against this proceeding. If the electrical trade and profession allow their brains to be put up to auction in connection with small schemes of this kind, it cannot be either for their own benefit or for the benefit of the public, whom they are supposed to serve. In this instance I trust that respectable engineers will not compromise their position by entering into such an undignified and useless competition.'[6]

By 1904, the plan was coming to fruition and an inquiry was held in the courthouse to justify the scheme. The scheme was estimated to cost £3,350 with an annual income of £625 per annum, although the final cost was £4,830. The scheme provided for 500 16-candle power lamps lighting at the same time with a provision for a further 250 lamps if necessary. It was funded by a loan of twenty years, repayable from rates obtained in the town and immediate environs. The area to be supplied with electricity was the town of Kildare and townlands of Whitesland, Collaghknock Glebe, Curragh Farm, Bisopsland, Crockanure Glebe, South Green, Loughminane, Knockshaugh Glebe, Loughlion and Grey Abbey, all in the Parish of Kildare and some lands in the parish of Tully.[7] A number of ratepayers, Denis Flood, Thomas Boland, Henry Brereton and J.E. Dunne objected to having to pay towards the cost of the scheme on the grounds that they did not live in the town.

The military, however, when pressed, would not commit to taking electricity in from the scheme, as indicated by the following letter to the council.

> With reference to your letter dated 30[th]ult, and previous correspondence respecting the proposed lighting by electricity of Kildare hut barracks, I am directed to inform you that although current may be taken in the future for the barracks of Kildare, the War Department can make no promise, and cannot consent to be committed in any way. Doubtless your council can so arrange their present scheme without additional expense to admit of expansion in the future.
>
> J.B. Sharpe, Lieutenant-Colonel[8]

Despite the difficulties with the military, the town lighting was switched on in November 1904.

> On Thursday night a large company assembled in the new power house, Kildare to witness the switching on of the new electric light. There is no doubt that the town required lighting; the visitor on Thursday night could well realise that fact.[9]

William Cooney was appointed to operate the electricity generator under the control of the Kildare Electric Lighting Committee who would remain responsible for electricity in the town until the ESB took over in April 1933 when the Shannon Scheme began to provide electricity. The military stood firm on their decision until at least 1910 – they were still not taking electricity from the town supply.[10] By 1914, the barracks was being supplied by the scheme as shown by an altercation between Mr Cooney the electrician and a Captain Reynolds of the Royal Artillery in which Mr Cooney threatened to cut off the barrack electricity supply unless the military carried out some rewiring work. Cooney had remarked that the council did not particularly want the military's business. Captain Reynolds wrote to the Naas No. 1 District Council repeating the allegation that Cooney had reported that the council were not at all interested in dealing with the officers of the Royal Artillery. Cooney wrote to the *Kildare Observer* defending his position and denying that he stated this to Reynolds and denying other charges about his work. Nevertheless, he was dismissed by the Kildare Electric Committee.[11] Cooney had previously been in trouble with his employers when he sent a boy around the town to read the electric meters even though he was not up to the task.[12] A welcome side effect of electricity in the town was the improvement in social activity and the Kildare Electric Palace opened in 1913 to provide entertainment for the town.

Water Supply and Waste-water Treatment

To cater for the erection of the barracks, the district council agreed to build a water storage tower in the town. There was some difficulty in drawing down the loan and as a result, the council did not expect to have the work completed for the opening of the barracks. Consequently, the War Department was requested to construct its own water tower and service tank in the barracks.[13] It should not have been a surprise to the council to get a frosty reception from the military, considering the intransigence shown by the council on the issue of electricity supply that was ongoing at the same time.

The supply of water to the town was not properly resolved until 1909 when agreement was reached with Lord Frederick FitzGerald for permission to erect a water tank in the People's Park, which was one of the highest points in the town. The Town Engineer, Mr Bergin, estimated that the laying of related piping in the town would cost £85. The War Office estimated that Kildare Barracks would require 40,000 gallons of water per day and agreed to pay the County Council, administered by Naas No. 1 District Council, for this amount. The water tower erected in the barracks was built to contain 40,000 gallons of water. As it transpired, the War Office had grossly overestimated the requirement for water and wrote to the Council in September 1904:

> With reference to the agreement for the supply of water to the War Department for the Kildare hutments, I am directed to enquire whether you are prepared to supply water at the rate of 9d per 1,000 gallons for actual consumption in lieu of, as at present, the fixed minimum of 40,000 gallons a day. Such alterations would of course, only take effect after 12 months' notice.
> Colonel A. H. Thomas, Royal Engineers, Curragh[14]

The district council was having none of it. The council engineer reported that the military were presently using about 28,000 gallons of water per day and the agreement was for five years. Having spent a considerable sum on upgrading the town water supply, the council was not for turning and agreed to revisit the matter after the expiration of the agreement. The military did not make the same mistake twice. When improvement works were carried out in Newbridge in 1904 in respect of the barracks, the military ensured that they would only pay for what they consumed in a separate agreement. At Kildare, they paid £547 per annum for five years. There was dreadful waste of water as a consequence and the military used a quarter of the water for cleaning their guns and wagons at Kildare.[15]

The War Office also contributed to general road maintenance works, but were slow to pay. The secretary of Kildare County Council reported at a council meeting in August 1904 that the War Department had agreed to pay £280 towards the improvement of roads around Kildare town owing to the increased military traffic, although they had only paid £70 to date. The county surveyor had applied on a number of occasions for the balance but was advised by the War Department that the matter was under consideration.[16]

The treatment of waste water commenced in 1900 with the construction of the Kildare Sewerage Works which was the first purification system introduced in Ireland.[17] The works were originally intended to drain onto the lands where the barracks was erected but once plans for the barracks were agreed, the War Office agreed to fund part of the works with a contribution of £300. The Kildare

Waterworks and Sewerage Committee was established to provide services for houses in the town and Albert Payne, contractor, carried out much of the work.[18]

Kildare Infirmary

The prospect of a large military barracks in the town prompted the people of Kildare to seek to the reopening of the Kildare Infirmary in 1901. There was some resistance from the county council which did not want to fund the project, so a local committee was established to seek subscriptions.[19] However, the Duke of Leinster was willing to offer the former infirmary premises and made the building available to the committee established to develop the project. The committee persevered and under the chairmanship of Charles Bergin wrote to the county council demanding that:

> The Local Government Board be requested to send one of their architects or engineers to report as to the repairs, alterations, and additions, if any, for the re-opening of the Kildare Infirmary as a county infirmary, and that the following be appointed a sub-committee to meet the persons appointed by the Local Government Board – C. Bergin, Fr. Campion, J.E. Medlicott, James Sunderland, John Healy, Rev R.S. Chaplin, and report to the committee.[20]

Tenders were invited and the position of surgeon was advertised by the Infirmary committee in December 1901. Louisa Brennan, Athy and Julia McGuinness, Boston were appointed as wardsmaids; Thomas Dillon, Rathangan was appointed porter and John McHugh, Kildare was given the position of apothecary, in preparation for the reopening which occurred in 1903. Daniel Power was appointed as medical officer but did not last long as he died of a heart attack while visiting London at the age of 48 in 1906. The coroner reported that the deceased doctor's heart was 130 per cent too heavy and was the largest he had ever seen.

The infirmary was rarely used by the military as they had their own hospital in the barracks, although in one instance two soldiers were admitted following an accident and the colonel contributed £5 to their treatment from his own resources. The infirmary proved expensive to keep open and fundraising events were organised in late 1902 to pay for its debts. One of the first contributors to the fundraising campaign was Lieutenant-Colonel A.C. Bailward, the most senior officer and brigade commander at Kildare Barracks, who contributed £5 towards the fund in November 1902.[21]

Gordon Bennett Race

In June 1903, County Kildare was the location of the first motor race held in Ireland when the Gordon Bennett race was held on a course around Counties Kildare, Carlow and Laois. The course passed through Kildare town and the railway station was busy with over 2,000 spectators arriving from all over Ireland to see the spectacle. There were a number of incidents during the week of the race. A French competitor, Mr Gabriel, killed a sheep on the road between Ballymany and Kildare at high speed cutting the sheep in two. Mr Gabriel informed the police in Kildare of the accident and subsequently paid twenty-five shillings to the owner of the sheep, Mr Farringdon, a Wicklow grazier. On the day of the race, a boy named Sheridan was knocked down by a touring car while crossing the square in Kildare and had his collar-bone broken, while another lad named Arthur Jones who was watching the race from the top of a tree, fell sustaining severe injuries to his back.[22]

At Kildare Petty Sessions, Mary Anne Parnell was charged with being drunk and disorderly on a public street on the night of the race and appeared before Mr J.E. Medlicott. Sergeant McGrath who prosecuted stated that the defendant's conduct was very bad and it occurred at 11 o'clock at night. This was her fourth offence within the twelve months. She was very noisy and drunk; she had plenty of drink taken. She was making an exhibition of herself on the street before some soldiers previous to that. The defendant replied that 'it was on the night of the Motor Race and it was ginger wine I took'. The Chairman said that 'I need not ask what her character is when it is her fourth offence within the twelve months.' She was fined 10 shillings or seven-days imprisonment. [23]

Demographics

The most significant change with the arrival of the barracks was in population. A comparison of census figures demonstrates the changes that occurred during this period in the town's history.

Year	Population	No. of houses
1881	2,152	440
1891	2,016	423
1901	2,430	541 (70 empty)
1911	3,608	-
1926	2,116	387 (20 empty)

The change in the religious composition of the population in the town reflected the new arrivals, as does a comparison with the town from the next available census after the British vacated the barracks:

RC	Protestant	Presbyterian	Methodist	Other	Total
1901					
2,202	170	16	14	28	2,430
1911					
2,307	1,080	44	44	43	3,518
1926					
2,047	61	5	0	0	2,113

The barracks alone had 1,020 residents in April 1911, 800 of whom were military personnel.

In 1901, the population of Kildare was 1,576. By 1911, out of a population of 2,639 persons, 808 were soldiers of the Royal Field Artillery stationed at the barracks. The accommodation available there catered for 892 officers and men with stabling for 614 horses. The occupations listed for Kildare show a marked change in the ten years between the construction of the barracks and its occupation, with the builders recorded in the 1901 census replaced by those stationed at the barracks in 1911.[1] In 1901, there were no officers and three soldiers living in the town but by 1911 there were twenty-seven officers and 781 men. The construction workers disappeared, but the increased business brought more publicans and commercial businesses to the town. The increased population brought a boom for local business as hackney drivers, shoemakers, saddlers and photographers, amongst others, were in demand. The media at the time commented that the local traders were not prepared for the increase in business and some outside capitalist might take advantage. There was also a property boom as the military authorities had not catered adequately for the number of married soldiers and their families who needed accommodation. Rents increased and those not lucky enough to be accommodated in the barracks immediately set to work seeking rented accommodation for their families.

By May 1902, it was clear that there was not enough accommodation to rent in the town. The 133 Battery vacated the barracks and was sent to Belturbet, County Cavan to make way for married soldiers and their families. They would rotate with other units from the brigade between Belturbet and Kildare. There was also a lack of suitable accommodation for officers and one of the building contractors, Albert Payne who came over from Croydon, London, to work on the construction of the barracks bought a plot of land at Curragh Farm in 1903 and proceeded to build a number of houses there over the next few years. The properties were primarily wooden houses like the barracks, and one property, ('The Nook') was built remarkably like the officers' mess in the barracks. The contractors at Curragh Farm got a surprise during excavation work when they unearthed three skeletons on the site, most probably dating from the famine era. These were reinterred in Grey Abbey cemetery. Albert Payne built a number of lodges on the site known as Leinster Walk including 'The Manse', 'The Nook', 'Ulster', 'Munster', 'Connaught' and 'Leinster' Lodges. [24] There were also a number of larger houses built during this period. The commanding officer's house was situated across the road from the barracks with a separate entrance for his use. A photograph of officers and NCOs of the XXXIII Brigade RFA at the house in 1905 survives. A number of other houses were also built at the turn of the century in the town. 'Lucknow' and 'Simla' on the Curragh edge were built before 1900 and General Allenby resided for a period at the latter. 'Gordon' and 'Bennett' houses were also built in the early 1900s more than likely called after the famous race of 1903 which passed through the town.

There was some rented accommodation available in the town but its condition was an ongoing problem, one that sanitation officials had been attempting to address for many years. With the arrival of the military, the sanitary authority, Naas No. 1 District Council, took a more proactive interest in improving the quality of rented dwellings in the town. In February 1903, J.E. O'Grady, Sanitation Officer, reported that a lane from Claregate Street to the church was spread out with heaps of rubbish from houses and that Chapel Hill was in a bad way. O'Grady recommended that the owners be made to connect their properties to the main sewer. John Breslin, Sanitation Officer also reported that the laneway at Shrawd was in a terrible filthy condition.

Despite these works there were still problems in the town and in July 1909, there were reports of unsanitary dwellings in Hospital Street and Bride Street. An advertisement appeared in the *Kildare Observer* in June 1903 for a lot of twelve cottages for sale opposite the military barracks with a weekly gross rent of £1 11 shillings.[25] Accommodation problems were also alleviated by the construction of a row of seven houses at Palacefield Terrace on Station Road in about 1905. The military eventually dealt with the problem of accommodation themselves and built accommodation for their married soldiers. A tender was invited for the construction of twenty married soldiers' quarters, and building commenced in early 1907.[26] As with terraced married quarters built in the Curragh, there were connecting doors between the houses and larger families could make use of rooms in adjacent units where necessary. Married quarters were subject to military inspection and soldiers could be severely reprimanded if their accommodation was not in good order.

The number of houses in the town grew from 250 in 1891 to 343 houses in 1901, 57 of them uninhabited in anticipation of the arrival of the military. The original tenants are not recorded but the 1911 census provides details of the families in the barracks and in these quarters. The men who lived in these married quarters were recorded separately in the census with their respective batteries. The variety of birth locations of the children of the barracks demonstrate the movement of troops around the Empire with children born in India, England and at other artillery stations in Ireland including Dundalk, Fermoy in County Cork and Cahir in County Tipperary:

Married Quarters – Kildare Barracks 1911
No.1: David Joel (England)
No.2: Beatrice Barret and Reginald (4, England)
No.3: Alice Jones and Caroline (11, India), John (9, India)
No.4: Sophie Butler

No.5: Florence Kinch and Frances (14, India)

No.6: Laetitia McGowan and Henry (7, England), Eliza (4, Tipperary), William (2, Kildare)

No.7: Bertha Allan (30) and Derwood (6, England), Aileen (5, England), Jeanette (2, Kildare), Stella (0, Kildare)

No.8: Clara Bendelow (28) and Bernard (4, India), Dulcie (2, India), Eric (1, India)

No.9: Annie Russell (35) and James (5, India), Dorothy (2, England), Annie (1, England), John (0, England)

No.10: Elizabeth Neal (37) and Joseph (7, England), Thomas (5, Tipperary)

No.11: Alice Denby (33) and Alfred (8, Cavan), William (6, Cavan), Leonard (4, Cork), Harold (2, Tipperary)

No.12: Agnes Isaac (33) and William (6, Tipperary), Ethel (3, Tipperary), Marjorie (1, Kildare)

No.13: Kate Mattock (34) and Hector (10, England).

No.14: Catherine Floyd (30) and Catherine (7, Scotland), Harold (6, Athlone), George (4, Athlone), Charles (2, England), Doris (0, Curragh).

No.15: Bessie Sharpe (35) and Hilda (10, England), Jack (7, Dundalk)

No.16: Minnie Lane (36) and Charles (11, England), Kathleen (9, England), Aileen (5, England)

No. 17: Henrietta Jones (25) and Kathleen (0, Kildare), Eileen (0, Kildare)

No. 18: Teresa Hilton (29) and William (0, Cornwall)

No. 19: Rachel Duggan (32) and Mary Doyle (20, Cork, Sister in Law)

No. 20: Isabel Coomber (30) and Ernest (5, Tipperary), Kathleen (4, Tipperary)

The soldiers of the barracks were on hand in June 1908 when a fire broke out at Colonel Hall-Walker's Stud Farm at Tully. The fire brigade attached to the barracks came to his aid and succeeded in stopping the fire from spreading from a hay barn to other buildings in the stud farm.

A plucky rescue of horses from a fire occurred on Sunday at the Tully Stud Farm, Kildare, the property of Colonel Hall Walker, M.P. The fire, which began in a large hay barn, was fanned by a strong breeze and spread rapidly. Close by were the stables for the farm horses, and their thatched roofs had already taken fire. Mr. Michael Costigan, a local resident, entered the burning stables, and not without great difficulty and danger managed to unloosen the horses and get them out. The rescuer was badly scorched about the hands and face. The Royal Field Artillery Barracks, Kildare were called in, and after a hard fight, lasting nearly two hours, the fire was got under control and allowed to burn itself out. It was afterwards discovered that a horse and a cow and calf perished in the flames. The horse, which was over twenty years of age, won a first prize at Chicago some years ago, and was a favourite of Colonel Walker's.[27]

There was another fire in October 1914 at the Stud Farm and the fire brigades from the barracks and from the Curragh were on hand to assist in putting out the fire which destroyed one hay barn and a rick of hay valued at £400. Constables Mathews and Bruce of the Royal Irish Constabulary arrested two men at Newtown in connection with the fire.[28] The barracks itself suffered its own fire in June 1914 when three cookhouses were burned to the ground before the flames were finally subdued with the assistance of the fire brigade from the Curragh Camp.[29] The barrack fire brigade also played its part in putting out a very serious fire in December 1917 at the Town Hall and Brothers' House in Kildare.[30]

Business in the town improved dramatically with the arrival of the barracks, with numerous army contracts available and various types of employment available for civilian contractors in the barracks. An advertisement from 1907 gave an indication of the type of material sourced through town suppliers:

Oats, Hay, Straw, required for Mr. O'Callaghan's Contract at Kildare Barracks. Highest prices given - Apply R. Brazil, Palacefield, Kildare.[31]

Military contracts meant that local contractors did not get the opportunity to provide goods and services. Major General Herbert Chermside wrote to business interests in August 1901 over the issue of canteen contracts in the Curragh district to advise that:

> 'The tender accepted offered better quality at more favourable rates than those that were declined.' The correspondent went on further to state that 'I must point out that, in view of the free trade system which prevails in the United Kingdom, it is quite beyond my local competence to adopt such a measure of protection. The military authorities here will of course consider all future tenders on their merits, and would be glad to find successful Irish competition. It is possible that the separation of the contract for porter from that for ale might favour the acceptance of Irish contracts.'[32]

There were some concerns raised about the increased volume of traffic in the town and lack of street lighting in the evenings.

> The danger to vehicular and pedestrian traffic is very great, and considering the large and constant stream of cars and baggage wagons which pass between the artillery hutments and the town and railway station, it is a wonder that frequent reports of accidents are not heard of. The principal roads leading from the town are all downhill, and consequently the danger of collision with an incoming vehicle is intensified.[33]

In 1914, local papers described some trouble in a public house. When a military policeman attempted to have the place vacated, he was given abuse by a soldier's wife.

The majority of soldiers in the barracks were Church of England. However, there is a notable increase in the number of conversions to Catholicism in the early years of the barracks, largely due to soldiers intending to marry local Catholics. The following is a list of soldiers baptised as Roman Catholics at St. Brigid's Parish Church, Kildare from the construction of the barracks to 1910.[34]

Name Occupation	Home	Date of Baptism
Robert Davison 132 Bty RFA, Kildare	-	1 Aug 1903
George Newman 137 Bty RFA, Corp.	-	15 Nov 1903
Thomas Gibbs 138 Bty RFA Gunner	Oxfordshire	21 Nov 1903
George Edward 131 Bty RFA	London	26 Dec 1903
George Ernest Browne 137 Bty RFA	London	3 Jul 1904
John Jackson 137 Bty RFA	Cumberland	28 Jun 1905
Richard Donovan 139 Bty RFA	London	25 Jun 1905
William Uracles 138 Bty RFA	Berkshire	22 Oct 1905
William Robinson 139 Bty RFA	Yorkshire	12 Nov 1905
Peter Parfitt Soldier 71 Bty RFA	Bath	28 Oct 1906
Thomas Hurst 71 Bty RFA	London	7 Nov 1906
Percival Foster Soldier, 48 Bty RFA	Lincoln	7 Nov 1906
George Newton 15 Bty, RFA	Norfolk	3 Apr 1907
Edward Butterfields 71 Bty EFA	Bedfordshire	3 Apr 1907
Henry Emery 135 Bty RFA Kildare	Somerset	8 Sept 1907
Thomas Judge 135 Bty Kildare	Cambridgeshire	20 Oct 1907

Joseph Honeyburn 134 Bty	London	20 Oct 1907
Arthur Coote 137 Bty	Cambridgeshire	20 Oct 1907
John Sherrard Ex-sold. 131 Bty RFA	Coleraine, Derry	24 Nov 1907
Charles Teirle 134 Bty RFA	London	19 Apr 1908
Henry David Tills 135 Bty RFA	London	31 May 1908
Albert Henry 135 Bty RFA	Derbyshire	5 Jul 1908
Edward Payne 136 Bty RFA	Lewes	5 Jul 1908
David Morgan Driver 117 Bty RFA	Glamorgan Wales	25 Oct 1908
John Rees ASC Kildare	Wales	14 Mar 1909
Herbert Bullimore 116 Bty Kildare	Nottingham	14 Mar 1909
Edward Joseph Haitley Bomb 141 Bty RFA	Hackney, London	5 Sept 1909
William Williams Gnr 118 Bty RFA	Southampton	24 Oct 1909

The file of Henry Emery survives and shows that he enlisted on 7 January 1902 with the regimental number 21302. He was described as 19 years old and his religion was Church of England. He was posted to 135 Battery on 26 February 1902 as a Driver. The explanation for his baptism at Kildare is evident from the file as he married Teresa Doogan at the Roman Catholic Church at Belturbet, County Cavan on 20 November 1907. Driver Emery had served in Belturbet from Kildare in August 1905 and was posted back to Kildare in April 1907. Herbert Bullimore, a former drayman, enlisted on 8 July 1901 at Nottingham and was given the regimental number 16551 and was sent to 116 Battery for training, being posted with the battery to Kildare in November 1907. The details of his marriage are nor recorded, perhaps because he was not accepted onto the marriage establishment. The military operated a system whereby married quarters were only provided for a particular number of men. A soldier, therefore who got married may not be accepted onto the married establishment by the authorities as this would prioritise his position for married accommodation. In order, therefore, to live with his wife, the soldier would have to obtain private lodgings elsewhere.

Diseases

Disease, in men and horses, was also a problem that had to be kept in check. Veterinary officers carried out regular inspections of the horses. The senior veterinary officer of the Seventh Division was at Kildare on 9 December 1904 carrying out inspections following a visit to units at the Curragh and Newbridge during the same week. These inspections were a follow up to an outbreak of epizootic lymphangitis in November 1903 at the Curragh. One case was confirmed in Kildare and another in Newbridge with eleven horses being destroyed and horses suspected of having disease being segregated from others and their bedding and manure collected and burned.

It was not only the horse that suffered disease. There was an outbreak of scarlatina at the barracks in 1906 with twenty men ill and ten further cases in the town. Dr Rowan reported to Naas No.1 District Council in April 1906 that:

It has been reported to me today by the medical officer in charge of the troops at Kildare barracks that seven cases of scarlatina have occurred there since 17th inst. They have all been, as soon as diagnosed, removed to the isolation hospital in the Curragh Camp. Disinfection of the quarters occupied by the affected persons has been adequately carried out by the medical officer in charge, which is instituting inquiries as to the probable source of the outbreak.[35]

The disease was a major source of concern in the town and the schools were all closed. A De La Salle Brother, Brother Timothy, died from the disease. Dr Rowan reported on 29 April that:

I regret to have to report to the Naas Guardians the extension of the outbreak of scarlatina which I mentioned in my letter of last week as having first come under observation at the military barracks here. About thirty cases in all have been so far ascertained – twenty of these having occurred in the military quarters. Of the ten among the civil population in the town who were attacked, one Brother Timothy of the Monastery National School died this morning after three days' illness.[36]

CHAPTER 4

MILITARY ACTIVITY AND TRAINING

Each year during the Summer the Artillery did firing
practice, brigades taking their turn to go to Camp for
about a fortnight and fire their guns on a range situated
at the foot of the Wicklow mountains.

GUNNER PERCY WHITEHOUSE[1]

137 Battery, Royal Field Artillery demonstrating a 15-pounder field gun in the Glen
of Imaal, County Wicklow, May 1903. (Courtesy of Paul Skingsley)

Life for those stationed with the Royal Field Artillery at Kildare revolved around the horse and the guns. The comfort of the men in the barracks was eased when the 10p.m. roll call was discontinued in May 1902, so that once the men had finished their stable duties in the evening, they were free until the next morning, making the town much busier at that time of day.

Gunner Percy Whitehouse who served with the VIII (Howitzer) Brigade recorded barrack life at Kildare in the early 1900s:

> We were roused each morning by a trumpeter sounding 'reveille' at 6.30 a.m. Our first duty was to clean out our stables, brush down the horses, who were then watered and fed. Half an hour was allocated to morning stables then we were dismissed to our quarters where we shaved and washed, tidied up our beds, swept around and then had breakfast. We ate in our own quarters, not in dining hall, the room orderly and helper brought the food from the cook house in containers we called 'dixies' and it was served out on to plates arranged on one of the tables, the NCO would inspect to ensure that the food was fairly shared out, then would give us the signal to 'carry on', we each secured our portion and sat down for the meal. Tea was brought in a tea bucket and poured into fairly large basins from which we drank. There were no cups and saucers, the basins were plain and rimless holding about a pint which was usually ample. The food was plain but quite good, we had a fairly regular diet having certain items on certain days.[2]

The Gunners

Thousands of gunners would pass through Kildare as the various units came and went. No records survive that show all of their names but an insight into the type of people who served in the barracks can be gleaned from newspaper reports and surviving service records.

Two soldiers of the XXXII Brigade at Kildare in May 1906 were presented with long service and good conduct medals by Lieutenant-Colonel A.B. Helyar, officer in charge of troops at Kildare. The local newspaper gave some information on the two recipients:

> Sergeant Major Tommy Rishworth – a typical Yorkshire soldier both in nature and habits, not to refer to his sporting proclivities – is a native of Wakefield, has completed his 20 years' service, has seen service in India and South Africa, is a possessor of the late Queen's medal for service in the latter country, has quite an array of clasps attached thereto, and is one of the most popular Sergeant-Majors extant. He is an enthusiastic cricketer and billiard player, and it is safe to assert that in no corner of the earth has his distinguished county a keener or more loyal supporter in all that affects it.
>
> Quartermaster-Sergeant Harry Hemmings has seen 18½ years' service with the colours, of which 2½ has been spent in India and 3 years in South Africa for which he is decorated with the late Queen's and the King's medals, to which he has appended four and two clasps respectively. He has in addition had the distinction of being recommended in Lord Roberts' dispatch of 10th September, 1901 as 'having rendered special and meritorious service,' QMS Hemmings is a native of Hindlip, in Worcestershire, is a keen angler, and is a thoroughly nice fellow.[3]

The entire XXXII Brigade was drawn up for parade on three sides of the barrack square for the presentation of medals to the two recipients, Sergeant Major Rishworth of 136 Battery and Quartermaster-Sergeant Hemmings of 134 Battery. Three other members of the XXXII Brigade also held good conduct medals – Regimental-Sergeant-Major Morrison, Wheeler-Quartermaster-Sergeant Dawes and Sergeant W.A. Harrison.

A rare surviving photograph taken by Charleton & Son photographer of Newbridge, Curragh, Kildare and Glen Imaal shows the senior gunners of the

XXXIII Brigade at Kildare in November 1905 relaxing outside the commanding officer's house across the road from the barracks. The photograph shows Lieutenant-Colonel H.K. Jackson DSO and Captain H.E.T. Kelly together with Regimental Sergeant-Major W.G. Presbury, Battery Sergeant-Majors Voce and Scoffield, BQMS Sandilands, Smith and Lee, FQMS Barnes, Saddler Staff-Sergeant Longmore, Farrier-Sergeants O'Neill and Daly, Saddler-Sergeant Mealyer and Sergeants Lucas, Skingsley, Uphill, Dobbs, Everest, Paterson, Chalmers, Murphy, McCorkindale, Prince, Gildon, McDonald, Wilson, Law and Perry. Except for the brigade commander, every other gunner in the photograph sports a moustache, which typified the sergeant of the British army.

Joseph Michael Mealyer

Joseph Michael Mealyer (1870–1913) was born in Wexford in 1870. He enlisted on 15 March 1889 at Colchester aged 18 years and 8 months and was described as a labourer.[4] Like all soldiers, he signed up for seven years with the colours and five years in the reserves, which meant that he could be called up again if required. Mealyer was Roman Catholic but converted to Wesleyan in 1898.

He service records gives a typical outline of army careers of the time. The term 'home' used in military records included service in Ireland, which was part of the United Kingdom at the time:

Home:	15 March 1889 – 29 September 1890
India:	30 September 1890 – 12 December 1896
Home:	13 December 1896 – 29 September 1899
South Africa:	30 September 1899 – 1 April 1902
Home:	2 April 1902 – 1 April 1913

The army educated him with a third-class certificate on 5 November 1891 and a second-class certificate on 24 October 1892. Mealyer started as a driver with the III Brigade, reorganised as 75 Battery on 1 July 1889. He was posted to 34 Battery on 8 September 1890. He got a pay increase on 15 May 1895 having completed six years and extended his service in June 1896 agreeing to complete twelve years with the colours. On 1 October 1896 he was posted to 39 Battery and appointed a bombardier collar-maker on 4 October 1897 before transferring to 68 Battery in the same month. Driver Mealyer had completed a collar-makers course in September 1893.

On 7 October 1899 he was posted to an ammunition column in South Africa and promoted to the rank of corporal on 1 April 1900. He was sent to Pretoria on 1 January 1902. On 21 June 1902 he was re-engaged to complete twenty-one years with the colours and posted to 126 Battery before transferring to 138 Battery on 1 June 1903 as a saddler-corporal.

On 1 October 1904 he was promoted to the rank of saddler-sergeant. Mealyer should have completed his service in 1909 after twenty-one years but was permitted to continue in service, dying of diabetes at Devonport on 1 April 1913.

He had served for twenty-four years and eighteen days. He had extensive service in South Africa being awarded the Queen's Medal with clasps for 'Delmont', 'Neadder River', 'Relief of Kimberley', 'Paardebereg' and 'Johannesburg'. He was also awarded the King's Medal with clasps. He married Martha Stickley on 4 May 1902 at Portsmouth and was brought on to the married strength of the brigade on 1 June 1903 meaning that his wife could live in the barracks at Kildare.

Alfred Passfield

Alfred Passfield (1874–1948) was born in Ilford, Essex in 1873 and enlisted in 44 Regiment on 24 February 1891 at 18 years of age.[5] He transferred to the Royal Artillery in June 1896. His service record gives the following details:

Home:	24 February 1891 – 19 February 1893
India:	20 February 1893 – 23 March 1904
Home:	24 March 1904 – 20 September 1906
India:	21 September 1906 – 23 February 1912

He held the following appointments or ranks:

Private:	24 February 1891	44 (Essex) Reg Extended to complete 12 years
	20 May 1896	44 (Essex) Reg
Gunner:	1 July 1896	54 Battery
Acting Bombardier:	28 August 1896	54 Battery

Bombardier:	21 January 1898	54 Battery
Corporal:	1 July 1898	54 Battery
Sergeant:	24 September 1899	54 Battery
Battery-Sergeant-Major:	1 October 1903	57 Battery
Battery-Sergeant-Major:	25 February 1904	Depot
Battery-Sergeant-Major:	22 May 1904	137 Battery
Battery-Sergeant-Major	20 September 1906	38 Battery
Battery-Sergeant-Major:	22 July 1908	No.6 Ammunition Column

He was discharged on 23 February 1912 following the completion of his second period of engagement. Passfield married Violet Tresham on 2 October 1900. Their son Aubrey was born in India in July 1901 and their second son Alfred Lancelot was born at Kildare in October 1904 and baptised by Dean George Cowell in St. Brigid's Cathedral. On completion of his military service in 1912 he was awarded a pension for life.

Augustus William Skingsley

Augustus William Skingsley (1872–1941) of Chelmsford, Essex, enlisted in the Royal Artillery at Woolwich on 21 July 1891 for seven years with the colours and five in the reserves.[6] He was 19 years and 3 months old and worked as a gardener. His service record indicates that he served in the following locations:

Home:	21 July 1891 – 5 December 1892
India:	6 December 1892 – 28 November 1902
Home:	29 November 1902 – 20 July 1912

Skingsley undertook the following courses during his military career.

3rd Class Certificate:	14 July 1894
2nd Class Certificate:	30 March 1895
Qualified for promotion to Corporal:	2 April 1896
Passed course of Equitation at Kirkee:	17 October 1897
Passed for promotion to Sergeant:	11 May 1900
Passed short course of gunnery Shoeburyness:	2 April 1907

His file notes that he married Anna Dix on 3 August 1903 and had five children, two of whom were born at Kildare – Alfred in 1904 and Millicent in 1905. His service record indicates the units that he served in and the dates when he served. The military always use the term casualty when a soldier is transferred to another unit or position:

Date	Battery	Casualty	Rank
21 Jul 1891	Depot	Attested	Gunner
6 Dec 1892	55 Battery	Posted	Gunner

Granted good conduct pay from 1 July 1893

11 Jan 1898	Appointed	Acting	Bombardier

Extended service to complete 12 years with the colours

14 Jul 1897		Promoted	Bombardier
3 Apr 1900		Promoted	Sergeant
5 Nov 1902	No. 4 Depot	Posted	Sergeant
16 Jan 1903	137 Battery	Posted	Sergeant
7 Jul 1903			

Re-engaged at Kildare to complete 21 years service

28 Jun 1908	Promoted	BQMS	
28 Jun 1908	134 Battery	Posted	BQMS
20 Jul 1912	Discharged after termination of 2nd period of engagement		

Horace George Parnell

Gunner 96321 Horace George Parnell (1878–1916) of Worlingworth, Suffolk enlisted in the Royal Artillery at Great Yarmouth on 3 March 1893. He was only 14 years and 11 months and just under 4 ft 11 inches, which was of some concern to the military authorities as the medical officer who examined him noted that he was a 'growing lad (special)'. When finally mustered as a gunner he had grown to nearly five foot six inches. His service record shows a typical career path for a boy in the army as he moved to being a trumpeter before becoming a gunner.

Unit	Promotion	Rank	Date	Location
Depot	Attested	Boy	3 March 1893	Home
Depot	Appointed	Trumpeter	29 Sep 1894	Home
19 Company	Posted	Trumpeter	10 Oct 1894	Home

Having completed two years' service Trumpeter Parnell was granted good conduct pay at one penny per day, and on reaching 18 years of age on 13 May 1896 he was now formally mustered as a driver and sent to an artillery battery.

86 Battery	Mustered	Driver	13 May 1896	Home

He was disciplined for some unknown reason in January 1897 and lost his good conduct pay but got it back six months later. He suffered another punishment and was imprisoned for 56 days from October 1897 before returning to duty in December 1897.

69 Battery	Posted	Driver	29 April 1898	S Africa
69 Battery	Mustered	Gunner	26 July 1901	S Africa

At this point after more than three years in South Africa where his unit had participated in the Siege of Ladysmith, Parnell was posted to India in October 1901 where he remained until he joined 140 Battery at Kildare.

69 Battery	Appointed	A/Bombardier	24 March 1904	India
Depot	Reverted	Gunner	9 July 1904	Home
140 Battery	Posted	Gunner	17 Feb 1905	Home
Discharged	Gunner		5 July 1911	

He was discharged from the Royal Artillery at Kildare after eighteen years' service. This would not be the end of his military service. He married in 1912 and settled into civilian life but like many other men of his generation, he re-enlisted in August 1914 and was killed in action in France on 27 June 1916 while serving with 5 Battery.

Transfers and Rotations

British Army personnel were in constant rotation as Royal Field Artillery batteries moved on to their next station in Ireland or abroad and their places were taken by other units. Units did not spend very long in the same place as they rotated between the home bases in the United Kingdom (including Ireland), India and anywhere else were the army was required, such as South Africa in the early 1900s.

The transfer of officers between units was more common than the movement of NCOs or gunners. This was particularly the case in the years immediately after the Boer War. By 1904, while the same units were still at Kildare, other officers of the batteries had changed almost entirely:

XXXI Brigade Royal Field Artillery Kildare

Brigade Headquarters
Brigade Commander: Lieutenant-Colonel E.J. Phibbs-Horby
Adjutant: Captain W.R. Eden
131 Battery, Royal Field Artillery
Major: C.C. Owens
Captain: O. de L'E. Winter
Lieutenant: L.M. Bucknill
Second-Lieutenant: W.A. Nicholls
Second-Lieutenant: J.A. Don
132 Battery, Royal Field Artillery
Major: H.D.W. Thomson DSO
Captain: A.M.R. Mallock
Lieutenant: R.C. Reeves
Second-Lieutenant: Hon H.G.O. Bridgeman
Second-Lieutenant: J.A. Bowles
Second-Lieutenant: A.W. Purser (attached)
133 Battery, Royal Field Artillery (At Belturbet)
Major: R.F. Ellice
Captain: H.L. Lithgow
Lieutenant: C.W. Bardon
Second-Lieutenant: A.S. Barnwell

XXXIII Brigade

Brigade Headquarters

Brigade Commnader Lieutenant-Colonel C.B. Watkins

Adjutant: Captain H.E.T. Kelly

137 Battery, Royal Field Artillery

Major: Brevet Lieutenant-Colonel C.E. Coghill

Captain: Brevet Major H.M. Thomas

Lieutenant:

Second-Lieutenant: L.E.O. Davidson

Second-Lieutenant: A.J.R. Kennedy

Second-Lieutenant: C.B. Blake

138 Battery, Royal Field Artillery

Major: H.S. White

Captain: A.E.M. Head

Second-Lieutenant: R.C. Dodgson

Second-Lieutenant: H.G. Lee Warner

Second-Lieutenant: C.J.B.Clibborn

139 Battery, Royal Field Artillery

Major: G.S. Duffus

Captain: F.W. Mackenzie

Lieutenant:

Second-Lieutenant: R.F. Parker

Second-Lieutenant: C.E. Boyce

Second-Lieutenant: L.W.L. Jackson

The following list is a sample of movements of officers recorded during this period:

Lieutenant R.C. Dobson, 138 Battery, Kildare on draft for India, 12 Dec 1904.

Captain A.E.M. Head, 138 Battery, Kildare appointed to XIII Brigade, Farnborough, 31 July 1905.

Captain W.M. Warburton posted to 138 Battery, Kildare 20 October 1905.

Second Lieutenant A.E. Deprez posted to 48 Battery, Kildare 16 March 1907.

Captain E. Harding-Newman, 137 Battery RFA Kildare appointed staff Captain RA Newbridge 30 Oct 1905.

Captain H.D. De Pree, 137 Battery has been appointed a Staff Captain at Army Headquarters 10 Mar 1906.

Lieutenant-Colonel C.H.Hutchinson transferred from 134 Battery, Kildare to command XXVI Brigade, Kildare, 13 May 1908.

Second-Lieutenant C.H.Getto Lancashire Royal Artillery Reserve officer for 6 months training to 142 Battery, Kildare, 12 May 1909.

Lieutenant R.W. Wynniatt, Pembroke Royal Field Artillery Reserve Officer to Ireland for 6 months training to 116 Battery, Kildare. 12 May 1909.

Lieutenant C. Holland posted from Woolwich to 68 Battery, Kildare, 23 February 1910.

Lieutenant E.M.Mansell-Pleydell posted from 116 Battery, Kildare to S Battery RHA Lucknow, 23 February 1910.

Lieutenant-Colonel S. Lushington, transferred from Command of XXXVI Brigade, Athlone to LXVII Brigade, Kildare.

Captain H. Ward selected to attend Gunnery Staff Course at Woolwich on 3 October 1911.

Major Higgins RFA posted on promotion from 110 Battery, Newbridge to 124 Battery, Kildare, 27 November 1911.

Captain H.A. Boyd posted from 140 Battery, Kildare to 110 Battery, Newbridge,
27 November 1911.

Second-Lieutenant E.H.P. Jackson posted to 122 Battery, Kildare from 21 October on first appointment after completing of course at School of Gunnery, Shoebury, 12 October 1911.

Second-Lieutenant Jackson posted from 122 Battery, Kildare to 39 Battery Deepcut and relieved by Second-Lieutenant L.G. Lutyens, 19 October 1911.

Lieutenant-Colonel E.C. Cameron posted on promotion from 142 Battery, Kildare to command XXVIII Brigade, Kildare with effect from 1 November 1911.

Major H.F.E. Lowin posted from Glasgow to 142 Battery, Kildare[7]

The first unit to serve at Kildare, the XXXI Brigade, left in August 1905 and was posted to Fermoy, County Cork. It was replaced by the XXXVI Brigade, consisting of 15, 48 and 71 Field Batteries. The XXXIII left in July 1906 for Sheffield and was replaced by the XXXII Brigade consisting of 134, 135 and 136 Batteries who arrived from Dundee. Prior to their departure from Kildare a cricket match was held between Sergeants' Mess XXXII Brigade and the Sergeants' Mess XXXIII Brigade followed by a social evening held in the Sergeants' Mess of the XXXIII Brigade before their departure under Regimental Sergeant-Major Presbury. The event was held two weeks before the departure of the unit to Sheffield, as their last action in Ireland would be two weeks annual practice at the gunnery camp at the Glen of Imaal.[8] The arrival of new artillery batteries in Kildare apparently caused an outbreak of Scarlatina in the town in May 1906. The disease first made its appearance in the barrack huts. Dr Rowan suggested that the children of the town got it from playmates in the tin huts in the barracks and noted that the outbreak had nothing to do with the sanitation in the town.[9]

The officers and units stationed at the barracks in 1908 were as follows, with 134 Battery about to go to Belturbet and 135 Battery returning from there to Kildare:

XXVI Brigade, Royal Field Artillery, Kildare
Brigade Headquarters
Brigade Commander: Lieutenant-Colonel E.M. Perceval
Adjutant: Captain F.A. Buzzard
116 Battery, Royal Field Artillery
Major H.J. Brock
Captain H.C. Simpson
Lieutenant G.A. Hare
Lieutenant E.M. Mansel-Pleydell
Lieutenant A.W. Van Straubenzee
117 Battery, Royal Field Artillery
Major G.H. Sanders
Captain N.H.C. Sherbrooke

Lieutenant A.A.S. Younger
Lieutenant C.L. Ziegler
Second-Lieutenant B.P. Almack
118 Battery, Royal Field Artillery
Major A.R. Bayley
Captain H. Ward
Lieutenant G.T. Strickland
Lieutenant G.B. Stopford
Lieutenant J.E. Marston

XXXII Brigade
Brigade Headquarters
Brigade Commander: Lieutenant Colonel A.B. Helyar
Adjutant: Lieutenant P.G. Yorke
134 Battery, Royal Field Artillery, (Kildare for Belturbet)
Major C.H. Hutchison
Captain C.C. Baines
Lieutenant L. St. J.R. Clutterbuck
Second-Lieutenant G.P. Leach
Second-Lieutenant E.F. Budden
135 Battery, Royal Field Artillery (Belturbet for Kildare)
Major M. Campbell-Herbert
Captain H.G. Pringle
Lieutenant H.A. Hamilton
Second-Lieutenant C.M. Longmore
Second-Lieutenant R.T. Hammick
136 Battery, Royal Field Artillery
Major F.A.G.Y. Elton
Captain:Vacant
Lieutenant K.M. Potter
Lieutenant J.N. Diggle
Lieutenant R.S. Ellis
Lieutenant D.W. Roberts
Kildare Riding Master: Lieutenant J. Hagan

Gunner C. Morrisson of 134 Battery died on 26 July 1906 and was interred at the military cemetery on the Curragh. Gunner Ockwell of 52 Battery died at the Curragh Military Hospital on 14 July 1913. It was noted that Gunner Ockwell 'had nearly twenty-one years' service, was very popular amongst his comrades, and especially the children in the barracks, a number of whom were present'.[10] The funeral service was held at Kildare Cathedral and he was interred in the grounds of the Cathedral. A large number of men from the 52 Battery under the command of Colonel Prescott-Decie attended the funeral and a volley was fired over the grave.

Several other soldiers were killed in training incidents on the Curragh. On combined artillery and cavalry manoeuvres in front of the Standhouse at the racecourse, the 19 Hussars charged at the guns protected by 11 Hussars. The result was 'men and horses became entangled in the artillery guns, and the scene was one of indescribable confusion. The two squadrons were thrown into a state of panic, and all struggled to get clear of the heavy ordnance'. The result was a Private Sanderson of B Squadron, 19 Hussars killed by breaking his neck and Private Blensley suffered a broken ankle. A horse was also killed.[11]

Hart's Directory of 1908 records the senior officers of the barracks as follows:

XXVI Brigade Royal Field Artillery

Brigade Commander:	Lieutenant-Colonel J.W.G. Dawkins
Adjutant:	Captain A.A.S. Younger
116 Battery:	Major C. Prescott-Decie
117 Battery:	Major G.H. Sanders
118 Battery:	Major A.R. Bayly
Riding Master:	Lieutenant J. Hagan

Lieutenant-Colonel J.W.G. Dawkins, a veteran of the Sudan campaign of 1898, remained in command of the XXVI Brigade until August 1909. Major Abigdon Robert Bayly was posted to Kildare in October 1907 from 90 Battery stationed at Brighton.[12] He was still in command of 118 Battery at the battle of Mons in August 1914 when his battery was overrun and he was wounded in action and taken prisoner by the Germans. While a prisoner of war in Germany, his wife filed for divorce.

Major Sanders of the 117 Battery was stationed at Kildare for five years. He joined the army in 1888, beginning his military career at Woolwich military academy as did all artillery officers. He served in Africa during the Boer War and in France during the First World War. He returned to Ireland to train new artillery batteries being formed during the war.

The Army issued an order in February 1908 giving the intended reliefs between stations in the United Kingdom, the colonies and India during the year 1908-09. The rotation of artillery brigades relating to Ireland was as follows:[13]

LXII Brigade RFA	India to Cahir
LXVII Brigade RFA	Cahir to Kildare
XXXII Brigade RFA	Kildare to Bordon
VII Brigade RHA	Ipswich to Newbridge
VIII Brigade RHA	Newbridge to Aldershot

At the time of the 1911 census, the following officers were at Kildare Barracks:

XXXXVII Brigade, Royal Field Artillery
Brigade Commander: Lieutenant-Colonel Stephen Lushington
Adjutant: Captain Edward Gilliat Langford
RSM:RSM S.G. Haggett
140 Battery, Royal Field Artillery
Major Robert Darell Wylde
Captain Henry Alexander Boyd
Lieutenant Edward Boyd Maxwell
Lieutenant John de Blaquiere Tindall Lucas
Lieutenant Charles Bennett Spence
141 Battery, Royal Field Artillery
Major Edward Charles Walthall Delves Walthall
Lieutenant W.C. Rait-Kerr
Lieutenant Derek Charles Stephenson
Second-Lieutenant Frederick Angus Wanklyn

Battery-Sergeant-Major Alfred John Wark
142 Battery, Royal Field Artillery
Major Evan Cornwallis Cameron
Captain Frederick E. Brousson
Second-Lieutenant S. Atkinson
Second-Lieutenant P.H.L. Playfair
Battery-Sergeant-Major W.G. Sharp

XXVIII Brigade, Royal Field Artillery
122 Battery, Royal Field Artillery
Captain Robert Arthur Jones
Lieutenant Maurice Gordon Soames
Lieutenant Edward Poulton Almack
123 Battery, Royal Field Artillery
Major George Herbert Sanders
Captain W.P. Poynter
Lieutenant J. Carlyon
Lieutenant C. Dowling
Second-Lieutenant R.B. Miller
Sergeant J. Burns
124 Battery, Royal Field Artillery
Major Charles Frederick Stevens
Captain Charles Hunter Browning[14]
Lieutenant Maurice Vernon Plummer
Lieutenant Richard Meadows Rendel
Lieutenant Robert Hallam Studdert

In January 1912 the LXV Brigade arrived at Kildare, having travelled from India to England and then on to Ireland:

The 5th Brigade of Royal Horse Artillery (G and O Batteries), from Secunderabad and Bangalore, are to arrive at Southampton in the transport Dongola tomorrow, to be stationed at Ipswich. The same vessel is bringing home the 45th Brigade of Royal Field Artillery (11,

62 and 80 Batteries) from Jubbalpore to be stationed at Kildare.[15] Gunners also arrived in small numbers to batteries following their initial training in artillery depots throughout the United Kingdom. Gunner Percy Whitehouse in his memoirs described the journey to Kildare in 1913:

> We were to journey to Ireland to join the 8th Howitzer Brigade R.F.A. which was stationed at Kildare about 30 miles from Dublin.
>
> We were escorted by a sergeant, an old soldier, and travelled via London, midnight train to Holyhead, to Dublin by steamship, where we arrived fairly early next morning and were soon in a train to the nearest station to Kildare. We finished our journey by Jaunting Car, a horsedrawn light vehicle on which one sat sideways; quite an experience. [16]

The Glen of Imaal, County Wicklow

Every gunner who passed through Kildare spent some time training in the Glen of Imaal in the Wicklow mountains. The Glen first opened as an artillery firing range in May 1899. The army spent a number of years searching for a suitable location for artillery practice and finally settled on the purchase of the Glen from the Earl of Wicklow. The War Department had to buy out the tenants who resided on this part of the estate with the payment of twenty-five times the value of the annual rental payment.[17] An annual camp was held at the Glen in County Wicklow from April each year and the batteries of the Irish Command took their turn on the artillery ranges.

The Kildare units first went to the Glen in August 1902. Photographs from the time show that the men wore the 'slouch' hat that the army had adopted in South Africa and continued to wear while on manouevres at home until 1905. They also wore a pouch at the hip to carry ammunition: this was replaced in 1903 by a bandolier which made handling and accessing ammunition for rifles easier – something that artillerymen also had to master. The Naval and Military Intelligence column of the London *Times* noted that the XXXI and XXXIII Brigades from Kildare were scheduled to arrive on 7 May 1904 for their annual camp. The scale of operations in the Glen of Imaal is demonstrated by the 1912 schedule for training:[18]

XXII Brigade RFA (104, 105, 106 Batteries), Cahir	11 May – 30 May
XXVII Brigade RFA (119, 120, 121 Batteries), Ballincollig	11 May – 30 May
XXIV Brigade RFA (110, 111, 112 Batteries), Newbridge	5 June – 25 June
XVIII Brigade RFA (122, 123, 124 Batteries), Kildare	5 June – 25 June
II Brigade RHA (D, E Batteries), Newbridge	29 June – 25 July
2 Brigade RFA (21, 42 Batteries) Fermoy (53 Bty) Waterford	29 June – 25 July
IL Brigade RFA (145 Bty) Fethard, (147 Bty)	29 June – 25 July
Clonmel (148 Bty) Kilkenny	29 June – 25 July
XXX Brigade RFA (128, 129, 130 Batteries) Dundalk	1 Aug – 21 Aug
LXV Brigade RFA (11, 52, 80 Batteries) Kildare	1 Aug – 21 Aug

In 1912 IL Brigade RFA were tasked with detailing a depot battery from 20 April until the close of the camp in late August except during their own practice when the Fifth Divisional Artillery were similarly responsible. The work of the depot battery was explained as follows by Gunner Whitehouse in his memoirs:

> Each year during the Summer the artillery did firing practice, brigades taking their turn to go to camp for about a fortnight and fire their guns on a range situated at the foot of the Wicklow mountains. One battery had to be 'depot ' battery for the whole firing practice and in that year of 1913 my battery had this particular job, which meant that we went to camp in advance to prepare the targets on the range. Consequently we spent about ten weeks under canvas near the mountains, living fairly rough and spending most of the time out in the open. It was a change from barracks and quite exciting at times especially when on duty on the range, not very far away from where the shells burst. We built splinter proof shelters of lumps of rock for protection. In these circumstances we experienced the sensation of

very nearly being under shell fire hearing the screech of approaching shells and being not very far from where they were bursting, both shrapnel and high explosive percussion, quite a change from routine parades.[19]

For the comfort of the soldiers, Elise Sandes, was given permission to use two marquees during the 1901 season and she was given the use of a lodge in the glen by Walter Tighe for her co-workers and herself. Elise Sandes (1851-1934) was born in Tralee, County Kerry and provided soldiers homes throughout Ireland and India to give some sort of a family life to soldiers and turn them away from the poor conditions and vices that had given the army a poor reputation over many years. The soldiers' home at the Glen of Imaal was built in 1902. Prior to the completion of the facility, the soldiers were left to their own devices but the provision of a home offered the men somewhere to go in the long summer evenings. The home was described in detail by one of Elise Sandes's fellow workers:

The home is full tonight, every chair is occupied; all sorts and conditions of men are here, from the old soldier who has done a bit of service on the N-W Frontier, or seen many a stiff scrap in South Africa, to the young fresh-faced lads who are going through their first camping season. Look round the rooms! There is Bob, the champion chess player, playing a comrade for all he is worth.

In 1904, a further soldiers' home was added at Knockanatgan Camp two miles from the Glen. In 1912 the military purchased an estate at Coolmoney Park as a result of the requirement of a longer range to deal with new guns and Elise Sandes added a further home at the camp there.

There were a number of accidents in the Glen of Imaal. Sergeant Russell, 71 Battery Royal Field Artillery based at Kildare, was seriously injured in September 1904 when he was struck on the head by a large rock during blasting operations and was brought to the Curragh Military Hospital where he was operated on.[20]

Horse Training

The life of a gunner in the Royal Field Artillery revolved around the horse. Gunner Whitmore recorded in his memoirs about his time at Kildare that:

> We recruits were soon initiated into the many duties, how to groom a horse etc. We had many lectures on many subjects. The horses were all-important and had to be considered and cared for before anything. We were lectured on the subject of horses very thoroughly and had to know how to diagnose various ailments and treatment, how to properly water and feed him, how to fit the bridle and bit, saddle and other harness.[21]

Although many came from rural backgrounds and had worked with horses before, many gunners were also from urban backgrounds and had never dealt with horses previously. While infantrymen concentrated on marching and learning to shoot, artilleryman had to master horsemanship before anything else.

> Before commencing actual riding instruction we were taken to the gymnasium and grouped round a dummy horse, a replica, life-size of a horse which could be rocked to simulate the horse's movement when walking, trotting etc. We were taught to fit bridle and saddle on this dummy over and over again, until we could almost do it with our eyes shut, the same with the saddling up. Then we were taught how to mount correctly, how to sit in the saddle and grip with our knees, how to hold the reins and when the apparatus was rocked, how to keep our seat and be in command.

Following intensive repetitive training on the dummy horse, the gunners were finally let loose at the real thing:

> A rough riding school was made near the camp in the open and various jumps improvised. It was here that I first rode over a jump and first found it rather difficult, falling off quite a few times in the

first stages but as time went by becoming more efficient and eager to have a go at higher and more difficult obstacles. A lot depended on one's mount, we did not ride the same horse but had to cope with whatever was detailed for us. The conditions were rough but I think encouraged greater efficiency.

There was also specialist training in the different disciplines of artillery such as gun laying, observation and signalling. Gunner Whitehouse was selected for training as part of brigade training for signallers.

Signallers were the so-called 'nerves' of the artillery and were chosen from the more intelligent and most promising material. It was a long course of quite six months at the end of which both qualified and trainees had to undergo an examination. The qualified had a month refresher course before the exam. It was most important that signallers should be capable and up to the mark, their function being so important to artillery.[22]

Those on courses were generally exempt from parades and picquets while undergoing training but continued with other types of training such as riding instruction and gunnery.

We had lectures most days and endless hours of flag drill, morse and semaphore had to be learned and the various means of using it. The training was very thorough and it sunk in from endless repetition . . . The apparatus we used then consisted of Flags, large and small, Heliograph, Lamp, Shutter, Field telephone (buzzer and speech). We were taught elementary electricity so that we could understand the circuits of the telephone and find faults to maintain it. We went out on various schemes and exercises to put our training to practical test. The months went by and the time came for the examination. Old and young signallers joined for the final tests, there were first and second class signallers, according to percentage of marks gained. One man in my quarters with quite a few years' service made a few bets backing me to get a first, something regarded as unusual for a young chap. This fellow was a signaller and had seen me during the final stages. He won his bets because when the results were posted on the order board, much to my embarrassment and pleasure I was in the first few being about third in the whole brigade as far as I can remember. I think some of the older men thought I was a bit of a freak, but a few days were enough to eliminate such thoughts. I was now entitled to wear the crossed flags on my lower sleeve being a qualified signaller.[23]

Horse training also played an intrinsic part of sporting activity in barrack life with the various mounted arms of the British Army – in particular the artillery and the Army Service Corps – competing in various mounted competitions such as tent pegging and jumping. These sports were a crucial part of military life and the same traditions continued into the Irish army until the horse lost its prominence with the mechanisation of the army in the late 1930s.

Inspections and Parades

The commander in chief of the army in Ireland visited Kildare on 17 April 1902 to inspect the new barracks in operation before inspecting the facilities at Naas.[24] The senior veterinary officer of the Seventh Division carried out the following inspections in 1904:

11 Hussars, Curragh	2 December 1904
6 Dragoons, Dublin	3 December 1904
19 Hussars, Curragh	6 December 1904
Royal Horse and Field Artillery, Newbridge	7 December 1904
Royal Field Artillery, Kildare	9 December 1904
60 Battery, Royal Field Artillery, Ballinrobe	13 December 1904

In May 1905, Colonel H.A. Rochford, Inspector of the Royal Horse and Royal Field Artillery carried out artillery inspections throughout the Irish Command.

The schedule included:

VIII Brigade, Newbridge	10-11 May 1905
XXXIII Brigade, Kildare	12-13 May 1905
XXXI Brigade, Kildare	15-16 May 1905

The Duke of Connaught reviewed the troops stationed at the Curragh, Newbridge and Kildare. The parade was under the command of Major-General Sir G. de C. Morton. The total force of 129 officers and 1,785 non-commissioned officers and men included 11 Hussars (317 officers and men), 19 Hussars (268 officers and men), XIV Brigade RHA (145 officers and men), XXXI, XXXIII and XXXV Brigades, RFA (427 officers and men), 54 and 57 Companies RE (158 officers and men), 4 Battalion, Lancashire Fusiliers (528 officers and men), and Army Service Corps (60 officers and men).[25]

CHAPTER 5

MILITARY DISCIPLINE, CRIME
AND PUNISHMENT

This is to command you to whom this warrant is
addressed to execute the said order against the said
Person as follows:- To deliver the said Thomas Bowers [sic]
gunner in the 132 Battery RFA Kildare into the custody of
his commanding officer.

PETTY SESSION DISTRICT OF RATHANGAN, FEBRUARY 1904

Non-commissioned officers and men of the Royal Field Artillery in dress uniform at
Kildare, 1902. (Author's collection)

M ilitary discipline was an adjustment for many men and some found themselves in trouble more often than others. Frederick James Banks of Trowbridge joined the army at Cardiff on 7 December 1902 and was posted to 138 Battery, Royal Field Artillery at Kildare with the rank of Driver. He found himself in front of the military authorities on numerous occasions.

3 May 1903: Absent from sick lines when stablesman
Driver Banks was given three days CB (confined to barracks) for this offence. His next offence was over the Christmas period 1903 when he most likely went home for a few days but did not get back to barracks on time, arriving over twelve hours late.

> 31 December 1904: Overstaying furlough from 10 p.m. 31.12.04 till 10.10 a.m. 1.1.05 (about 12 hours, 20 minutes.)

He was admonished for this offence and Captain Head took two days pay from him as punishment. His next offence cost him seven days confinement to barracks (CB).

> 2 March 1905: I. Mistreating a horse II. Making an improper reply to a NCO – 7 days CB

The combination of offences meant that his next offence went before the brigade commander, Lieutenant-Colonel Jackson, and he forfeited a good conduct badge as a consequence.

> 29 March 1905: I. Making an improper reply to a NCO II. Volunteering for the Guard Room – 8 days CB

Driver Banks improved his behaviour after this and did not have any further charges against him.

Another gunner who found himself in trouble at Kildare was 21585 Gunner Thomas Bowes, a 19-year-old carter who had enlisted at Hartlepool on 22 January 1902 and was sent to No. 2 Depot Glasgow before being posted to 132 Battery on 27 February 1902. He arrived with them at Kildare when they moved in April 1902. Gunner Bowes had a long list of offences.

19 November 1903: Insolence to a NCO

Witnesses were Sergeant Barker, Acting Bombardier Gade and Battery Sergeant-Major Seymour. He was given ten days CB, which was approved by Major Owen.

30 March 1904: Refusing to obey an order.

Witnesses were Corporal Coy and Acting Bombardier Allan. Gunner Bowes got fourteen days CB. Punishment was approved by Lieutenant-Colonel Dunlop, the brigade commander.

2 August 1904: Overstaying leave from 1 a.m. till 12.45 p.m.

Witness was Bombardier Howden. Major Owen gave him eight days confined to barracks and he forfeited two days pay.

1 April 1903: I. Absent from signalling parade at 2 p.m. II. Drunk at evening stables

Witnesses were Sergeants Mahon, Wilson and Ash. Major White-Thompson gave gunner Bowes seven days confined to barracks.

30 November 1903: Drunk in town about 9.40 p.m.

Witnesses were Corporal Burrell and Acting Bombardier Reeves. Bowes was confined to barracks for five days by Major White-Thompson. Gunner Bowes was also picked up in Rathangan as a deserter by the Royal Irish Constabulary in February 1904 but there is no record of this on his charge sheet.

> Whereas upon the hearing of a complaint, that on Saturday the 27th day of February 1904 at Rathangan, in the said County of Kildare, the said defendant was found to be absent from his regiment without leave.
>
> An Order was made on the 28th February 1904 by the Justice, against the said Gunner Thos Bowes of Kildare RFA to the following effect, viz:- To be delivered up to the custody of his Commanding officer.
>
> This is to command you to whom this warrant is addressed to execute the said order against the said Person as follows:- To deliver the said Thomas Bowers [sic] gunner in the 132 Battery RFA Kildare into the custody of his Commanding officer.
>
> And for this present warrant shall be sufficient authority to all whom it may concern.
>
> Simon Malone
Justice of Said County
This 28th day of February 1904

Desertion was a relatively common occurrence. New recruits were often unprepared for the rigours of military discipline. Drafts of new recruits for units at Kildare were generally obtained from Number 4 Depot in England. The military authorities took a serious view on desertion and rewards were offered for the capture of deserters who were generally locked up following their recapture and returned to their unit. The Royal Field Artillery had only arrived in Kildare two weeks when one gunner deserted in April 1902. He was picked up in Athy, County Kildare by the Royal Irish Constabulary. John Price appeared before M.J. Minch at Athy Petty Sessions charged by Sergeant Ruttell with desertion from 131 Battery stationed at Kildare. He was ordered to be handed over to the military authorities and Sergeant Ruttell was awarded 15 shillings for the capture of a deserter.[2]

Two gunners ended up in Tullamore Gaol for desertion following court martial at the Curragh. John Mackey a 20-year-old groom and soldier with the RFA at Kildare, originally from Dublin, was arrested for 'I. desertion II. loss of kit III. Larceny and IV. Receiving'. He was court martialled at the Curragh on 9 December 1904 and sentenced to seventy-two days with hard labour at Tullamore Gaol.[1] Another deserter, Herbert Parker, age 23 described as an electrician and soldier of Kildare Barracks and originally from Yorkshire, was sentenced to 112 days by a court martial at the Curragh on 20 June 1905 for I. desertion II. loss of kit and III. stealing the property of an officer.[2]

The financial bonus for catching deserters ensured that the Royal Irish Constabulary kept a close eye on suspicious characters. At Sallins railway station in October 1902, Constable Lavelle spotted a man who got off the Kildare train to change for Dublin. He claimed to be John Rae of Newbridge. Constable Lavelle promptly arrested him despite the man's protests until he eventually admitted that he had deserted from the Royal Field Artillery at Kildare. A railway ticket from Kildare to Dublin was found on the man and he was handed over to the military authorities in Naas.[3] Some deserters did manage to evade the constabulary but found that they were not safe in England. Alfred Johnson of Anesbury, Huntingdonshire was charged in September 1903 with being a deserter from the Royal Field Artillery at Kildare[4] while John Storey of North Shields was also arrested in September 1903 and charged with desertion from the Royal Field Artillery at Kildare.[5]

A strange incident was reported in May 1907. While most of the batteries were in the Glen of Imaal on firing practice, it was suggested that the body of a deserter was in the barracks water tank. Personnel in the barracks began drawing water from the town until the tank was drained but no body was found.[6]

Some soldiers, rather than desert, hoped that being convicted for a minor crime would be enough for them to be put out of the army. Driver Frederick Coram, stationed at the barracks, broke the window of Alice Fitzpatrick. Coram admitted to the Royal Irish Constabulary that he had broken the window to get out of the army. He was fined £5. Two of his colleagues appeared before the courts the same day. Drivers Arthur Gardner and Thomas Wilkins were charged with breaking the windows of the post-office.[7] Coram had enlisted as a 15-year-old boy soldier in 1898 and deserted in September 1901 from 132 Battery at Trowbridge. He was tried and convicted for desertion in December 1902 and forfeited all previous service. He was back on duty in February 1903 and moved with his battery to Kildare. In addition to the fine issued by the court at Kildare for breaking a window, the military locked him up for sixty days. He deserted again in September 1903 and served further imprisonment before rejoining his battery. He came to a tragic end as his service file noted that he was killed (accidentally) on duty on 13 September 1905.[8]

One soldier suspected of desertion, Albert Bricknell of 134 Battery was arrested by police in December 1903 in Derby. He successfully argued in court that he was on furlough from Kildare from 2 November to 1 December and had an extension until 5 December although he had lost the paperwork. He went to the railway station to return to Kildare on Friday night but left the train for a moment and it departed without him. There was no point in getting a train on Saturday as no boat sailed to Ireland on a Sunday. Bricknell was released to return to Kildare.[9]

With time on their hands, many men fell foul of the law. The batteries were not long in Kildare before they started to appear before the courts. Gunner Grey appeared before the civilian authorities in July 1902 for stealing three pounds from the adjutant's office. A penknife inscribed with his regimental number was found beside the petty cash box and he was subsequently apprehended in Dublin.

The barrack canteen operated by Sir B. Dickson was broken into and a sum of money and other items were stolen at the beginning of June 1902. The police were called to investigate and Head Constable Roche, together with some constables carried out a search of the barracks: they located the stolen material in a hut and established that the robber had cut himself entering the premises. The Constabulary at Naas were notified and arrested a Yorkshireman named William Shepherd acting suspiciously, who, when examined was discovered to have blood on both of his hands. He was arrested, brought back to Kildare and charged with the robbery.[10]

Two artillerymen from the barracks, William Taylor and Roland Helley, were charged with stealing from the shop of J.J. Moran in Kildare town on 6 February 1903. The men purchased a shirt for 3s 3d and a cardigan for 3s 6d. The shop manager Edward Gallagher parcelled the goods for the men and they ran off with them without paying. Gallagher and a shop assistant, Patrick Conway, chased them. An officer of the battery testified that the men had some offences against them, and they were sentenced to three months imprisonment.[11] A day earlier, two other men of the same battery had stolen two alarm clocks from the premises of Joseph Dunne. Anne Casey, an assistant in the shop, heard a window break and when she went to investigate found a clock missing. Sergeant Naughton, RIC, went to the barracks and Lewis Rankin admitted the offence. In the course of the investigation, William Broadhead also admitted theft of a clock. Both men were sentenced to three months imprisonment. Another gunner, Driver Abel was charged with theft in April 1907:

> A court-martial was held in the Kildare Military Barracks on Monday to investigate a charge brought against Driver Abel of the 137th Battery RFA, for the alleged stealing of a pair of boots from one of his military comrades. Major Hutchinson presided. Mr. Kearns, pawnbroker, Newbridge, gave evidence of the pawning of the boots by defendant who pleaded not guilty. The Court found the defendant guilty and sentence was deferred.[12]

An ex-gunner, named Chadwick, of 137 Battery, was discharged at Kildare on 13 February 1905 as not likely to become an efficient soldier. He was arrested in Mountmellick in May 1906 and charged with obtaining lodgings and food by false pretences and using the name John Delarey and claiming to be the son of a Boer general named Delarey. He was identified by Quartermaster-Sergeant Lee of 137 Battery at Kildare.[13] In 1908, the soldiers' home in the barracks was broken into and a large quantity of goods stolen; and the newsagent's shop of Mrs Malone in the town was broken into with gold and silver taken from the cash box.[14] A pre-war deserter was Edward A. T. Heather (with the regimental number 73613), age 20, born in London and stationed with the RFA at Kildare.

He was handed over to the military authorities on 18 December 1913.[15]

A gunner who suffered under the influence of drink was Patrick Cassidy, aged 19, who broke a window valued at £12, which was the property of Mary Anne Cleary in the town. Cassidy had deserted previously from the army and had served forty-two days detention as a consequence. Judge Barry remarked that the Royal Field Artillery seemed to be above representing their men in court and did not think it worth saying anything about them, whereas a few weeks previously in a case involving a Connaught Ranger, his Colonel, Major and Captain had attended to assist the court. A constable from Kildare testified that Cassidy carried out the crime to get out of the army. The man was sentenced to eight weeks and told to return to the army.[16]

Soldiers were also subject to the same vigorous rules that applied to the local population. A gunner from Kildare, Alfred Hawker, who was visiting friends in Naas was arrested there by Constable McCarthy in Naas for cycling, on 17 August 1910, on the public pavement twenty-five minutes after lighting up time. He was fined three shillings and six pence.[17] Driver Frederick Virtue, stationed at Kildare was brought before Major Thackerry at Naas Petty Sessions in December 1909 for cycling without a light on his bicycle in Naas and giving a false name to the arresting policeman, Sergeant Clarke, who testified that Virtue had ridden up and down the street 'eight or ten times' before he (Clarke) finally caught up with him.[18] Cyclists, who often took to using footpaths to avoid poor road surfaces, would face the local magistrate if caught. Bombardier George Fox was fined 2 shillings and 6 pence, and costs, in August 1906 for riding a bicycle on the footpath in Kildare while Lieutenant Kenneth Mitchell Potter, Royal Field Artillery was fined one shilling and costs for using a motorbicycle after sunset without a lamp attached.[19] Driver Michael Grace, age 21 and a native of Ballinhassig, County Cork stole a bicycle worth £6 in Kildare and appeared before William Thackerry at the Kildare Petty Sessions on 6 October 1910. He was sent to Mountjoy Gaol for six months hard labour.[20] Another gunner at Kildare, Alfred J. King, age 19 from Belfast got a lighter sentence a month earlier when he was charged with stealing a bicycle, tyre and mudguard (check if this is a tyre and mudguard for a bicycle, as distinct from three separate items; and if so the punctuation needs amendment) worth 7/6 and was sentenced to one calendar month with hard labour in Mountjoy Gaol in September 1910.[21]

Suicide was also, unfortunately, a common occurrence. An inquest was held in the barracks in 1910 following the tragic death of a soldier who killed himself with a rifle.

> A very deliberate suicide took place at Kildare Barracks last Thursday, when a corporal wheeler of the Royal Field Artillery, named Peter Merron, shot himself through the heart. It would appear that Merron placed a rifle in a vice in his workshop, and removed his boots and outer clothing, after which he opened his shirt front, and having pointed the rifle at his breast, pulled the trigger with his toe.

The inquest was presided over by Dr Kenna, Coroner for South Kildare with Dr L.F. Rowan and Captain Irwin, Royal Army Medical Corps in attendance. The coroner noted that this was the sixth or seventh similar inquest that he had attended and added that no one ever seemed to know where the victims got the ammunition. Corporal John Crombie identified the body and advised the inquest that he had found Gunner Merron with his boots off.

Gunner George Cricheton, RFA, gave evidence that:

> The deceased slept in the same room with him, and in the next bed. He last saw him at 5.12 that morning, and Corporal Merron was then up and dressed. Witness thought it was a bit strange, and rather early to see him getting up, but did not speak. Witness knew him well, as far as soldiering was concerned, and never noticed anything strange about him. He did not complain of any severity or anything of that kind. He was a good soldier, and was never drunk.

Constable O'Grady of the Royal Irish Constabulary at Kildare remarked that he examined the box of the deceased, where he found several letters, but they were only the usual letters from the man's mother and sisters in London. There was nothing in them that would tend to throw any light on the act of the deceased. Peter Merron's military file also survives. It confirms that he had enlisted at Woolwich in December 1899. He had an exemplary service record and was with 140 Battery. The file simply notes 'Died at Kildare 11 Aug 1910 (Gunshot wound self inflicted)'. The register of Mountjoy Gaol also records a soldier from Kildare Barracks. John Parker Price, a 30-year-old army private [sic] with the Royal Field Artillery, regimental number 26824, was sentenced to twelve months hard labour on 19 June 1912 at the Kildare assizes for attempting to 'commit suicide by cutting his throat with a razor'.[22] Drownings were also, unfortunately, common. Drivers Francis Holland, Evans and Daiken went for a swim at Ardenode on the river Liffey on 11 July 1910. Driver Holland stumbled on a rock and drowned and his body was recovered later by Lieutenant Maxwell.[23] Of course crime and tragedy were not exclusive to the military. There was a murder in Kildare town on 2 January 1904 when John Kelly killed his wife. He was executed at Kilkenny on 15 April 1904.

A number of gunners at Kildare were also convicted of homosexual acts, which were illegal in the early twentieth century. Two gunners from Kildare barracks appeared before the Naas quarter sessions on 17 October 1911 and were charged with 'attempt to commit buggery'. Both men were sentenced to three years penal servitude and were sent to Mountjoy Gaol. Another gunner was convicted of buggery in July 1914 but got the lighter sentence of three months in Mountjoy.

One gunner who was on duty over the Christmas period in 1913 was courtmartialled for being missing from duty. Sergeant Henry Heffernan was charged with 'failing to appear at the place of parade duly appointed by his commanding officer on the 25 December'. Major Wilson RFA acted as President of the court and Sergeant Heffernan had a solicitor, Mr M.J. Crowe defending. Lieutenant M.H. Monckton testified that he was barrack orderly on 25 December and went to see the horses fed at 3 p.m. and 4.30 p.m. Sergeant Heffernan was absent on both occasions, and was was put under arrest the following morning. Heffernan testified that he had performed the duties of battery orderly sergeant on 22, 23 and 24 December and had attended stables at 7 am, 12.30 pm and 3 pm. It transpired that he had served twelve years in the army and had a wife and children in the town. His wife was unwell and there was no one else to mind their eight-month-old baby.[24] The outcome of the case is not known but the military was not known for leniency in the early 1900s.

CHAPTER 6

SPORT AND ENTERTAINMENT

Kildare Town v 137th Battery RFA
Played on the Kildare Garrison ground on 20th instant. The
match lost much of its interest owing to a hastily formed
decision to play it after a deliberate arrangement for its
abandonment had been made, coupled with the scratchy
aspect it assumed through the inclusion of substitutes hastily
summoned for the completion of both teams.

KILDARE OBSERVER, 23 JUNE 1906

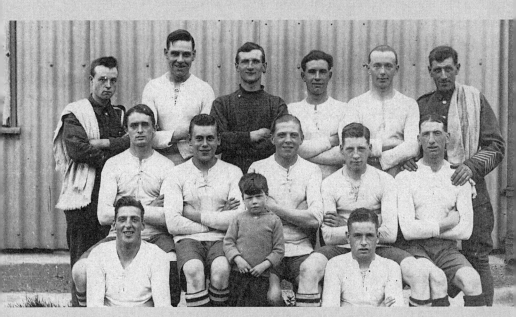

A football team at Kildare, circa 1910. Sport played an important part in military life.
(Author's collection)

Sport formed a major component of army life and the barracks was the location of numerous events including cricket matches, athletics, boxing, association football and military sports particular to army units who relied on the horse, such as tent pegging and jumping competitions.

Association football was a popular recreation and artillery teams in the Irish Command competed for the Knox Challenge Cup, a trophy made from a used shell from the Boer War. At a match in Kildare Barracks in March 1904, the 137 Battery defeated 134 Battery by four goals to nil. The goal scorers were Bombardier Brinklow and Driver Towers. Best for the winners were the brothers Beach, Bombardier Brinklow and Gunner Higgins.[1] Kildare Barracks won the trophy in April 1912 when they defeated a team from the Athlone Royal Field Artillery by one goal to nil.[2]

In November 1905, Bohemians Football Club travelled to Kildare to play against the Barrack team. They arrived two men short and took substitutes from the Royal Artillery. The Artillery team won two goals to nil.[3] There were also opportunities to play in the Irish Command completion. In the 1909–10 competition, the XLVII Brigade at Kildare made good progress represented by Sheldrake, Morgan, Hale, Rogers, Mitchell, Williamson, Pye, McKenzie, Jones, Long and Morgan.[4] A newspaper columnist had some comments on the refereeing of Mr G.H. Impey of the Royal Sussex Regiment when Artillery's two goals to nil win over the Royal Engineers from the Curragh was assisted by two offside goals. In the third round of the 1912 competition, played at Kildare, the Connaught Rangers defeated the XXVI Brigade RFA Kildare by two goals to one. The reporter commented that 'with the referee, I would not agree at all at times, but I suppose his position to see the game was better than mine'.[5] Boxing was also popular in the army. At an event held in the Riding School in January 1911, Captain H. Webber, Battery Sergeant-Major A. Wark and the 141 Battery organised a boxing tournament.[6] The highlight of the event was the six-round bout in which Driver Pindar (141 Battery, Kildare) knocked Driver Murphy (RFA Athlone) out with a right hook to the jaw. A well-known boxer 'Sandie' McKillop served with the artillery in Kildare but died in a mine explosion in England in November 1905.[7]

A cricket ground was opened in the barracks in June 1906 and the first match was between the XXXII Brigade at the Curragh and the XXXVI Brigade stationed at Kildare.[8]

> XXXII Brigade v XXXVI Brigade
>
> This, the first match played by the 36th Brigade since the concentration of its batteries at Kildare, was played at the Curragh District Cricket ground on the 6th instant. The sides were not fully representative owing chiefly to the absence of Major Hutchinson from the losing side and of Captain Twidale from the winners' side. Counting these abstentions as of equal importance, it would seem that the 36th Brigade have much the better team. Captain Parsons is undoubtedly an excellent bat, and so is Driver Molloy, and to the batting contributions of these two players, coupled with the excellent bowling performances of the latter, and of Captain Mahon, who owing to an accident was compelled to retire 'hurt' unfortunately failed to demonstrate his fine battling capabilities, the victory of the 36th Brigade is clearly attributable.
>
> XXXVI Brigade
>
> | | |
> |---|---|
> | Captain W. Parsons c Diggle b Graver | 30 |
> | Driver Molloy c Barnes b Graver | 52 |
> | Captain M.H. Mahon c Harrison b Arthurs | 3 |
> | K. Parburby b Arthurs | 1 |
> | Captain E.H. Harper retired hurt | 0 |
> | Gunner Wickens c Harrison b Arthurs | 0 |
> | Gunner Geoghegan c Arthurs b Graver | 19 |
> | FQMS Butler c Harrison b Arthurs | 3 |
> | Corporal Holmes hit wkt b Arthurs | 5 |
> | Gunner Court not out | 0 |
> | Extras | 2 |
> | Total | 112 [sic] |

XXXII Brigade

Captain C.C. Barnes c Geoghegan b Mahon	8
Sergeant Whittle run out	8
J.N. Diggle b Molloy	3
Captain A.H. Harrison b Molloy	37
Major F.A. Elton b Molloy	0
R.T. Hammick c Court b Mahon	1
Gunner Arthurs b Mahon	4
Bombardier Graver b Mahon	1
Gnr Grover b Mahon	
Gunner Patterson run out	0
Bombadier Swinnerd not out	0
Extras	2
Total	64

Army units also played against local teams and Kildare town fielded a team on the opening of the new grounds in June 1906. The first game involving local players was held on 13 June 1906 and the *Kildare Observer* noted the lack of practice in the Kildare side. The 139 Battery played an internal match a week earlier when Major Sandars's side played Mr Boyce's side.[9]

Kildare town v 139 Battery RFA
Played on the Royal Artillery ground, Kildare on 13th inst. The Kildare team showed signs of want of practice, and it is especially regrettable that there is no remedy for that disadvantage, as there is no ground on which practice can be obtained. Their bowling and fielding were by no means to be despised, there being some very creditable analyses in the first named department. F. Burke secured 3 wickets for 20 runs, J. Kelly three for 29, J. Murphy two for 17, and W.H. Gallagher one for thirteen. The work of H. Buxton in the out-field was quite brilliant, whilst that of J. Cosgrove at long leg and cover and C. Heffernan at point was remarkably fine. For the military Gunner Wheeler and Gunner Blick played

good cricket and Corporal Wilkins 5 wickets for 21 and Gunner Dobson 5 wickets for 11, bowled exceedingly well throughout.

Score:

Kildare

T. Harte b Dobson	0
W.H.F. Gallagher c Bond b Wilkins	10
J. Kelly b Wilkins	7
J. Hazlett b Dobson	0
C. Heffernan b Wilkins	0
F. Burke b Dobson	1
J. Murphy b Wilkins	11
C. Burke b Wilkins	3
J. Cosgrove b Dobson	0
H. Buxton b Dobson	0
J. Mahon not out	0
Extras	3
Total	35

RFA

Gunner Wheeler b. Kelly	25
Diver Dobson b F. Burke	1
Gunner Bradford lbw b Kelly	1
Bombardier Bond run out	5
Gunner Philpotts c Heffernan b Murphy	5
Bombardier Roe b Murphy	6
Corporal. Wilkins b F. Burke	4
Gunner Blick c Murphy b F. Burke	18
Gunner Sands c Murphy b Kelly	3
Dr. Fisher st Hazlett b Gallagher	6
Gunner Cooke not out	0
Extras	12
Total	86

The sporting columnist of the *Kildare Observer* was never short of an opinion on sporting matters and the second match that the Kildare town side played was not as well organised:

Kildare Town v 137 Battery RFA

Played on the Kildare Garrison ground on 20th instant. The match lost much of its interest owing to a hastily formed decision to play it after a deliberate arrangement for its abandonment had been made, coupled with the scratchy aspect it assumed through the inclusion of substitutes hastily summoned for the completion of both teams. The chief features were the batting of Lieutenant Walker for the military, the bowling of Kelly for the civilians and the crude fielding of both teams. A finer regard for the game and greater preparation are required than were here vouchsafed.[10]

Kildare Town did not have a cricket team prior to this and attempted to organise a club in the town.

An informal gathering of some of the Kildare players was held, and the question of the formation of a cricket club discussed. The opinion that such a step is desirable in the interests of the town, as well as that of individuals, held predominance. It was conceded that several fitful efforts had been made in the past to establish such a scheme, but that all such had failed to attain fruition through the fact that the question of ground never received its due share of recognition. Putting aside the personal aspect of the question, it is clearly manifest that a community of the importance that the inhabitants of Kildare constitute should not be devoid of the health-giving means of ordinary recreation, whilst it seems distinctly apparent that a cricket ground would have a strong tendency towards attracting people to the town, either to play or to witness matches, and be a valuable help towards the improvement of the town's trade. A meeting is being organized for Tuesday evening next at the Railway Hotel, Kildare, when it is hoped that all who are interested in the scheme will attend and give the benefit of their opinions.[11]

There is no record of what occurred at this meeting but Kildare town fielded a cricket team against Kildangan a few weeks later. It was noted that Kildare town was hampered by the absence of J. Murphy, J. Kelly, C. Burke, P. Talbot and T. Harte. Nevertheless the game was very enjoyable and keenly contested with T. Talbot securing five of the Kildangan wickets for eighteen runs. Kildare won by fifty-two runs to forty-four.[12]

In August 1907, the season ended with a flurry of activity at the cricket ground in the barracks with the gunners from Athlone playing against the Kildare artillery:[13]

RFA Kildare v RFA Athlone
At this match, played at Kildare on 26th inst, the visiting batsmen were impotent before the bowling of Captains Mahon and Bond, the former of whom had the remarkable analysis of 5 wickets for 9 runs, whilst his partner in the attack also performed most creditably by securing 5 for 21. On the other hand, the home batsmen displayed effective opposition to the visitors' attack, and some capital innings were played by Captains Harpur, Mahon and Parsons and Driver Molloy. Score:

RFA Kildare

Lieut Deprey b Richards	0
Sgt Major Risworth b Richards	8
Capt. Bond c Richards b Cheeseman	7
Capt Harrison c Holland b Butler	16
Capt. Parson c Holland b Butler	16
Capt. Harpur b Richards	34
Driver Molloy c Walthall b Soames	29
Lieut. Diggle c and b Butler	12
Capt. Mahon c and b Cheeseman	18
Lieut Gordan c Cheeseman b Richards	14
Sgt Irving not out	2
Extras	11
Total	167

There were also internal barracks matches between the various batteries such as 15 Field Battery RFA v 48 Field Battery RFA in July 1907.

This interesting fixture was contested on the Garrison ground, Kildare on 11th instant, and won by the 48th Battery. The bowling on both sides was of such excellent quality that the batsmen were kept very much in subjection, the only serious resistance being offered by Gunners Geohagan and Harrington on the winning, and Lieut. Gordon on the losing side. Lieut. Gordon and Gunner Stewart [best] for the latter, and Captain Mahon and Driver Molloy [best] for the former.[14]

The teams played against each other a month later in August 1907 with the result reversed, owing to the arrival of a new Captain to the battery:

15 Battery RFA v 48 Battery
The debut of Captain Bond on the team of the Battery which he had recently joined was a fortunate event for his side, as it was his score which practically determined the issue in this match. Lieut. Hall also played excellent cricket for his runs, whilst QMS Coles and Driver Stewart were very helpful. Gunner Stewart's bowling (8 for 47) completed the task of the 15th Battery. For the 48th Battery Gunner Geoghegan, Sergt Irving, and Bombardier Clarke all struggled hard to avoid defeat. It looks as if Captain Mahon's services were much needed by his side, although Sergt Irving (4 for 35) and Bombardier Clarke (5 for 35) were both very efficient substitutes in the bowling department.

15th Battery: 125
48th Battery: 74

The complications of keeping scores in cricket were demonstrated by a report on a match held in 1907:

71 Battery RFA v 135 Battery RFA
The all round form of Bombardier Graver and Lieutenant Wallace, good innings by Bombardiers Deacon and Fox, and some useful

bowling by Gunner Radbourne and Gunner Fox, were the more important features of this game, which was supposed at the time to have been won by the 135 Battery, but which owing to the subsequent discovery of an error in the score book, was found to be a 'draw'.

Score:

71 Battery: 1st Innings, 63; 2nd Innings (8 wickets), 79

135 Battery: 1st Innings, 54; 2nd Innings (8 wickets), 88

The RFA team stationed at Kildare played against County Kildare on a number of occasions, including a draw between the two teams in a twelve-a-side match held at Oldtown, Naas in May 1911 and another draw at Oldtown in July 1911. The Royal Artillery stationed in Ireland also held an annual match again the County Kildare cricket club. In the Regimental Cup held at the garrison grounds on the Curragh in September 1912, fifteen teams participated with a high-scoring final between the RFA Kildare and the RFA Newbridge held on Friday and Saturday, which was a draw. As it was so late in the season, the game was not replayed and the trophy was shared between the teams.[15]

Annual Sports

There were also annual sports days held at the ground behind the barracks:

On the RFA sports ground, Kildare in beautiful weather, the above sports were held yesterday. The prizes were plentiful and valuable, which induced great keenness in the various competitions. During the progress of the events the band of the 3rd Dragoon Guards discoursed a pleasant selection of music, and at the close of the programme the prize winners received their awards from Mrs. C.H. Hutchinson. Details:

Quarter-mile race: 1st prize 15s., Bombardier Smith (134); 2nd, 10s,. Driver Conway (48); 3rd, 5s., Bombardier Hurst (71).

Tent Pegging: 1st prize, 15s., Sergeant Tingley (48); 2nd, 10s., Sergeant Woolmer (48); 3rd, 5s., Bombardier Begrie (136).

100-yards Race: 1st prize, 10s., Bombardier Smith (136); 2nd 5s., Bombardier Hurst (71).

Section Jumping (1 section per battery): 1st prize, £2, 136th Battery, Sergeant Baseley, Bombardier Harrison, Bombardier Begrie, Gunner Parks; 2nd £1, 15th Battery, Driver Sizzey, Bombardier Francis, Bombardier Sims, Saddler Halfnight.

There were also specific artillery competitions with the Knox Rifle Trophy for batteries of Royal Horse and Field Artillery galloping over fences to firing points over distances of 300, 400 and 500 yards. These events were not without risk and Gunner Underhill-Barton of the 112 Battery, RFA was killed at Newbridge on 21 September 1912 when engaged with a number of men of different batteries at an exercise for the forthcoming gun carriage competitions at the annual sports when a sudden jolt caused him to be thrown from his seat to the ground where he was run over by a wheel of the gun carriage and killed instantly.[16] He was interred at the military cemetery at Stepaside on the Curragh.

There was also time for some fun at the annual sports days. Lieutenant W.C. Rait Kerr of the 141 Battery won the donkey race in costume at the All-Ireland Military Athletic Meeting held on the Curragh Cricket ground in June1909.[17] The lieutenant was a native of Rathmoyle, Edenderry. He was killed on 10 November 1914, aged 28 years old while his brother, Sylvester Rait-Kerr, also serving with the Royal Field Artillery, was killed on 13 May 1915 at 27 years old.

For the entertainment of the troops, Elise Sandes established one of her soldiers' homes in the barracks. The superintendents in 1911 were Mary Constance Stoney and Frances Birney. Wherever soldiers served far away from their own homes and had time on their hands, there were invariably problems as young men got into difficulty. Elise Sandes writing in 1915 on the purpose of her soldiers' homes said:

> In our work we come very close up to drunkenness and sin. The soldier's temptations are terribly real to us, and we know that he cannot stand the test of these fierce temptations, that he is not safe in the hard battle of life unless he is linked on to the Divine Guide and Helper.[18]

Officers also participated in outings with the Kildare Hunt, not without incident. Mr Wanklyn stationed at the barracks broke his collarbone when he fell off a horse while riding with the Kildare Hounds at Celbridge in February 1910.[19] The Hounds meets in January 1903 included one at the Royal Field Artillery Barracks, Kildare.[20] One of the last acts held in the barracks during the British years was a meeting of the Kildare Hounds in April 1922. For soldiers, the Curragh racecourse offered a source of entertainment. Betting on horses in the town was illegal and became the subject of a court case in December 1907 when Bridget, John and Charles Bourke were charged with using a premises for betting on horses. There was some debate in court as to how it was legal to bet at the Curragh racecourse but not in Kildare town. The case was subsequently dismissed.[21]

The most popular sport amongst the civilian population in Kildare at the time was Gaelic Football. The local team, Round Towers Gaelic Football Club, did not have its own grounds at this time. On one occasion, in April 1914, no pitch was available for a number of matches due to be played in the South Kildare League hosted by the local club. The organising committee contacted the British military:

> Mr. Bob Byrne (Chairman) and Shaun McCormack (Hon. Sec.), as a last resort agreed to wait on Regimental Sergeant Goble who is in charge of recreational grounds attached to the RFA Barracks. Having explained their predicament, he, in sportsmanlike manner gave the key of the field just outside the town. Your many readers, even the most bigoted, will surely appreciate the broadminded action of the Saxon soldier.[22]

As a sign of impending changes and conflict in the country, there was little gratitude from the author of the letter, John Donnelly, Claregate Street:

> We must keep on hoping that some of our many land holders will see their way at least to granting a field for matches arranged by the county committee south Kildare League on a Sunday fixed for Kildare; and by so doing would obviate the necessity of our enterprising Gaels from humiliating themselves to the British Army.

The service records of soldiers and other institutional records often give descriptions of tattoos on soldiers. No publication on a military barracks could omit mention of some of these descriptions:

James Seddon, age 19 (enlisted: 1908) 'Buffalo Bill's head with American flags'
Samuel Lester, age 21 (enlisted: 1910) '4 swallows and butterfly'
Patrick Byrne, age 27 (enlisted: 1921) 'jockey on horse'

'The Duke of Killicrankie'

In March 1914, on the eve of the political crisis that was the Curragh Incident, officers of the Royal Field Artillery took part in a performance of 'The Duke of Killicrankie' at the Palace Theatre, Kildare. The concert was organised by George Maxwell, District Inspector, Royal Irish Constabulary, to raise funds for an X-Ray machine for the Kildare Infirmary.[23] Major Graham Dooner, Royal Field Artillery was stage manager assisted by QMS-Wheeler Slater 80 Battery, Royal Field Artillery and Private Norman of the Manchester Regiment. His wife played the difficult part of 'Lady Henrietta Addison' in the performance while Mrs Duffus played the role of 'Mrs. Mulholland'. The male characters were played by:

'Duke of Killicrankie'	Captain Trueman, Manchester Reg
'Henry Pitt Welby, M.P.'	E.G. Earle, RFA
'The Postman' and 'Mrs. Macbayne'	R. MacLeod RFA
'Macbayne'	R. Scott-Watson RFA
'Butler'	J. Dallas-Edge RFA
'Footman'	J.H.K. Richardson RFA

The reporter noted that Mr Scott-Watson RFA spoke glorious Scotch and was a marked success and that the music was supplied by the 'Beechgrove Orchestra'. The attendance on the night included Sir Charles Fergusson, General Headlam and General Rolt.

CHAPTER 7

THE CURRAGH INCIDENT: 1914

In view of the possible active operations in Ulster, all officers domiciled in Ulster will be allowed to disappear from Ireland till the operations are over. Any officer who, from conscientious reasons, refuses to take part in these operations will send in an application by 10 a.m. tomorrow.

SECOND-LIEUTENANT W. SCOTT-WATSON. 20 MARCH 1914

Officers and men of 80 Battery, Royal Field Artillery in the Glen of Imaal including Lieutenant Roderick MacLeod. (Courtesy of the Council, National Army Museum, London)

The Curragh Incident, or Mutiny as it is often called, caused tensions to emerge in the British army amongst those who had sympathies with the unionist population who did not want to be part of an Ireland governed under Home Rule from Dublin.

Despite a series of negotiations between the Irish nationalist leader John Redmond and the Ulster unionist leader Sir Edward Carson during the course of 1913–14, unionists were against the implementation of Home Rule in Ireland. The bill to implement Home Rule was pushed through the British House of Commons in January 1913 and designed to become law in June 1914. When the bill reached its second reading on 9 March 1914, Carson opposed it and maintained that Ulster must be excluded. In 1913 a volunteer force had been formed in Ulster and nationalists in the south had begun to form their own force. With the threat of civil disturbance and possible civil war in the case of the bill being implemented, the British troops that formed the Irish Command faced the prospect of having to enforce law and order in Ulster.

A document circulated by the War Office in March 1914, outlining what would happen if the army had been requested to move on Ulster to maintain law and order and implement Home Rule, was circulated and interpreted as an order to move. A provision was included to allow officers who were domiciled in Ulster to disappear, while anyone else who refused to carry out orders would be dismissed from the service. General Hubert Gough, commanding officer of the III Cavalry Brigade at the Curragh, outlined his objection to the scenario presented and declared that he would resign rather than carry out military operations in Ulster. While the cavalry were the main focus of the affair, the impact was also felt at Kildare Barracks.

On 20 March 1914, the men of the XV Brigade and VIII Howitzer Brigade were confined to barracks and on 21 March, their howitzer shells were prepared, two days' rations were served out, the horses' feed packed, and blankets and kits packed and put on the wagons ready to travel to Ulster. The fear of the army barracks being raided for weapons by either unionists or nationalists prompted an increased level of alertness. Roderick MacLeod wrote to his father in Cambridge to let him know that:

> All our guards now parade with arms and ball ammunition as I believe the authorities are afraid the nationalists might make an attack on the barracks. Up in the north 80% of the Special Reserve are unionists, as all their arms and mobilization equipment are stored up there, the one battalion up there has to provide guards over all the depots. Consequently the wretched men only get every other night in bed. They will probably send more troops from the Curragh.[1]

Roderick MacLeod (1892–1984), who in his later career was involved in the planning of the 1944 D-Day deception, was a second-lieutenant serving with 80 Battery in Kildare at the time and was a witness to the situation. He wrote to his father on 23 March 1914 about the ongoing events:

> You may be interested to hear about everything that has happened but it must be strictly confidential.
>
> On Friday afternoon I returned from playing golf at the Curragh about 6.40. As soon as I arrived in barracks my Major [Birkley] told me that I should have to decide that night whether I would obey orders to march and take part in operations in Ulster. If not, I would have to resign. At 7 we were called to the Colonel's office and we had a document read to us, which it was said was sent from the Army Council and sanctioned by the King. This said:
>
> Officers whose homes were in Ulster would be allowed to 'disappear' provided they took no active part in the operations. Any officer who for conscientious or other reasons objected to service in Ulster would be instantly dismissed the service. All other officers would have to obey implicitly all orders issued them. It further stated that it was hoped that there would be very few

officers who would elect to be dismissed. There were no doubts in the minds of all present that active operations in the field were contemplated.

When the question was put to us 7 out of 15 officers, myself included, elected to be dismissed. Some others might have gone but could not afford to go as dismissal would entail loss of pension and all other privileges. We were given till 8 next morning (Saturday) to reconsider our decisions. We discussed the matter till late that night but I did not alter my views.[2]

An officer who took a different view was Second-Lieutenant W. Scott-Watson. He wrote home from Kildare on 20 March 1914:

This evening I and the other officers of our Regiment were called upon to make the most momentous decision of our lives. We were assembled in the Colonel's office, and he read out the following proclamation from the War Office. In view of the possible active operations in Ulster, all officers domiciled in Ulster will be allowed to disappear from Ireland till the operations are over. Any officer who, from conscientious reasons, refuses to take part in these operations will send in an application by 10 a.m. tomorrow. Any officer doing so will be dismissed the service. This we are all agreed is the greatest outrage that has ever been perpetrated on the Service. We have had to make this decision without any opportunity of discussing it with our people.

The words 'domiciled in Ulster' have been underlined, and under penalty of court-martial our Colonel has to state whether a man is domiciled in Ulster or not.

I had hardly time to wire for your opinion, so I have decided to carry on. Seven in my Brigade have decided to refuse, and will probably be dismissed the Service either tomorrow or very shortly. I have decided to stay on for the following reasons: Although, as you know, my sympathies are absolutely with Ulster, I think that at a time like this the Army must stick together. If we once start to disintegrate the Service, then goodbye to the Empire and anything else that matters.

Moreover, in case of strike duty, the men whose sympathies are fairly obviously with the strikers have to carry on and do their duty, so that now it is up to us to do the same.

I hope and pray that I have done the right thing, but anyway it is now too late for anything else, for if you don't avail yourself of this opportunity of quitting, and then later on you want to do so, it means a court martial, with a possibility of being shot.

Altogether, it is the most diabolically ingenious thing that has ever been brought in. What we especially detest is being dismissed, and not allowed to resign.[3]

Major-General Sir Charles Fergusson was involved in discussions with members of the General Staff and in preparing plans to bring troops from England to deal with unrest in Ulster. In the surviving correspondence of the period, he gave a detailed account of his actions and the events of March 1914. On 25 March 1914 Fergusson wrote from his headquarters at Ballyfair, Curragh that following the initial action by the officers of the III Cavalry Brigade, their counterparts based at Curragh, Newbridge and Kildare had decided to follow the lead and threaten to resign their commissions. Fergusson visited the various units under his command and addressed the officers and men of the Artillery at Kildare and Newbridge.

Roderick MacLeod in his correspondence from Kildare was able to give a full account of a meeting with General Headlam on 21 March 1914:

General Headlam addressed all the Artillery Officers at Kildare in the Mess. He said that he hoped no one would apply to be dismissed. He said that soldiers had sometimes to shoot down strikers with whom they sympathised, and it would be a bad example if we did not do so when ordered.

Major-General Fergusson addressed the officers at Kildare after Headlam. He advised the officers that:

He was a Conservative and all his sympathies were with the Ulster people. But he was going to see the thing through, and he hoped we would all do the same. He had seen General Sir A. Paget the day before and had it from him that the notice we had on Friday came from the Army Council. General Fergusson said the ultimatum was an insult to any officer, but he did not know who was responsible. Four divisions were to be sent to Ulster. We were to stand as much punishment as possible without replying. All strategic points had already been seized. If the Army split up on this question, it would be the end of the Empire.[4]

To the ordinary gunner, the event was of little consequence:

There was a bit of trouble in Ulster in about June or July of 1914 and we were put on the alert and partially mobilised. I remember there was some unusual activity in connection with the guns and ammunition in our sheds. The ins and outs of this matter were not of great interest to us but we knew something was going on. It seemed to blow over and other events were soon to happen eclipsing the Ulster Rising. War was coming![5]

History records that the army were never requested to march on Ulster and none of the officers were forced to make the choice. There never was a mutiny but it was not the last time Kildare town would play a role in national policy only the next time, there would be real mutiny and not a British soldier in sight.

CHAPTER 8

THE FIRST WORLD WAR

A couple of large detachments of the Royal Field Artillery
left Kildare Barracks early on Sunday and Monday
mornings, they on each occasion being played out of
the town by the band of the Kildare Volunteers, which
rendered such tunes as 'Come back to Erin', etc.

KILDARE OBSERVER, 22 AUGUST 1914

The 25 Mobile Section, Army Veterinary Corps, part of the Tenth (Irish) Division
formed at Kildare in early 1915. (Courtesy of Paddy Newman)

On 4 August 1914, Britain declared war on Germany and by 7 August the first elements of the British Expeditionary Force had landed in France. The onset of the war brought great excitement to the town. Military leave was cancelled and military intelligence occupied Kildare railway station. Two foreigners were arrested at Kildare as spies, and on 14 August an aeroplane passed over Kildare Barracks and hovered for a while before proceeding in the direction of Tully, causing quite a stir throughout the town. It was reported that a large airship had been seen flying over the Curragh Camp, and had alighted in a field at Tully, the property of Colonel Hall-Walker and which is situated about a mile outside the town. The available constabulary, Head-Constable Daly, Sergeant Ryan, Constable McWeeney, Constable Morrissey and Constable Matthews turned out immediately and cycling quickly to Tully where the aeroplane had been seen alighting, they could find no trace of the machine or its occupants. A large number of the National Volunteers proceeded to Tully and scoured the fields in the neighbourhood, but could find no trace of the mysterious aeronauts who had disappeared.[1] Mr Lynch of Tully claimed to have seen the aeroplane as did a number of other witnesses who saw it fly over Kildare Barracks and the newspaper reported that the local RIC barracks was strengthened and there were increased nightly patrols by the police on all local roads. The South Kildare Agricultural Society abandoned their annual show on 15 August owing to the war and the absence of horses and military from the district.[2]

For the batteries of the Royal Field Artillery at Kildare and Newbridge, the order to mobilise came on 4 August 1914. All leave was cancelled and the different brigades worked to bring the batteries up to strength and to prepare supplies for the impending departure for France.

There were two brigades of the Sixth Division stationed at Kildare: VIII (Howitzer) Brigade consisting of 37, 61 and 65 Howitzer Batteries and XV Brigade consisting of 11, 52 and 80 Field Batteries and being the divisional artillery were under the command of the Sixth Division and would depart for France with them. A diary kept by Colonel F.A. Wilson of the 61 (Howitzer) Battery stationed at Kildare on mobilisation recorded the following:

> 4 August: Orders received by the battery stationed at Kildare to mobilize for active service. The battery at this time was on the higher establishment.
>
> 5 August: Mobilisation equipment issued and marking commenced.
>
> 6 August: All marking and issuing of equipment finished. The battery suffered severely by promotion losing two sergeants and the majority of the battery staff. It is important that in the future the various grades of NCOs for the ammunition column should be maintained in peace.
>
> 7 August: Reservists commenced to join. The gunners are good, drivers indifferent, bad horsemen and unaccustomed to riding, driving for years.

The British Army in mobilisation was a well-disciplined machine, with experienced gunners who had seen action in the Boer War over a decade earlier. Gunner Whitehouse recorded the mobilisation:

> The reserves were called up and very soon our numbers doubled, men were sleeping in all sorts of places including the riding school. Horses were commandeered and many had to be quickly broken into army ways. Things seemed rather chaotic for a few days but were soon sorted out. The various units were soon made up to war strength in men and horses and all unnecessary kit was handed into the stores. We only needed service stuff, all the ornamental gear was handed in and goodness knows what happened to it.
>
> All those posh helmets, jackboots and tight fitting gold red and blue uniforms suddenly became surplus, not required. We stood up in most of our kit. A spare pair of socks, a field dressing, our iron rations only to be used in an emergency on orders from an officer, these were the important items now.[3]

A diary for one of the XV Brigade units, the 80 Field Battery, records in detail the changes in personnel at Kildare as the unit was brought up to strength with promotions, additions and men transferring to other units in the early days of the war, and it demonstrates the momentous changes that occur on mobilisation.[4]

1st Day of Mobilisation
Joined Artillery Headquarters 5/8/1914 out of rations 6/8/1914
at Newbridge
32851 Gunner M. Colgan
72694 Gunner T. Buckley
55405 Driver S. Allen
71232 Driver G. Kennerley

Joined Brigade Headquarters at Kildare 5/8/1914 out of rations
6/8/1914
73619 Dvr. Taylor Brigade
       Trumpeter attached
70085 Gnr. Cairns, E.
66294 Gnr. Evans, J.
72891 Gnr. Gilbert, A.G.
69964 Gnr. Goldswain, S.W.
73615 Gnr. Baker, E.H.
72191 Dvr. Hannon, M.
74139 Dvr. Eden, G.G.
46134 Cpl. Lawlor, R.W.

Promotions with effect from 5/8/1914
24538 Cpl. Hughes, J. to Sergeant
24518 Cpl. Patchett, W. to Sergeant
56936 Bdr. Reilly, C. to Corporal

Joined Brigade Ammunition Column 6/8/1914
22754 Sgt Edmundson, G.R.
24518 Sgt Patchett, W.

56936 Cpl. Reilly, C.
69092 Gnr. Robb, W.
67772 Gnr Tanner, W.C.
67040 Dvr. Flemmington, G.T.
73621 Dvr Thorn, W.

The first officer transferred to join 80 Battery RFA with effect from 6/8/1914 was Captain Higgon. His groom and servant, Driver Sharpe, was posted from 69 Battery to 80 Battery on the same date.

56934 Lance Bombardier Cocking rejoined Battery from Gymnastic Course 5/8/1914

Captain A.W. Bartholomew left 80 Battery to join 5 Divisional Headquarters, Newbridge, as Staff Captain 5/8/14

55755 Driver Tilbury, A. classified 1st class Driver, and granted 1st Class proficiency pay at 6d per diem, with effect from 7/8/14.

51501 Driver Butler. T rejoined bty from furlough 4/8/14

68514 Bombardier Hemmingway, C classified 1st class gunner and layer, granted 1st class pay at 6d per diem with effect from 7/8/14

66870 Trumpeter S.W. Swaine, appointed Trumpeter with effect from 7/8/14

62308 Trumpeter E.A. Jarvis mustered driver, on attaining age of 18

29151 Corporal E. Shuttlebottom promoted Sergeant with effect from 7/8/14

51288 Bombardier J. Thendall promoted Corporal

68514 Bdr. Hemmingway, P. posted to 52nd Bty RFA with effect from 7/8/14

52185 Dvr. Dalton, F. posted to 26th Bde RFA Aldershot as Fitter, effect from 5/8/1914

Joined 80th Battery RFA, ASC Reservists, 7/8/14

25453 Dvr. Devaney, J.

26231 Dvr. Thuose, J.

20412 Dvr. Parkinson, reservist admitted Curragh hospital 7/8/14

The following men were ordered to stay at Kildare as a base detail, because they were sick or under 19 years of age, with effect from 11 August 1914. The British Expeditionary Force did not initially allow those under 19 to serve overseas, although this would change quickly.

72919 Gnr. Charnich, hospital
74112 Gnr Moody, R. under 19 years of age
75899 Gnr. Meyler, T. under 19 years of age
78077 Dvr. Gunn
20412 Dvr. Parkinson
64418 Dvr. Hargreaves
39303 Dvr Robson
62308 Dvr. Jarvis

Another gunner was left as a base storeman at Kildare with effect from 4 August 1914:
3927 Gnr. Christopher Base Storeman

Three more gunners were dispatched from the VI Reserve Brigade at Glasgow to Kildare to bring the unit up to strength, arriving on 8/8/14:

54118 Corporal Leslie
59131 Bombardier Meuir
59251 Bombardier Sparkes

60645 Gnr. Foster joined 80th Battery RFA 10/8/14, in exchange for No. 68649 Gunner Snelling, A.T. transferred to 1st Reserve.
52445 Lance Bomdardier Glover J.B. promoted Bombardier
56934 Lance Bombardier Cocking, T. promoted Bombardier
With effect from 11/8/14.

30372 Gnr. Bland posted to 80th Bty
43069 Gnr. Brierley posted to 80th Bty
With effect from 11/8/14 reserve men from the Officer in command detail.

One of these men, Gunner Brierley, would be noted as killed in action just two weeks later.

> Private Cochrane 11th Hussars attached to 60th Bty for rations from 12/8/14
> 42719 Gnr. Blois, J.S. transferred to 80th Bty from OC i/c Details
> 45865 Gnr. Bell, R. transferred to 80th Bty from OC i/c Details
> 51501 Dvr. Butler, R. admitted hospital on 14/8/14
> 46295 Bombardier Hoyler admitted to hospital 15/8/14
> 31221 L/Bdr Hayes promoted Bombardier with effect from 15/8/14

As the 80 Battery was now on active service, any misdemeanors that occurred were treated very seriously. Corporal Leslie who had arrived at Kildare on 8 August 1914 was reduced to the rank of gunner for I. Neglect of duty whilst in charge of the dismounted party and II. Absence.

On 16 August 1914, the officers and men of the 11, 52 and 80 Batteries of the Royal Field Artillery, which together formed the XV Brigade, left for France with the British Expeditionary Force. The *Kildare Observer* recorded that:

> A couple of large detachments of the Royal Field Artillery left Kildare Barracks early on Sunday and Monday mornings, they on each occasion being played out of the town by the band of the Kildare Volunteers, which rendered such tunes as 'Come back to Erin', etc. Though it was 2 o'clock on Sunday morning, nevertheless a large crowd of Kildare townspeople assembled to cheer them off and this was repeated on Monday morning at 7 o'clock. Such warm demonstrations must have helped to bring gladness to the hearts of those men who were going forth to defend our nation's right, and also to their wives and relatives from whose presence they have been called for an indefinite period.[5]

The departure of the troops left the barracks virtually deserted until new drafts of volunteers were recruited to form new artillery batteries in the barracks during the course of the war. The mixed political feeling that was emerging in Ireland at the time was evident when the Irish Volunteers had to place a notice in the newspaper in respect of the use of their band at such an occasion:

Irish Volunteers Kildare Branch – The committee of the above unanimously passed the following resolution at their weekly meeting on the 5th inst., and directed that copy of same be sent to the Press for publication: 'That although we have no control over the Kildare Band, we thoroughly approve of their playing off the military from Kildare on the 16th and 17th inst.'[6]

The XV Brigade marched out of Kildare on 16 August and camped at Rathcoole, County Dublin 22 miles away. On 17 August they marched into Dublin to the North Wall where 52 and 80 Batteries were loaded onto the *SS Cornishman* and sailed for Le Havre. Gunner Whitehouse of the VIII Howitzer Brigade recalled the departure:

I remember riding through the streets of Dublin, people cheering and our horses being rather restive on the cobblestones. We spent the night on Phoenix Park sleeping on our groundsheets under the open sky, beneath our greatcoats.

Gunner 57867 Hannon, 80 Battery decided that soldiering was not for him and deserted in Dublin before his unit embarked. He was not the only soldier from Kildare to desert during the war. John Dwyer, a 29-year-old, originally from Manchester and stationed with the RFA at Kildare and with the regimental number 90792 was picked up by the authorities on 10 May 1915, was brought to Mountjoy Gaol and handed over to the military authorities on 18 May 1915.[7] Cornelius Groucott, aged 31 and born in Stafford, was arrested in Dublin on 19 April 1915 for being absented from His Majesty's army and was handed over to the military on 23 April 1915.[8] Discipline was now a priority and gunners were severely punished for military crimes. Trumpeter S.N. Swaine, regimental number 66870 was given Field Punishment No. 1 section B for being absent from 6p.m. on 19 August until 8p.m. on the same evening, a mere two hours, by Captain Higgon. Gunner H. Hazell, number 72912 and

Gunner A. Hitchcock, number 67766 forfeited two days pay for being absent from 9 p.m. on 23 August until 10.40 a.m. on 24 August and both were given Field Punishment No. 1, Section B. Field Punishment No. 1 involved being tied to an immoveable object – often the wheel of a gun – for long periods of time.

Whitehouse recorded his unit's departure from Ireland:

> Next morning we were roused early, had breakfast, our last on British soil for many a day, and marched to the docks soon becoming involved in embarking on to a troop ship called 'The Crown of Toledo'. The horses were slung aboard. It was quite exciting to see them lifted high into the air by crane and gently dropped aboard where they were soon tied up to lines in the hold, watered and fed. It was surprising how quickly and smoothly everything was done without any fuss. Discipline and drill were responsible.[9]

First Action and Casualties

The XV Brigade suffered one of the first British casualties of the war on 21 August 1914 when, on reconnaissance at Le Cateau, 63852 Bombardier James William Ketteridge, 11 Battery, was shot by the French in a 'friendly fire' incident. He was married at Kildare Parish Church in 1914 and his first daughter Rosary Annie Le Cateau Ketteridge was born in Kildare on 20 December 1914. He had arrived in France with 11 Battery on 19 August 1914. The battery suffered many casualties in action ten days later at the Battle of Le Cateau. On 26 August 1914, the 11 Battery lost Lieutenant Coghlan, Bombardier Jarman and Gunner Mackay. The 52 Battery lost Sergeant Woolger, Corporal Hyde and Gunners Fry, Lake and Lyons. Their commanding officer, Major P.W.B. Henning, was wounded in the leg during the Battle of Le Cateau.

An account of the action and the death of Captain Buckle of 11 Battery was reported in the *Aberdeen Journal* of 17 December 1914.

> The death is announced as having taken place on 4th October at St. Vincent Hospital, Duisberg, in Germany, of Captain Henry Buckle, 11th Battery, Royal Field Artillery. Captain

Buckle received a wound in an action on 26th August, in which he greatly distinguished himself. The battery put eight German guns out of action, but the fighting was so severe that the major, three subalterns, the quartermaster-sergeant and sergeant-major were killed, wounded, or missing. He stayed to the last, and had the satisfaction of completing the task set the battery. He was then badly hit by a bullet, and he, with many other wounded was subsequently captured by the Germans. Blood poisoning supervened, with fatal result, the exposure and long journey to hospital probably having unfortunate consequences. Deceased was 34 years of age. He saw considerable service in the South African war, 1900-02, including the actions at Johannesburg, Diamond Hill, and Wittebergen. For that campaign he had the Queen's medal with four clasps and the King's medal with two clasps. His battery was at Kildare when the war broke out. He was the eldest son of Mr. Henry Buckle, Burma Commission and the late Emma Buckle, and, as the nephew of Mrs. George, Aibyn Lodge, was a frequent visitor to Aberdeen.[10]

Captain Buckle was prominent on the social circuit in pre-war Kildare, playing with the Kildare Lawn Tennis Association and attending numerous functions in the area.

The 80 Battery lost Gunners Brierly and Grant and reported at least 36 men wounded on the same day, including their commander Major R.A. Ohrley. More were killed the next day and many more would be killed over the coming years in the conflict on the Western Front. One gunner, 76567 John Williams was reported in the newspaper as stating, in hospital, 'I had two horses shot under me, and on the second occasion was scrambling over a trench into safety when I was shot in the thigh.'[11] Corporal Albert Jubb of the 37 Battery was reported by the War Office to be missing on 27 August 1914. His local newspaper reported as follows on his situation on 20 October 1914. 'The last his parents heard from him was that he was with his battery at Kildare, Ireland. Albert Jubb had been in the army six years, and is 26 years old. He was formerly employed by Hull Corporation.'[12] Jubb had gone overseas on 19 August 1914 with his battery as part of the VIII Howitzer Brigade. He had enlisted on 16 April 1909. There was good news for his family as the medal rolls note that he was discharged from the army on 2 March 1919.

Farrier-Sergeant William Sanderson, 80 Battery was awarded the Distinguished Conduct Medal and the Order of St George – a Russian award. The media reported correspondence sent by his commanding officer to William Sanderson's wife: 'Your husband bears a charmed life. He goes about his duty with the bullets following around him like snow.'[13] Sanderson, who was later reported as being a corporal, wrote a letter that was reprinted in the Dundee Courier.[14] 'I am very pleased to say that Sergeant Shufflebottom and myself were congratulated by General Headlam, Fifth Division Artillery for our bravery.' Another gunner who survived the war was Patrick Dalton from Waterford. He served with the VIII (Howitzer) Brigade in India in 1912 and returned to Kildare until the war broke out. He served throughout the war with the Royal Field Artillery, returning to Ireland in 1919.

The Home Front

An advertisement in the *London Times* on 24 September 1914 stated:

> Miss Mary G. Campbell, Riverside, Parkgate, Cheshire, appeals for magazines and illustrated papers for the troops now stationed at Kildare. Lantern slides of interesting places or things would greatly assist. Parcels may be sent as above or to Miss Sandes, Soldiers' Home, Kildare, Ireland.[15]

There was also local support for the artillery units that had been stationed at Kildare on the outbreak of war:

> Kildare ambulance and working guild[16]
> The committee of the above desire to gratefully acknowledge the following additional subscriptions:

Mrs. Mahon (Lackagh Glebe)	£1	0	0
Miss Medlicott	£1	0	0
Mrs. Waller	0	10	0
Mrs. Bratton	0	10	0

Mrs. Neale	0 10	0
Mrs. Logan	0 2	0
Mrs. Morrissey	0 0	6

The committee have already been enabled to forward for the soldiers at the front:- 16 red flannel bed jackets, 17 white do., 8 dozen pairs of socks, 5 dozen pocket handkerchiefs, 6 dozen pillow cases, 13 nightingales, 4 accident jackets, £10 for woollens for the 11th Battery, £5 for woollens for the 37th Battery.

Further subscriptions gratefully received by the Hon. Treasurer, Mrs. F. Bergin, Kildare.

There was a somewhat bizarre incident in Liverpool in September 1914 when Michael Keogh, a postman from Charleville, County Cork was arrested for impersonating a soldier. Keogh testified in the County Magistrates Court in Liverpool that:

> I am not a soldier, although I have these clothes on. I am a civilian postman attached to Charleville, Ireland, and got in company with some artillerymen, who took me to Kildare Barracks and put these clothes on me. I afterwards went to Dublin and came across to Liverpool on a boat. We went into a public-house, where the other man left me.[17]

The Superintendant in Liverpool contacted the military at Kildare who informed him that the prisoner had not enlisted. No charges were brought against Keogh when he confirmed that he now intended to enlist in the army.

The *Kildare Observer* reported in August 1914 that 'in consequence of the departure of troops to the war, numerous families and cottage occupiers find it difficult to provide the means of subsistence. In nearly every street and house vacant rooms can be found, and in many cases the occupiers find themselves penniless.'[18] Kildare did not have to wait long for new units to arrive. With the rapid expansion of the British army in 1914, the creation of six new divisions was authorised in August 1914, including the Tenth (Irish) Division. The Artillery of this division was immediately established at Kildare and Newbridge. The batteries and commanding officers were as follows:

September 1914:

10th (Irish) Division, Divisional Artillery

LV Brigade

Brigade Commander:	Colonel A.H.C. Philpotts	
Brigade Adjutant:	Vacant	
175 Battery	Major Howden	Newbridge
176 Battery	Vacant	Newbridge
177 Battery	Major R. Casement	Newbridge

LVI Brigade

Brigade Commander:	Colonel J.H. Jellett	
Adjutant:	Captain J. Hagan (also Riding Master)	
178 Battery	Major Battine	Kildare
179 Battery	Major W.S. Wingfield	Kildare
180 Battery	Major L.A. Bryan	Kildare

These batteries were part of the Tenth (Irish) Division and were predominantly Irishmen. Ultimately these batteries left for Alexandria, Egypt in July 1915 and on to Gallipoli. Major W.S. Wingfield, battery commander of 179 Battery participated in a concert at Kildare in November 1915.

A man named William Fraher was charged with the theft of nine bandoliers from the barracks and Daniel Molloy was charged with the theft of groundsheets from tents pitched at the Standhouse, Curragh. Both men were acquitted.[19] Gunner Fraher also claimed that he had only left Kildare Barracks three times since he arrived at Kildare and was due to go to the front the next day. He had come from Athlone and was originally from Dublin. Major Thackerry, hearing the case at Kildare Petty Sessions declared: 'There is absolutely no evidence against this man. If we were to shut up everybody on such evidence it would be strange and I might as well be shut up myself in such a case or my friend, General Waldron.'[20] Another gunner, Walter Fry assaulted his superior officer at Kildare. Fry was 28 and originally from Somerset and had the regimental number 47466. He was court martialled at Kildare on 7 January 1915 by Lieutenant-Colonel J.H. Jether and sent to Mountjoy on 10 April 1915.[21]

The primary concern for Kildare was not the war but the loss of business when the Royal Field Artillery went to France. The civil authorities curtailed the opening hours of public houses in Newbridge, Kildare and Kilcullen for the duration of the war, although this restriction was not extended to Naas for an unknown reason and army canteens operated under their own regulations under the control of the military. In May 1915, in Dublin, licensed premises were closed to military personnel at all times by order of the Dublin Metropolitan Police.

> Everyone is anxious that soldiers should be provided with every possible means of enjoying themselves while undergoing training, but this enjoyment does not include laxity, moral or physical, and any pandering to the weakness for drink would be a huge mistake, and as unjust to the soldier as to the nation. It is a pity that similar regulations to those made in Dublin could not be applied everywhere to the cases of drinking by soldiers' wives.[22]

Soldiers in Trouble

One man, born in Kildare but living in Dublin, Daniel Coleman, aged 20, enlisted in the Royal Field Artillery on 29 August 1914 and was sent to the Depot at Athlone. He was then posted to the 179 Battery in his home town of Kildare for training. This battery was formed in August 1914 as part of the divisional artillery of the Tenth (Irish) Division, which was also formed at this time. He found himself in trouble in Kildare when he took an unauthorised visit out of the barracks into town.

> 90855 Gunner Daniel Coleman
> I. Breaking out of barracks
> II. Improperly dressed in town about 10.15am

Witness to the event was Bombardier Leavy, 69 Battery at Kildare. Coleman found himself in trouble again a short time later:

> 90855 Gunner Coleman, 179th Battery, Kildare
> Absent without leave from 12 p.m. 20/09/1914 until found at 11.30 p.m. 23/09 1914.

Witnesses were Corporal Taylor and Sergeant Davis. Coleman was given seven days confined to barracks. Army life was clearly not for Gunner Coleman as he forfeited fourteen days' pay from 14 November 1914 and received twenty-one days imprisonment on 7 December 1914. He never completed the sentence as he was discharged from the army on 21 December 1914. The story of soldiers breaking out of barracks was nothing new and not uncommon for new soldiers who were not accustomed to military life. Three gunners from 176 Battery in training at Newbridge, Gunners James Taylor, Chas Poole and Driver Andrew Johnson went to Naas for a few drinks in early November 1914 and appeared before Colonel De Burgh as a consequence. The men testified that they had just gone out for a ramble and a few drinks, although Lance-Corporal Dooley, RFA Newbridge testified that Johnson was missing a few days. Colonel De Burgh was more concerned about the disgracefulness of publicans serving drink to men without passes during this time of national emergency.[23]

Soldiers' wives received a separation allowance while their husbands were on military service and the incidence of alcoholism amongst women during the war years became an issue of some debate also.

The consumption of alcohol got one old soldier into trouble before the local magistrate in August 1915. With the arrival of the Lancers in Kildare, Major Thackerry inevitably had more soldiers before him at the Kildare Petty Sessions. The unit was only in Kildare a month when Private Daniel J. Cobbe, 5 Lancers was charged with the theft of field boots, spurs and ankle boots, the property of Lieutenant McElwain and the theft of a blanket, the property of the War Department on 6 August 1915.[24] Cobbe sold the spurs to a Lance Corporal Ure, 5 Lancers. Ure handed the spurs over to Lance-Sergeant Goodliff of the squadron office after seeing Cobbe trying to sell a pair of ankle boots to another soldier, which aroused his suspicions. Private John Ryan who was servant to Lieutenant McElwain reported that the items were stolen from the hut occupied by him in the barracks and subsequently Private George Fowler, Regimental Police, searched the kit of Cobbe and found some of the missing items. Daniel Cobbe in his defence, said that this was the first time he was ever in trouble, having served for 13 years, including the South African war and re-enlisted in September 1914, serving in France where he was invalided home blind as a result of continuous wettings. He had no recollection of breaking into the hut as he was drunk at the time. Cobbe, a 46-year-old married Londoner, got off relatively lightly owing to his previous military service and good conduct in the barracks as a storeman and a recommendation from an officer. He was sentenced to one month's imprisonment rather than the six-month sentence that Major Thackerry felt would be the norm in such cases.

The main concern in respect to the loss of business in the town was alleviated by the arrival of elements of the V Cavalry Reserve Brigade to Kildare.

> For a long time since the opening of the war the people of Kildare have felt the financial loss which followed the departure of the artillery from their midst. For a number of years up to the call of war there were 1,100 members of the RFA, stationed at the barracks attached to the town of Kildare, but the town has practically been deserted some time past. The people of the town will be pleased to learn that the 5th and 12th Lancers will be stationed in the barracks to the number of 1,100 in a few days.[25]

Although the Lancers did not stay very long in Kildare, two members never left Ireland. Private John Ashbie 12 (Prince of Wales) Lancers died on 9 August 1915 and Private George Evans, 5 (Royal Irish) Lancers died on 28 August 1915 – both part of the VI Reserve Cavalry Brigade. Both were interred in the grounds of Kildare Cathedral. Private Ashbie was a married man, 45 years old. He died having fallen down the stairs outside his quarters in Kildare Barracks during the night. Private John Fleming who shared a room with him and Shoeing-Smith Sydney Baxter who was in the next room testified at the inquest that they had heard nothing until he was found at the bottom of the stairs the next morning.[26]

Despite the war, the units stationed in the barracks still had time for sport. A Squadron, Kildare Barracks played D Squadron, Newbridge barracks in the semi-final of the Curragh Garrison Regimental Cup in football, in which the Newbridge team were victorious.[27] When the rising against British rule broke out in April 1916, British army units were rushed to Ireland. The Fifty-ninth Division was posted to Ireland and part of this included the CCXCV Brigade, Royal Field Artillery. An unknown gunner of their ammunition column was stationed in Kildare during this period and described the town as a 'nice place' in a postcard home prior to a rumoured move to Newbridge.[28] This unit returned to England in January 1917 before heading to France in February. One soldier who served in Kildare for a period during the war was Gunner Jarrold. He wrote in 1918 to advise his mother that 'I have landed safely after a very rough time, 12 hours in the train and 11½ hours on the water.'[29] One comment about Kildare was not very favourable. A letter appeared in the *North Cheshire Herald* from some men of the 3 Cheshire Yeomanry stationed at Kildare during Christmas 1915: 'We spent our Christmas at a little village called Kildare, where the houses are just like stables. You talk about being among the pigs, we are amongst them.'[30]

Although most of the soldiers were not local, many married local girls. Sergeant Edward John Hartley, Royal Field Artillery was posted with his unit overseas to Egypt on 31 March 1915 and died in hospital from wounds received at the Dardanelles on 7 August 1915 while serving with the 92 Battery, XVII Brigade Royal Field Artillery. The newspapers provided conflicting reports, and it was also suggested that he died at Ypres and his name was Ernest. It was noted that 'he was very popular while stationed at Kildare'. He was married to Elizabeth Thomas and they had married at Kildare in 1910. He was a brother-in-law of Ernest Thomas of Kildare and his widow and child lived at 25 Casey's Cottages, Kildare.

Kildaremen in the War

Many soldiers from Kildare or who were stationed there were taken prisoner, particularly during the early battles of the war. The ladies of the Kildare Guild collected weekly parcels of food, cigarettes and tobacco from townspeople for fourteen soldiers, formerly stationed at the barracks, who were prisoners of war at Doeberitz Camp in Germany.[31] The following men who were natives of Kildare town were reported as prisoners of war in Germany in 1916:[32]

> Treacy Pte P. (9417) Royal Dublin Fusiliers, Wustermark (Kildare)
> Snowden, Corpl C (7166/11104) Royal Irish Fusiliers, Munster Westphalia (Palacefields, Kildare)
> Forde, Pte Peter (10664) 2nd Connaught Rangers, Zosson, Brandenburgh (Kildare)
> Murphy, Pte John (137) 1st Leinsters, Limburg (Kildare)

Private Peter Forde was born in Kildare on 14 April 1896, the son of William and Brigid Forde living at Church Lane in the town. He had a brother Patrick in the Royal Field Artillery at Athlone, a younger brother John and two sisters Dina and Maggie at home. He was a farm labourer and enlisted as a special reservist in the Connaught Rangers at the Curragh on 20 November 1912 aged 17 and attested into the army on 15 March 1913 at the Curragh before being posted to Galway.

He went overseas with the Connaught Rangers on 13 August 1914 and participated at the Battle of Mons where he was captured by the Germans on 26 August 1914. The War Office wrote to his father on 23 September 1914 advising that Peter was missing in action and wrote on 16 February 1915 to advise that he was a prisoner of war. No doubt Peter would have written home before that informing his family of his circumstances. He did write to the army in 1915 from his prison in Limburg advising them to allocate nine pence per week from his wages to his cousin Josephine Forde, Tully, Kildare. Forde is of significance because he became a member of Casement's Irish Brigade. Sir Roger Casement attempted to raise an Irish Brigade from the ranks of Irishmen held as prisoners of war in late 1914 and early 1915. In the end, he only managed to convince fifty-five out of at least 2,200 Irishmen at Limburg and Forde was one of those who joined the brigade. Ultimately, the men were segregated from the other prisoners but nothing came of the scheme. Forde remained in Germany until he was repatriated in April 1919 and subsequently emigrated to Toronto, Canada after leaving the army in August 1920. Forde returned to Ireland in 1935 and attended a memorial service for Casement in Dublin.

A young teacher at Kildare National School, Harry Greene applied for a commission in 1915 and was initially posted to the Royal Munster Fusiliers before being posted to the Royal Irish Regiment in January 1917. He was killed in action on 29 April 1918. Captain Taylor wrote to Greene's father, Thomas, in Roscarberry, County Cork and gave him the circumstances of his son's death.

> Your son fell on 29th, when leading half a company to attack a hostile post. Being a young, gallant, and thorough officer, he

was selected for this duty and it was performed, as the post was captured, and a German machine-gun, too. Poor Greene – a friend of mine since January, 1917 – was sniped and instantly killed. His body was brought back and reverently buried on Hill Top Farm – our battalion headquarters – by the Revd. W. Hutchinson, the regimental padre.[33]

Although there were many men from Kildare town who enlisted in the army and served during the war, records for very few survive. The *Kildare Observer* reported in May 1915 that seven men enlisted in the previous week at Kildare in the Irish Guards and Royal Field Artillery.[34] Michael Dillon of Tully Road, Kildare had enlisted in the Irish Guards in 1911 and arrived in France on 8 August 1914 with the Second Battalion Irish Guards before returning home wounded on 16 October 1914. He was the son of Michael and Martha Dillon. His file records that he had three brothers, Patrick, Thomas and Joseph. He suffered mental difficulties as a result of active service, which would now be classed as post-traumatic stress disorder.[35] John Forde served with the 16 Lancers. He was an apprentice to Michael Dawson of Rathbride Manor, Kildare and enlisted at the Curragh on 9 March 1915 at 14 years old.[36] He was the son of Michael Forde, Church Lane, Kildare. He served for almost a year as a boy but was kept at the Curragh, no doubt because of his age. His age did not prevent him from being reprimanded for losing his kit on Church Parade when he was admonished by Sergeant Field and had to pay for his kit.

Patrick McDonnell, son of Kate McDonnell of No. 2 New Row, Kildare enlisted in the 16 Lancers at the Curragh on 27 March 1915. He was 16 years, 11 months old.[37] He was discharged on 24 November 1915, service no longer required.

Gunner Joseph Fyland, a farm labourer, 23 years old from Kildare town joined the Royal Field Artillery on 26 November 1913 and was posted to Athlone for initial training. He was fortunate enough to serve at home in Kildare with 65 Battery from 21 February 1914 for a period of time.[38] He fell foul of the military authorities at Kildare on a number of occasions. On 23 March 1914, he was charged with being drunk on gymnasium parade by Corporal Mitchell and Bombardier Pepper. He was given ten days confined to barracks by Lieutenant-Colonel E.J. Duffus, commanding officer of the VIII

(Howitzer) Brigade. He was back in front of his Commanding Officer for an offence on 4 April 1914 when he was charged with being improperly dressed in a public house at 5.45 pm; breaking out of barracks while being under arrest as a consequence of the previous event and deficiency of kit. He was deducted ten days pay for this offence. He was imprisoned for twenty-eight days later in April for failing to appear at parade and losing by neglect his personal clothing and as a consequence discharged from the Royal Field Artillery on 16 May 1914.

James Byrne[39], Bride Street Kildare, a former platelayer, 25 years old and son of Michael Byrne enlisted on 7 June 1916 in the Royal Engineers and was posted to Egypt with the 53 Railway Company, arriving in Alexandria on 16 September 1916 where he remained until May 1919, completing his service at Port Said. John Geoghegan, Church Street, Kildare, son of John Geoghegan, aged 22 years enlisted in November 1917 with the Royal Army Medical Corps serving until the end of the war. Jack Geoghegan was a 39-year-old stableman from Chapel Hill, Kildare. He enlisted on 28 December 1917 and was married to Ann Byrne since 1895.[40]

John Hanks, Church Lane, a 29-year-old labourer enlisted on 18 March 1915 at the Curragh and was posted to the First Battalion, Royal Irish Regiment, serving in Mudros. His wife was listed as Mary Shanks, Hospital Street, Kildare.

The end of the war in November 1918 was marked simply in Kildare. A young Welsh gunner Driver J. Davies of the CCCXXVI Brigade RFA stationed at Kildare who had received a gift of £1 from his local church in Merthyr Tydfil, Wales wrote to the church on 13 November 1918:

I have much pleasure in acknowledging your gift to we boys from home. It will go towards a better Christmas dinner than those what I had last year. I did not receive one you sent last year and I lost a few of my letters from home at the time so forgive me for not answering. We only have Church of Ireland here for place of worship so we have our little meetings in the soldiers' home. We are going to have a supper and concert this evening owing to the armistice being signed. Give my kindest regards to the members of the church.

Now that the war is at an end, I dare say we won't be long before being able to return home and I am glad to hear we still have a place in the church. [41]

The war may have ended, but for the majority of soldiers it would be 1919 before they were demobilised and allowed to go home. Gunner Charles William Hewett was stationed at Kildare with the 542 (Howitzer) Battery, RFA. He was 41 years old, had re-enlisted in the army in November 1916 after previously serving with the Imperial Yeomanry, and was sent to the CCCXXVI Brigade at Kildare. He was demobilised in March 1919 and allowed to return home by his commanding officer Major W.G. Fletcher.

CHAPTER 9

THE WAR OF INDEPENDENCE

...a special word of mention is due to the officers of the
Royal Artillery, Kildare, and the management of Messrs.
Todd Burns, Curragh Camp for having facilitated the
provision of essential furnishing equipment.

JAMES BERGIN, SECRETARY, KILDARE INFIRMARY, KILDARE
OBSERVER, 3 JANUARY 1920

Gunners of 14 Battery, Royal Field Artillery at Kildare, 1919. (Courtesy of Ian Jones)

With the end of the First World War, the Royal Artillery gradually returned to peacetime duties. This process continued throughout 1919 as units returned home from France and other gunners were demobilised to return to civilian life. Although the CCCXXV Brigade was disbanded in May 1918, its constituent batteries remained in Ireland as independent units, with 884 Battery in Limerick and 885 and 886 Batteries at Kildare. The batteries were disbanded in 1919 but not before 885 Battery was on hand to carry out a six-gun birthday salute to the King in June 1919.[1]

While the War of Independence did not have a huge influence in Kildare, there were a number of incidents involving the railway station in the town. In June 1920, the railway employees passed a resolution declaring that they would no longer handle military equipment or supplies.[2] A body of men from the barracks attempted to travel to Athlone in June 1920, but when they arrived and attempted to load their ammunition and supplies, the driver, fireman and porter would not deal with the train. In the end, the troops had to return to their barracks. Kildare was in an area deemed safe by the British and referred to as the Newbridge–Kildare–Curragh triangle, the details of which are outlined in the next chapter.

One serious incident in the town occurred in October 1920 when George Graham, owner of Graham's bakery was shot in the back and chest by a sentry as he drove past the barracks. Graham, whose son was also in the car but uninjured, made a full recovery. The military claimed that they issued a warning before opening fire, although Graham claimed that he heard nothing. [3] There was a local IRA unit active in the area. The south part of County Kildare formed part of the Carlow Brigade IRA. The Sixth Battalion was commanded by William Byrne of Ballysax, and Kildare town came under the auspices of F Company. The names of those who served in F Company were recorded after the campaign by their commanding officer as follows. The addresses listed below most likely relate to the 1930s, when nominal rolls were prepared for pension and service-related purposes.[4]

Strength of Company: 32 officers and men as at 11 July 1921

Captain Michael Mangan	Fair Green, Kildare
Lieutenant Jas Houlihan	Rathbride
Second-Lieutenant William Graham	Grey Abbey
Volunteer C. Conway	Cross Keys
Volunteer Jas Walsh	Lucan
Volunteer Thomas Graham	Darby's Cottages
Volunteer J. Kenna	Kildare
Volunteer Jas. Doyle	Dublin
Volunteer Patrick Domigan	Kill, Naas
Volunteer S. Aherne	Cork
Volunteer Val. Grady	Loosville, Kildare
Volunteer Jos. Kelly	USA
Volunteer M. Byrne	Bride St.
Volunteer Neil Byrne	Bride St.
Volunteer W. Colton	Abbey View
Volunteer W. Gannon	Bride St.
Volunteer A.J. Fitzpatrick	Darby's Cottages
Volunteer J. Hayes	Chapel Hill
Volunteer Chas. Murphy	Lackagh, Kildare
Volunteer S. Martin	England
Volunteer Jas. Lennon	England
Volunteer Bill Graham	Grey Abbey
Volunteer Tom Mangan	Fair Green
Volunteer T. McEvoy	Rathbride
Volunteer D. Nolan	Blakestown
Volunteer M. Breslin	Newbridge
Volunteer John Breslin	Newbridge
Volunteer P. Moore	Rathbride
Volunteer J. Ryan	Rathbride
Volunteer T. Walsh	Fair Green
Volunteer S. Reddy	Rathbride
Volunteer M. Murphy	Rathbride

William Gannon (1901–67) of Bride Street, Kildare represented Kildare in Gaelic Football throughout the 1920s and captained the Kildare team that won the All-Ireland Gaelic Football championship in 1928, having played for the team that also won the championship in 1927.

In 1919 the XXXI (later renamed XXX) Brigade (9, 16, 17 and 47 Batteries) and XXXVI Brigade (48 Battery with 15, 71 and 142 Batteries at Newbridge) of the Royal Field Artillery were stationed at Kildare. In July 1921, there were eighteen officers and 369 other ranks of the XXX Brigade stationed in Kildare, together with three officers and 101 other ranks of 142 Battery, the remaining members of the brigade being stationed at Newbridge. One soldier who did not like army life in Ireland was Gunner 110749 Reginald Wardle who enlisted in Newcastle, England on 19 May 1919 and deserted at Kildare on 13 February 1921.[5] An Irish gunner, Patrick Byrne 1032051 of the 9 Battery was dismissed with ignominy from the army for sending his commanding officer a threatening letter. He was tried by a district court martial at Kildare by Major Orr and dispatched to Mountjoy Gaol to serve one year with hard labour.

Royal Field Artillery – July 1920
Following on from the First World War, the strength of each brigade of artillery had been increased from three batteries to four. This meant that while in pre-war days there had been five batteries of artillery making up two brigades with one battery in rotation at other locations, the barracks had one brigade, with the other brigade being stationed at Newbridge, less one battery at Kildare. Newbridge also had L, M and N batteries of the IV Brigade, Royal Horse Artillery. At the height of the War of Independence, the senior officers of the two brigades between Kildare and Newbridge were as follows:

XXX Brigade Royal Field Artillery
Brigade Commander:	Lieutenant-Colonel C. St. L.G. Hawkes CMG DSO
Adjutant:	Major H.C. Lowry-Corry MC
9 Battery	Major R.J. Adams
16 Battery:	Major E.G. Langford DSO
17 Battery:	Major C.C. Colley

47 (Howitzer) Battery: Major D.R. MacDonald DSO
XXXVI Brigade Royal Field Artillery
Brigade Commander: Lt Col A. Hinde CMG
(Newbridge)

Adjutant:	Major S.R. Watson MC
(Newbridge)	
15 Battery	H.E. Thellusson
(Newbridge)	
48 Battery	G. Masters DSO
(Newbridge)	E.O. Anderson

(Newbridge)	
71 Battery	F.D.S. Gethin
(Newbridge)	
	J.L.C. White MC
(Newbridge)	
142 (Howitzer) Battery	F.B. Binney
(Kildare)	

During the course of the conflict in Ireland, it became apparent that the Royal Artillery were not being fully utilised in assisting in military operations. As a consequence, the Fifth Division formed a Royal Artillery Mounted Infantry Brigade to assist with operations in September 1921. A number of gunners of the 48 Battery were subsequently killed during the conflict and Lieutenant Wogan-Browne was killed after the truce, as outlined in the next chapter. The Royal Artillery Mounted Rifles reverted to normal duties in January 1922.

Nevertheless, military training did continue as normal. The artillery training camp at the Glen of Imaal opened in May 1920 and continued until September. Training consisted of a gunnery instruction course, run fortnightly, until the end of September. Section commanders, battery commanders, and 'No. 1s' from all over Ireland attended. In 1921, the glen camp opened in April which each battery in Ireland attending one weeks' instructional manoeuvre and gunnery training and one week's tactical training.[6] As late as March 1921, the military were preparing plans for the re-appropriation of adult and infant schools in the barracks as a sergeants' mess. The existing mess was too small following an increase in NCOs entitled to become members and the old mess in the west brigade was to be converted into a new adult and infant school. Plans were drawn up to include a liquor store and billiards room in the school. In addition, married quarters were built some time after the war, referred to in 1923 as 'recently built by the British War Department at the rear of Kildare Artillery Barracks'.[7]

Despite the difficult conditions in Ireland, there was still time for sport and the Royal Artillery Mounted Rifles played a football match against the Royal Dublin Fusiliers Depot in Naas on 10 December 1921, with the Fusiliers winning by four goals to nil. The artillery team were Lieutenant Parton, Sergeant Rastall, Lieutenant Maude, Bombardier Walman, Bombardier McKay, Driver Smith, Colonel Bouchier, Lieutenant Griffiths, Lieutenant Beaker-Jones, Lieutenant Rogers and Lieutenant Bower. Normal life continued in the town also. The Kildare Infirmary Ball was held in the Town Hall in January 1920. The secretary of the Kildare Infirmary committee James Bergin gave '…a special word of mention is due to the officers of the Royal Artillery, Kildare, and the management of Messrs. Todd Burns, Curragh Camp for having facilitated the provision of essential furnishing equipment'.[8]

In most respects, life in Kildare town was not disturbed by the continuing War of Independence. Dances and sporting events continued, the military continued to play a role in local society and the locals got on with their daily lives. There was a somewhat amusing court case in the town in September 1921 when Mrs Bell and Mrs Molly Hutton, Hospital Street, Kildare summoned Mrs Alice Kelly and Mrs Maggie Sindell of the same street for abusive language. The resident Magistrate, Major E.J. Dease remarked that 'all the ladies in Kildare seemed to be in court'. Two other women in court that day were Mary Ann Parnell and Ellen Davis of Chapel Hill, Kildare who were charged with stealing coal from Kildare railway station. Corporal Webb and Lance Corporal Alders hid in bushes close to where the coal was stored and apprehended the two women when they came to take the coal.[9] These cases were typical of Kildare during this time, perhaps indicating more than anything else the normality that existed in the area at the time.

CHAPTER 10

THE KILLING OF LIEUTENANT J.H. WOGAN-BROWNE

'...wilful murder against some person or persons unknown.'

CORONER'S INQUEST, FEBRUARY 1922

Medal Ceremony at Kildare, February 1922. The four officers at front centre are
Colonel-Commandant Sandys, Lieutenant-General Jeudwine, Lieutenant-Colonel
Marryat and Lieutenant de Robeck. (Courtesy of Paul O'Rorke)

On Friday, 10 February 1922, Lieutenant John Hubert Wogan-Browne of 48 (Howitzer) Battery, XXXVI Brigade, Royal Field Artillery stationed at Kildare Barracks, was robbed of £135 and shot dead on the main street of Kildare town. The murder was a shocking crime and caused considerable outrage at a time when the country was in a period of transition following the signing of the truce between Britain and the new Irish Free State, just two months before the departure of British troops from Kildare. The deed caused a flurry of activity between London and Dublin as the British suspended the evacuation of troops and the Provisional Government sought to reassure them that this was an isolated incident. No one was ever brought to account for the killing and over a relatively short period of time, the incident was forgotten. However, Wogan-Browne, was the youngest son of a prominent Catholic military family with Kildare roots dating back to the seventeenth century.

Francis William Nicholas Wogan-Browne (17 February 1854–11 April 1927) had a long and distinguished career in the British army serving as a sub-lieutenant from 3 December 1873 when he was known as Franz William Wogan-Browne of Kildare. F.W.N. Wogan-Browne served with the First West India Regiment as a lieutenant from 30 November 1876[1] before being posted to the Third Hussars in 1880.[2] He was given command of the Third Hussars in August 1898 and served in South Africa during the Boer War as Colonel-in-command returning to England in July 1902. He married Bridget (Beda) Costello, daughter of James Costello of Foxrock, Dublin on 2 August 1879. Francis and Beda had three sons and five daughters; Mary Charlotte (1880–1962), Francis Thomas (1882–1902), Henry Edward (1883–1886), John Hubert (1896–1922), Beatrice Judith (1886–1886), Judith Helen (1887–1966), Dorothea (1890–1910) and Claire Renee (1893–1955).

The Wogan-Browne's eldest son, Francis Thomas was commissioned a second lieutenant on 8 January 1901 having trained as a gentleman cadet at the

Royal Military College.[3] He served with the Second Battalion Scottish Rifles during the Boer War in South Africa with the rank of lieutenant at the same time as his father. He drowned on 4 October 1902 while swimming in the sea at Greystones, County Wicklow.

The Career of Wogan-Browne

John Hubert Wogan-Browne was born on 23 July 1896 at Hale Crescent, Farnham, close to Aldershot, England where his father was stationed as a major with the Third Hussars. John, or Jack as he was more commonly known, was educated at Cheltenham College from May 1910 to June 1914 where he was a keen rugby player, participated in the Officer Training Corps as a corporal and was a house prefect. Wogan-Browne was described as 'a very popular Irish boy' and a 'most attractive boy' by one of his contemporaries at Cheltenham.[4] He applied for a cadetship to the Royal Military Academy at Woolwich, the home of artillery in the British Army. He was successful in the examination and was admitted as a gentleman cadet on 11 July 1914 on the eve of the First World War. He served in France from September 1915 as a second lieutenant and in Salonika from 12 December 1915 with C Battery, LVII Brigade, Royal Field Artillery, part of the Tenth (Irish) Division and was promoted to the rank of lieutenant on 8 August 1916. He was appointed as adjutant to the Brigade in February 1917. He was mentioned in dispatches in November 1917 and appointed aide-de-camp to the general officer commanding the brigade in December 1917 as an acting captain. In May 1918 he was transferred to D Battery, CXVI Brigade and embarked from Varna, Bulgaria to Alexandria, Egypt in April 1919 returning to the United Kingdom in August. He was posted to the 48 (Howitzer) Battery stationed at Kildare in 1920 by which time he had reverted to the peacetime rank of lieutenant with the position of battery adjutant.

Jack was fortunate in being stationed relatively close to the family residence at Naas, County Kildare. He often served at mass in Naas in the mornings before travelling to duty at Kildare. He was an accomplished athlete, winning the 880 yards final at the Irish Command sports in June 1920 by 10 yards[5] and he played senior rugby for Lansdowne Rugby Club in Dublin as three-quarters, helping the club to win the senior championship in 1921. He had played a match for the British Army at Leyton on 26 January against a United Hospitals team in the back row.[6] He was scheduled to line out for Lansdowne the day after the robbery.

The Threat

Kildare town was in an area referred to by the British as the Curragh–Newbridge–Kildare triangle, a recognised safe area where the risk from republicans was deemed low. There had been no trouble in the town in the two years that the battery was in Kildare and relations with the local population were generally good. However, there were a few warning signs. On 8 January 1922, an intelligence officer, Lieutenant Bevin, in plain clothes was fired at from behind a hedge on the roadside 3.5 miles south of the Curragh near Suncroft, the bullet passing through his coat and lodging in his motorcycle.[7] There were also general occurrences of lawlessness with gangs of armed robbers operating around Dublin. A bread-van driver was stopped by armed men outside Naas and the driver was robbed of his cash takings.[8] The British military were anxious to evacuate troops and their families as soon as possible following the ratification of the treaty by Dáil Éireann and especially after the release of republican prisoners in December 1921, as the situation, in their view, began to destabilise.[9] Instructions were issued to all military stations on revised security measures but, as shall be subsequently seen, were not relayed to Kildare Barracks. Lieutenant-Colonel Lionel Edward Warren, commanding officer of the XXXVI Brigade viewed the situation in Newbridge and Kildare as so peaceful that he saw no reason to issue orders to battery commanders in either place that their officers should be armed or provided with an escort.

The Events of 10 February 1922

Local newspaper reporting of the inquest into the death of Lieutenant Wogan-Browne and information in his military file have assisted in the reconstruction of the events of 10 February.[10]

At 10.30 a.m., the lieutenant as battery subaltern on duty collected a cheque from Lieutenant Colonel Arthur Graves Leech in the amount of €135 which was the weekly pay of 48 Battery. He walked to the Hibernian Bank, which was approximately 500 yards from the barrack gate. He had carried out this duty since about May 1921, always went to the bank alone and was generally the first officer to collect his pay on Fridays with the other battery subalterns drawing their pay about 12.00 noon. Wogan-Browne entered the bank between 11.10 a.m. and 11.15 a.m. He gave the cheque to the cashier Charles Edward Swain, who issued him with £100 in Bank of Ireland £1 notes, £20 in silver and £15 in ten shilling treasury notes. He put the money in his haversack and left the bank by 11.20 a.m., walking back towards the barracks on the same side of the road as the bank.

Before these events, two young men walked into the garage of Mr Kennedy on Station Road and asked a young mechanic, 18-year-old Patrick Daly, about hiring a car to bring them to Kilcullen. Patrick went up to his employer, Mr Kennedy, who told him to agree a rate of fifteen shillings for the trip. The men agreed and arranged to be back at the garage at 11 a.m. Patrick testified to the coroner's court that he had seen the men on the town square from at least 10.15 a.m. The two men returned to the garage at 11 a.m. and another employee of Mr Kennedy, Thomas Graham, drove the Ford car. They left before 11.15 a.m. and once they passed the post-office, they told the driver to stop the car at the gates of the national school opposite the County Infirmary.

As Wogan-Browne came towards the gate of the national school, two civilians, armed with revolvers confronted him. One shouted 'hands up' and tried to grab the haversack containing the money. Wogan-Browne struggled with one assailant and was dragged across the road in the struggle. He dropped his haversack as he tackled one of the men, with both of them falling on the ground. The other civilian grabbed the haversack, threw it into the car, then shot Wogan-Browne in the head, over the right eye with a .32 automatic colt pistol and got into the front passenger seat of the car beside the driver. A third assailant sat in the car with the driver Graham during the entire incident.

One witness, a 14-year-old boy named Robert Neil who lived on New Row and whose father worked as a labourer on the railway, claimed that, at this point, a motor van owned by J.J. Parkinson, a well-known racehorse trainer based at Maddenstown on the edge of the Curragh, coming from Kildare knocked one of the civilians down but kept going. This was not mentioned by Bridget McCarthy, a second witness, who lived on Hospital Street and whose husband was an ex-soldier who worked as a civilian barber in the barracks, nor was it mentioned by Lizzie Flanagan, also of New Row who witnessed the attack and gave evidence at the coroner's court. She testified that Parkinson's car passed by immediately after the shooting. McCarthy also testified that the gunman pointed the gun directly at her before getting into the car.

Driver Harold Onions was on sentry duty at the gate of the Artillery Barracks and had observed the car parked outside the school with the hood up, approximately one hundred and fifty yards from the barrack gate. He testified to the military inquiry that the car was there about five minutes when he heard a shot and saw Lieutenant Wogan-Browne fall behind the car as it moved off. Driver Onions ran to the scene of the shooting and carried Wogan-Browne down to the barrack gate where Onions collapsed exhausted. He put the lieutenant into a cart and brought him to the barrack hospital where he was subsequently pronounced dead.

The car carrying the robbers drove around Infirmary Corner. Thomas Graham, the driver, testified that he was told 'Drive, or by God, we'll riddle you.' One of the gunmen remarked 'That fellow is done for anyway.' The car headed for Kildoon, a townland about three miles south of Kildare town where Graham left the three men. He drove back to Kildare and told the police where he had left them.

The Royal Irish Constabulary, Royal Artillery Mounted Corps (a rifle brigade formed by soldiers of the Royal Field Artillery in Kildare and Newbridge barracks) and Irish Volunteer Police immediately commenced a search of the countryside, setting up a cordon in the area in an attempt to apprehend the robbers. The military at Kildare notified London at 2.10 p.m. by telegram that:

10/2/1922 aaa Lieut J.H. Wogan-Browne 48th Battery 36th Brigade R.F.A. killed at Kildare aaa next of kin informed.[11]

The immediate response to the murder was an instruction issued by the War Office to suspend the evacuation of troops from Ireland. It was suggested that after the event, the people of Kildare would not assist and 'laughed and jeered' which subsequently resulted in a hostile demonstration by some of the military in the town that night and the withdrawal of passes from traders to the Curragh. The local doctor, Laurence Rowan, refuted the allegations in a letter to the *Kildare Observer* and advised that a public meeting was held in the town the day after the killing to express abhorrence of the crime and to offer sympathy with Wogan-Browne's family.[12]

The hostile demonstration reported in the *Kildare Observer* was a serious occurrence. According to the IRA Liaison Officer for County Kildare, Sean Kavanagh, who was based in Naas, it was suggested in the town that John Breslin, an ex-prisoner and former IRA captain in Kildare town would be a target for the military because of his position as a senior republican in the town.[13] The Royal Artillery and local IRA representatives closed the public houses early and a military police picket was placed on the streets. Sean Kavanagh reported that the local IRA Company was not a strong one and most of the men were employed in the pursuit of the killers. It would subsequently transpire that the local IRA had no involvement in the incident. Dr Rowan noted that 'the unceasing search for the perpetrators, day and night, by every man here who is permitted or authorised to do so, speaks for itself'.[14]

A party of former IRA members assisted Breslin armed with shotguns and some rifles. Breslin asked the local IRA commander named Graham for protection but he told him he would only protect him if they gave up the unauthorised weapons they held, which he declined.[15] At about 9.45 p.m. six soldiers from the barracks broke some windows in the Palace Cinema where Breslin was caretaker. Immediately, fire was opened up on them with three soldiers wounded and brought to hospital. A civilian named James Darcy got a pellet through the neck.[16]

Sean Kavanagh, made contact with General Skinner OC Fifth Division to get British soldiers at Kildare confined to barracks while he endeavoured to deal with unauthorised persons in possession of guns.[17] There was no reporting of this incident in the media except for correspondence from W. Doolin, private secretary at the Under Secretary's office at Dublin Castle to General Emmet Dalton, Chief Liaison Officer:

> The following extract from Police report of yesterday's date is transmitted for your information:
> KILDARE: At Kildare on night of 10.2.22 six soldiers from RFA Barracks fired on while breaking windows in private houses; three wounded, one civilian wounded. All by Volunteer Police Force. Soldiers were unarmed. (This occurred following on the shooting of a Military Officer. Soldiers taken to hospital.)
> Doubtless you have received a report from your local officer as to the circumstances in which fire was opened on these soldiers? I should be much obliged if you would kindly let me have your views on the matter.[18]

On the evening of 13 February, Michael Collins sent a telegram to Winston Churchill to advise:

> Have just been informed by telephone that we have captured three of those responsible for the attack on Lieutenant Wogan-Browne. Everyone, civilian and soldier has co-operated in tracking those responsible for abominable action. You may rely on it that those whom we can prove guilty will be suitably dealt with.[19]

Churchill spoke on the matter in the British parliament the next day and advised the House of the contents of Collins's telegram and said that three of the suspected murderers had been captured in an operation in which the RIC, IRA and civilian populations had combined. Churchill advised the British Parliament that: 'These persons have been captured and will be dealt with according to law in the most expeditious manner.' An unrecorded member of parliament replied: 'What law? There is no law there.'[20]

In the weekly survey of the state of Ireland presented to the British cabinet for the week ending 13 February 1922, Hamar Greenwood, Chief Secretary of Ireland, reported that:

> The murder of Lieutenant Wogan-Browne was entirely non-political. He was attacked by three armed men and shot dead while returning to barracks, the motive of his murderers being to obtain possession of a large sum of money (£135), which he was known by them to be carrying. I am glad to state this abominable crime has aroused feelings of strong indignation in all sections of the people, and that the local IRA are co-operating energetically with the Crown Forces in the search for the murderers. Three persons have already been arrested on suspicion.[21]

General Cecil Frederick Nevil Macready, remarking on the suspension of the evacuation of troops which was ordered on the day of the murder said:

> The suspension of the evacuation of troops from Southern Ireland

was no doubt ordered for very good reasons. I have not been informed what those reasons were. I hope, however, that when the evacuation is allowed to proceed it will be continued without interruption and with all reasonable expedition.[22]

The reports by Hamar Greenwood on 18 February and Macready on 21 February were a clear indication that the view from Ireland was that the killing was an isolated incident and that the British Parliament and War Office over-reacted. Wogan-Browne's murder was the first of a soldier since October 1921 although five policemen were killed the same week and three in the previous week. The kidnap and murder of Lieutenant Henry Genochio, Royal Engineers, in Cork on 15 February and the murder of Lieutenant William Mead and CQMS Thomas Cunliffe of the Royal Army Service Corps near Inchicore, Dublin on 20 February did not provoke as much outrage or reaction from the British. Greenwood noted that:

Breaches of the truce in the form of attacks upon the Crown Forces have again been frequent, especially in the South-Western counties, where the extremist element in the IRA is known to be strongest. The most obvious inference to be drawn from these attacks is that they were committed with the object of discrediting the Provisional Government and embarrassing its relations with the British Cabinet.[23]

It would seem that level heads in the military and on the ground in Ireland recognised the struggle between the new Provisional Government and the anti-treaty forces before Westminster did and were able to avert an over-reaction from there. The history of the Fifth Division noted 'for certain unknown reasons the evacuation of troops was held up between 12 February and 27 February'.[24]

The coroner's inquest was held at the Curragh Military Hospital on 11 February 1922 by Dr Jeremiah O'Neill, Deputy Coroner for South Kildare. The jury found that death was due to injury to the brain, caused by a gunshot wound, inflicted by some person or persons unknown, and returned a verdict of: '…wilful murder against some person or persons unknown.' [25] The British were also informed of the coroner's verdict as a demonstration of the feelings of the public to the killing.

The Kildare District Nursing Association, of which Wogan-Browne's mother had been an active member, issued their reaction through the *Kildare Observer* newspaper:

> We place on record our horror and abhorrence that unspeakable barbarians should violate and bloodstain the hitherto sainted annals of Kildare by the vile and cowardly assassination of a popular, innocent, gallant, young Irish gentleman on the public street of Kildare in open daylight.[26]

Military Inquiry

A court of inquiry was held at Kildare Barracks on 16 February 1922 to address the following issues:

1. The circumstances in which the deceased left Barracks.
2. Orders existing as to precautions to be taken for safeguarding parties and money.
3. Evidence of bank cashier regarding visit of deceased to Bank and to drawing of money; what article was used to carry the money and particulars of amount drawn.
4. Sentry on gate duty as regards the shooting of the deceased and the finding of the body with no haversack or money.
5. Medical evidence as to cause of death, subsequent post mortem examination and verdict of Coroner's Inquest.

The Court consisted of Lieutenant-Colonel Milton, presiding, Lieutenant-Colonel Hanbury and Lieutenant-Colonel Hodgson.[27] The witnesses who testified at Kildare Barracks were Lieutenant-Colonel Marryat RFA, commander of Troops at Kildare; Lieutenant-Colonel Lionel Edward Warren, DSO, commander of XXXVI Brigade RFA; Lieutenant-Colonel Arthur Graves Leech, battery commander of 48 Battery; Charles Edward Swain, Hibernian Bank; Robert Neil, age 14; Bridget McCarthy; Driver 1049365 Harold Onions and Edward Thomas Coady, Medical Officer. The main focus of the investigation from the military point of view relates to the orders that existed at the time in respect of officers carrying arms.[28]

On 22 February 1921 orders were issued by the general staff of the Fifth Division instructing that: 'Whilst in Ireland all Officers are to be armed at all times, until this order is cancelled.' Officers were issued with .32 colt automatic pistols rather than the more cumbersome standard issue Webley revolver, which was too bulky to carry.[29] This order was subsequently relaxed on 14 October 1921 when an order was issued stating that 'Owing to the acceptance of the Conference by the representatives of Sinn Fein, the divisional commander has decided that the orders issued for the safety of Officers, barracks, etc., may be modified in certain cases.'[30]

The situation changed again in January 1922 with a number of attacks on Crown Forces and Government property caused by 'the present lawless state of the country and to the return of released internees and convicts who no doubt will try to revenge themselves on those members of the Crown Forces who arrested them or gave evidence against them'.[31]

8. 5th Division No. 13990.G of the 16th instant [16th January 1922] laid down as a minimum an armed escort of two Officers or other ranks for a single military vehicle travelling outside the Curragh-Newbridge-Kildare triangle. Conditions may arise later or in certain areas where this number will be too small. Brigade Commanders will therefore issue any orders they may consider necessary in their areas increasing the strengths of escorts.

9. No order has been issued forbidding Officers to carry pistols or revolvers; except when proceeding on leave to some place in Ireland. The order that all Officers should be armed at all times was only suspended, and is still suspended.

The day before Lieutenant Wogan-Browne was killed, the following order was issued from the Curragh on behalf of the General Staff, Fifth Division.

G.O.C. – in Chief Irish Command wishes attention drawn to para 5.g.h.q. letter 2/32413.G dated Nov 27th 1920 regarding necessity Officers being at all times prepared to offer resistance to any attempt against their persons'. Ends.

Take necessary action. Letter referred to was forwarded under these H.Q. 3932/26 G. dated 28th November 1920.

Despite the existence of this order, which inexplicably had not reached Kildare, the military inquiry made the following finding:

…that no orders were at the time of the above events on the 10th February 1922 in existence either in the said officer's Brigade or Battery or in the artillery station at Kildare to the effect that officers should be armed or that they should be provided with an escort when proceeding to the Bank to draw public money or when returning there from.[32]

The General Officer commanding Fifth Division, Lieutenant-General H.S. Jeudwine, gave the following opinion:

I concur with the opinion of the Court.

It is certainly regrettable that in view of the duty on which he was employed, and the number of robberies which have lately taken place, Lieut. Wogan-Browne was not armed or escorted, but the evidence of Lt. Col. Margate shows the view held on this point, for which there is considerable justification. If it is held that blame is attributable for the want of predictive measures I must personally accept the quarter share of it, for although definite orders had been issued from these H.Q. that officers were to be armed at all times, these orders did not issue in time to reach the OC Troops Kildare before the murder took place.

The military inquiry did not record how the other batteries collected their pay each week and no recommendations were made in this regard.

Investigation of the Murder

Following on from the initial search for the assailants, the officer in command of the 1st Eastern Division IRA took control of the investigation which was carried out by the 7th Brigade IRA. Captains Guilfoyle and Saurin were sent from IRA GHQ to assist with the investigation. The IRA Liaison Officer for County Kildare based in Naas Courthouse, Sean Kavanagh reported 'most active inquiries and investigations are being made by me'. He also reported to headquarters in Dublin that:

> I might mention that the local Brigade OC Commdt Lawlor, and myself have received warnings in connection with the case from a source which helps to confirm our suspicions as to the organisers and motives of the crime.[33]

The first three men arrested in connection with the murder were Michael and William Howe, two brothers from Ballysax, Curragh and the car driver Thomas Graham who was arrested by order of the Minister for Home Affairs for complicity in the crime. All three were brought to Trim barracks within a few days of the arrests.[34] Kavanagh reported that 'I find more we are on the right track and have at least one of the guilty men in custody.'

Graham, despite denying any knowledge of the assailants at the coroner's inquest, reported in the *Kildare Observer*, admitted to the investigation that he recognised William Howe. Thomas Graham was from Crosskeys in the town and was 20 years of age at the time of the robbery. Following his imprisonment at Trim barracks, he was interned in Newbridge by the Provisional Government where he participated in a hunger strike. The windows of his house were broken by British soldiers on the night of the attack.[35] Graham had served with 'F' Company, 6th Battalion, Carlow Brigade IRA during the War of Independence which operated in the Kildare town area.[36]

Further investigations revolved around an anonymous letter received by District Inspector Queenan, Kildare on 15 February which was posted in Kildare town on 14 February. The letter, a copy of which, was forwarded on to the Chief Liaison Officer in Dublin by Commandant Kavanagh stated 'have good reason for believing mens [sic] names seen outside P Office with Graham "Friday"are Howe Ballysax, Byrne, Kelly Maddenstown'. Kavanagh reported that he was endeavouring to identify the writer. Following further investigation, Kavanagh established that those involved in the attack were part of a group of eight IRA men who attacked the house of a Mrs Belford at Ballyshannon near Kilcullen in

July 1921. Mrs Belford together with her son and daughter took refuge in the Curragh and in March 1922 she wrote to the Under-Secretary at Dublin Castle concerned about her safety once the British army vacated the Curragh. Her correspondence was passed on to Captain McAllister, Deputy Liaison Officer who was based at the Gresham Hotel, Dublin. He enquired with Kavanagh in Naas on the case and was advised of the details of the men involved in the attack and their apparent role in the murder of Wogan-Browne:

> I am aware that eight men were arrested last June on Mrs. Belford's information for being concerned in destroying her house. Five were subsequently interned in the Rath Camp and three were detained untried at Mountjoy until the general amnesty. Of these eight men three are at present in our custody for the murder of Lieut. Wogan-Browne at Kildare on 10th February – William Howe, Patrick Byrne and Patrick Kelly – and Mrs. Belford's daughter is also a witness in this case.[37]

Kavanagh reported that while the Brigade OC did not want the Belfords to be molested, he was not in a position to guarantee their safety in the area in which they previously lived.

The IRA unit operating in the Ballyshannon and Suncroft areas was C Company, 6th Battalion, Carlow Brigade IRA.[38] The youngest of the three men implicated in the killing, Patrick Byrne was a 21 year old carpenter from Suncroft. His neighbour Patrick Kelly of Newtown, Suncroft was 22 and William Howe of Ballysax was 21-years-old. Kelly and Howe were both labourers. William's brother, Michael another member of the column at Ballyshannon, was 20 years old.[39] This unit was an active one involved in a number of attacks on soldiers and policemen during this period and the killing of an informer, Michael Power, in June 1921. At the time of the truce, C Company had a strength of forty-six officers and men with seven others interned by the British.[40]

Patrick Kelly and Patrick Byrne were imprisoned at Mountjoy on 10 October 1921 together with a number of other men from County Kildare by Colonel F.W. Skinner following trial by court martial charged with various offences under the Restoration of Order in Ireland Regulations. The General Register of Mountjoy Prison includes the following information:[41]

Patrick Byrne, age 20, Maddenstown,   whiteboy offence
Patrick Kelly, age 21, Newtown, Suncroft   whiteboy offence
James Dowling, age 27, Carna, Curragh   whiteboy offence

Patrick Kelly was released on parole from Mountjoy over the Christmas period 1921 and was returned to Mountjoy on 7 January 1922. The three men were released from Mountjoy a few weeks before Wogan-Browne was killed. James Dowling of Carna is the third man held at Mountjoy, referred to above by Kavanagh in his report in respect of the attack on the Belford residence.

There are some uncorroborated suggestions that the three men suspected of the robbery and murder were held in custody by the IRA in the home of Eamonn O'Modhráin, officer commanding the 6th Battalion, for a short period.[42] The General Register of Prisoners for Mountjoy Prison confirms that the three men were committed to Mountjoy pending trial on 19 April 1922 charged with:

'Did unlawfully and with malice aforethought kill one Lieut Wogan Brown [sic].'[43]

The three men were committed from the Parish Court, Newbridge, County Kildare by Patrick Kelly, Justice of the County. The three were never brought to trial for the killing. They were released from Mountjoy by order of the Adjutant General on 29 May 1922. While the man who killed Wogan-Browne was never identified, the testimony of Bridget McCarthy to the military inquiry gave some further information. She stated that she saw two assailants on the road, the taller man getting knocked to the ground with Wogan-Browne and the smaller man being the one who shot him.[44] The Mountjoy Register recorded that Kelly was 5' 10", Howe 5' 7" and Byrne 5' 6".[45] This would suggest that Kelly was the taller man who accosted Wogan-Browne first and fell to the ground with him in the struggle while either Byrne or Howe, who are close to each other in height, must have fired the fatal shot. Wogan-Browne himself was recorded as 5' 7" in his military file.

The personnel file of Lieutenant Wogan-Browne notes that the Provisional Government authorities in the Curragh, in June 1922, state that the arrested men will be released due to the lack of evidence against them and the unwillingness of anyone to make a statement. The suspects were already released at this stage and were never brought to trial in respect of the events of 10 February 1922. The British authorities had treated the area known as the Curragh–Kildare–Newbridge triangle as a safe area and Lieutenant-General H.S. Jeudwine acknowledged that he should take a share of the blame in not insisting that appropriate measure be in place in his area of command. Clearly, the death of John Wogan-Browne could have been prevented by better security and implementation of orders that existed in other parts of the country. The fundamental difference between this death and many others was that this was a case of robbery gone wrong by opportunistic assailants rather than a politically-motivated act. However, it was unusual in that the victim, although a British army officer, was from a prominent Kildare family. A comparison between the case of Wogan-Browne and that of Lieutenant Henry Genochio who was kidnapped on 15 February and murdered two days later is noteworthy and reflects the difference between Kildare and Cork at the time. General Macready reported to the British Cabinet that military witnesses would not attend the Coroner's court for safety reasons while an offer to hold the inquest at Victoria Barracks was declined by the Coroner as he feared the jury would not turn up. Macready reported:

> The Provisional Government declined to help as they feared their orders would not be obeyed. The [IRA] Liaison Officer in Cork would do nothing as he did not recognise the Provisional Government. Finally the Coroner stated that he was acting on the instructions of a Competent Authority (whoever this may be, probably IRA) – so I gave instructions that a Military Enquiry was to be held in lieu of an inquest.[46]

In contrast, the commander of the XXXVI Brigade, Lieutenant-Colonel Warren wrote to Reverend Thomas P. Kelly, Kildare to say:

> On behalf of the Officers, Warrant-Officers, Non-Commissioned Officers and Men of the 36th Brigade, Royal Field Artillery, I thank the people of Kildare for their very kind and thoughtful act in passing a resolution of sympathy with us in our great sorrow for the loss of our beloved comrade, the late Lieut. John Hubert Wogan-Browne.

Aftermath

The file of Lieutenant J.H. Wogan-Browne makes for sobering reading considering the manner in which he was killed and contains a considerable amount of correspondence in respect of financial matters. The military authorities were concerned with two elements; the overpayment of wages to him for the period from 11 February – 28 February 1922 and the possibility of recovering the £135 from his estate. The British eventually wrote off the money that was stolen but a portion of the wages was recouped from his estate. A committee of adjustment, comprising of three lieutenants, assembled at Kildare on 9 March 1922 'for the purpose of the allocation of effects and payment of preferential charges of the late lieutenant'.[47] His sister, Mrs Lillis, paid his outstanding mess bill at Kildare Barracks and money found on his person was used to pay two days outstanding wages due to his groom and servant and to pay for clothes left with a tailor.

His father, Colonel Wogan-Browne died at Parame, France on 12 April 1927 while on a motor tour and was interred at St Iduc. His wife had died at Naas on 2 June 1920. He was the last of the holders of the Wogan-Browne name in Ireland.[48] The death of his son was referred to in his obituary:

> It was a crushing blow from which he never recovered, and shortly after he left his place, Keredern, near Naas, never to return.[49]

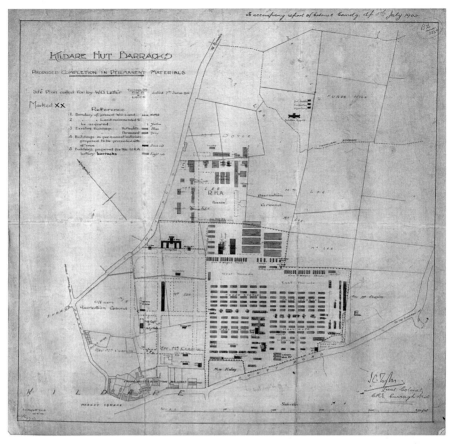

Image 1: Plan of Kildare Barracks as constructed showing proposals for expansion and completion in permanent materials, June 1902. (Courtesy of Military Archives, Dublin)

Image 2: Postcard view of Kildare Barracks, early 1900s. (Author's collection)

Image 3: Postcard view of Kildare Barracks, early 1900s. (Author's collection)

Image 4: Married Quarters, Kildare Barracks 1907 with Lena, daughter of the contractor Albert Payne. (Courtesy of Frank Goodwin)

Image 5: Internal view of Married Quarters showing the interlinked terraced houses. (Courtesy of Frank Goodwin)

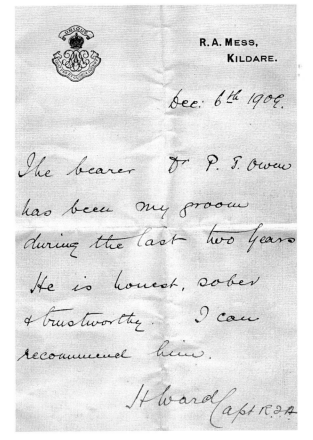

R. A. MESS,
KILDARE.

Dec: 6th 1909.

The bearer Dr. P. T. Owen has been my groom during the last two years He is honest, sober & trustworthy. I can recommend him.

H Ward Capt R.A.

Image 6: Reference for Driver Philip Owen of Swansea, signed by Captain Ward, 6 December 1909. (Courtesy of Angela Dauria)

Image 7: XXXIII Brigade Royal Field Artillery at Kildare, November 1905. This photograph was taken at the commanding officer's house across the road from the barracks.

Rear: Sergeants Lucas, Skingsley, Uphill, Dabbs, Everest, Paterson, Chalmers, Murphy, McCorkindale, Farrier-Sergeant O'Neill, Sergeants Prince, Gildon.

Centre: BSM Voce, Scoffield, Passfield, Barnes, Captain H.E.T. Kelly, Lt. Colonel H.K. Jackson, RSM W.G. Presbury, BQMS Sandilands, BQMS Lee, BQMS Smith, Saddler-Staff-Sergeant Longmire.

Front: Sergeants McDonald, Wilson, Law, Saddler-Sergeant Mealyer, Farrier-Sergeant Daly, Sergeant Perry. (Courtesy of Paul Skingsley)

Image 8: Kildare Barracks viewed from the Round Tower. (Author's collection)

Image 9: 15-pounder field gun of 137 Battery, Royal Field Artillery at annual training camp in the Glen of Imaal, County Wicklow, May 1903. (Courtesy of Paul Skingsley)

Image 10: Ceremonial shoot by 18-pounders of 885 Battery, King's Birthday, 4 June 1919. (Author's collection)

Image 11: Lieutenant-Colonel Arthur Charles Bailward (1855–1923) commander of the XXXIII Brigade at Kildare in 1902. (Author's collection)

Image 12: Gunner Robert Allan from Aberdeen enlisted in the Royal Field Artillery in 1903 and was posted to XXXIII Brigade at Kildare. (Courtesy of Alistair Allan)

Image 13: Sergeant George Edward Nurse, 131 Battery, winner of the Victoria Cross at Colenso, South Africa in December 1899. (Author's collection)

Image 14: Gunner George A. Jarrold, Suffolk who was posted to Kildare in 1915. (Courtesy of Jenny Smith)

MEMBERS SERGEANTS' MESS,
8th Bde. Royal Field Artillery,
KILDARE, 1913.

Image 15: Sergeants of VIII Brigade who were posted to Kildare in 1913. (Author's collection)

Image 16: 4.5-inch Howitzer Battery, Royal Field Artillery at Kildare 1916. (Courtesy of Reggie Darling)

Image 18: Civic Guards at Kildare town wearing the first ever issue of uniforms, 1922. (Garda Museum)

Image 17: Lieutenant John Hubert Wogan-Browne. (Cheltenham College)

Image 19: Civic Guards undergoing physical training at Kildare in 1922. (Garda Museum)

CHAPTER 11

THE EVACUATION – 1922

Provisional Government took over Kildare Barracks (RA) without incident at about 14.00hrs today.

WAR OFFICE, 15 APRIL 1922

The Irish Republican Army at Kildare during the handover of the RIC Barracks, April 1922. (Courtesy of Kildare County Library)

Following the War of Independence and signing of the Anglo-Irish Treaty of December 1921, the British made plans to vacate all barracks throughout Ireland. A conference was held by the military at the Curragh on 28 March 1922 to discuss the practicalities of evacuating the military stations under the control of the Fifth Division. In respect of Kildare, Lieutenant-Colonel Jeudwine confirmed that:

> KILDARE Barracks to be evacuated as soon after the evacuation of the married families from KILDARE. The 4.5" Howitzer Battery will then be accommodated at NEWBRIDGE Barracks and the dismounted RA personnel from KILDARE and NEWBRIDGE accommodated at the CURRAGH. Officers Mess furniture and Officers furniture for quarters to be withdrawn and despatched to Ulster. The remainder of the equipment, barracks and Ordnance stores, exclusive of regimental equipment be handed over to representatives of the Provisional Government as soon after the move of married families as can be arranged.[1]

The evacuation of Kildare Barracks commenced early in 1922. The newspapers reported:

> Two batteries of the Royal Field Artillery stationed at Kildare are under orders to leave for Bulford Camp, in England. These are the only batteries of the Royal Field Artillery at present in Kildare. The barracks there was built during the Boer War to accommodate six batteries.
>
> The departure of the troops is causing a great deal of unemployment among the civilian population at Kildare and in the Curragh district. Many civilian workers are under notice.[2]

The British military made some provision for civilian employees who worked in stores and the maintenance of essential services in barracks. Lieutenant-Colonel Jeudwine circulated a document to all stations noting that 'A guarantee of three months employment at a wage not less than now issued, or proportionately more if the responsibilities are more, to be given by the Provisional Government.'[3]

The civilian employees, who were employees of the Board Of Works, were not retained permanently as all of the staff involved in maintenance – eleven men – consisting of three carpenters, a bricklayer, a plumber, some labourers, a carter and an electrician were let go as the Provisional Government had over 100 men employed in works companies in the barracks in 1923.[4] The army offered civilian employees the chance to attest into the army to allow them to retain their positions but would not pay them as civilian employees. This led to a dispute in Athlone Barracks and similar issues arose in Kildare, Newbridge and the Curragh where some of the men were not willing to enlist in the national army. Senator Cummins who was also chairman of Newbridge Town Commissioners made representations to the Minister for Defence Richard Mulcahy. At Athlone and Mullingar, civilian employees were removed from their positions for failing to attest into the army. Mulcahy advised Dáil Éireann that civilian employees worked for the Board of Works but as the military took over barracks from the board 'civilians became disemployed'. At Kildare there were a 200 employees, made up of general workers, carpenters, plumbers and electricians. Representations were made to retain three carpenters, some labourers, a bricklayer and an electrician. The military took a different view:

> It was a question whether for day-to-day maintenance a staff like that was required at all, and certainly not when their own men were capable of doing the maintenance work required, especially when large work could be given to an outside contractor.[5]

However, at least one employee, John Higginbottam of Nurney, remained employed as a carter until September 1923.[6]

One soldier deserted from the barracks in its last days at Kildare. Frederick George Ware deserted 48 Battery, Royal Field Artillery at Kildare in April and was arrested over a year later in July 1923. It was noted that his battery was now in India.[7] Perhaps the thoughts of moving to a station in India prompted the gunner to give up military life. On 4 March 1922 the following units were at Kildare and Newbridge:

XXX Brigade Royal Field Artillery – Kildare
One battery XXXVI Brigade Royal Field Artillery – Kildare
XXXVI Brigade less one battery – Newbridge
Detail of I Brigade Royal Horse Artillery – Newbridge

The soldiers in Kildare held a dance at the end of March. While the dance was taking place, someone attempted to steal the safe from the canteen and it was later found unopened in a nearby field. There were a number of incidents around the town in the run-up to the evacuation as republicans flexed their muscle and the new Provisional Government tried to take control. Commandant Kavanagh, IRA Liaison Officer based at Naas reported in his weekly report for County Kildare to GHQ in Dublin that a wagon of hay was destroyed and:

On Wednesday night in Kildare town the residence and motor car of George Graham, a Protestant were destroyed by fire started by armed 'Republicans'. Graham, I understand, is a rather obnoxious character given to send the Pope to hell while drunk (Graham, not the Pope). This I presume is another 'Boycott' incident forgotten during the war.[8]

The military were concerned about getting their families out of Ireland and this was addressed by Lieutenant-Colonel Jeudwine on 21 March 1922 who advised that: 'All married families, both officers, NCOs and men to be evacuated from CURRAGH, KILDARE, NEWBRIDGE and NAAS by the 18th May.'[9]

The handover of barracks was also a complicated matter:

The question as to the disposal of KILDARE Barracks and HARE PARK Camp to be taken up with GHQ. If necessary HARE PARK Camp to be used to accommodate RA personnel from KILDARE, the latter station to be given up as soon after 1st May as can be conveniently arranged.

In other incidents on 12 April, Connaught Lodge, the home of Captain Ernest

Northern was burnt down by armed men and Leinster Lodge, the home of Margaret Chaplin was destroyed. Gunners of the Royal Field Artillery were on hand to assist with putting out the fire at Connaught Lodge. The local IRA dissociated themselves from the burning of houses in the Kildare district, and the commander of anti-treaty IRA forces, Thomas Harris, warned against persons interfering with meetings in favour of the treaty or the destruction of their property.[10] The difficult emerging situation in the country was well summarised by a note placed in the local newspaper by the IRA Brigade Commandant Thomas Lawler:[11]

> To all Officers and men of the 7th Brigade
> I hope to be able to visit all units of the Brigade in the next few days to put the present army position before all ranks personally. Meanwhile I rely on all officers and men to remain steadfast to General Headquarters and Dáil Éireann.
>
> Members of the Army in this area are relieved of the responsibility of obeying orders of former officers who have repudiated General Headquarters.
>
> Signed Thomas Lawler
> Brigade Commandant
> 7th Brigade
> Naas
> 6 April 1922

The two arson attacks and the attack on Graham were the subject of malicious injury claims received by Kildare County Council.[12] Before the British had left, the battle lines for the forthcoming civil war were being drawn as republicans attempted to undermine the new state and British forces attempted to stay out of trouble and leave the country as quickly and smoothly as possible. Unfortunately, as outlined previously, Lieutenant Wogan-Browne was the main victim in Kildare of this period of transition.

The British army now moved to evacuate stations as quickly as possible. Lieutenant-Colonel Jeudwine submitted revised plans for the evacuation of Kildare on 4 April 1922 to General Headquarters in Dublin: The Royal Irish Constabulary barracks at Kildare was evacuated the next day on Wednesday 5

April 1922 and taken over by General Headquarters.[13] Kildare artillery barracks was handed over to the Provisional Government on Saturday 15 April 1922 and was marked by a telegram to Dublin from the Curragh simply stating:

> Date: 15.4.22
> Provisional Government took over Kildare Barracks (RA) without incident at about 14.00 hrs today.[14]

The relatively short British Army occupation of Kildare Barracks had lasted a mere twenty years from April 1902 to April 1922.

Part II
The Irish 1922–1998

CHAPTER 12

THE CIVIC GUARDS AND CIVIL WAR 1922

In loving memory of
VICE-COMMANDANT SEAN NOLAN, KILDARE.
WHO FELL IN ACTION 6TH JULY 1922,
AT CURRAGHTOWN HOUSE, KELLS. AGED 24 YEARS

GRAVESTONE INSCRIPTION, TULLY, KILDARE

Training Staff of the Civic Guard Depot at Kildare, 1922. (Courtesy of Garda Museum)

Following the withdrawal of the British army, the barracks became a training camp and headquarters for the new civic police. An advance party of 300 men left the showgrounds at Ballsbridge, Dublin on 9 April and travelled to Kildare by train where they were joined by a further 600 new recruits for the force.[1] All the new Civic Guards, including Commissioner Mel Staines, Patrick Greenan, Assistant Commissioner and Joseph Ring, Camp Commandant, were in 'civvies' as new uniforms had not been tailored. They carried Lee Enfield rifles with bayonets fixed and came under attack from irregular forces within a week of arriving. There was some disquiet in the barracks because the new police force took on former members of the Royal Irish Constabulary as instructors, much to the annoyance of some republicans.

In February 1922 Michael Collins had established a committee to examine a replacement force for the RIC and within a month had decided on the establishment of the Civic Guard. Following the withdrawal of the British army, the barracks was selected as the site for the training of the new Civic Guard and 800 men were sent to their new headquarters at Kildare on 25 April 1922 where the new recruits engaged in drill instruction and route marches as far as Newbridge and Monasterevin. Within a week of arriving the Civic Guard was attacked by anti-treaty forces and soldiers were put on the gate to protect the barracks. There were simmering tensions in the barracks when the new recruits arrived as they found themselves being instructed by former RIC men. These experienced policemen were appointed over former republicans and tensions came to a head on 15 May 1922 when a former Cork IRA man, Thomas Daly, the leader of the mutineers presented an ultimatum to the commissioner of the Civic Guard demanding the expulsion of five named former RIC men. Commissioner Staines ordered a full parade of the barracks and when he ordered the signatories of the ultimatum to step forward, a shouting match ensued and the parade was abandoned in chaos.

The next day, Newbridge Barracks was handed over to the Civic Guard and while the commissioner was there, the mutineers in Kildare raided the armoury and seized rifles, revolvers and ammunition. Meanwhile, Staines had called for backup from the army, which had just taken over the Curragh from the British army to assist the Civic Guard. A unit from the Curragh arrived in Kildare but was prevented by armed civic guards from entering the barracks and a stand-off ensued with the army threatening, at one point to open fire and assault the gates of the barracks. The situation was so serious that Michael Collins came to Kildare and met the mutineers, agreeing to set up an enquiry into the mutineers' demands, provided that Commissioner Staines and other senior civic police were allowed back into Kildare Barracks.

However, when the senior policemen arrived at the gates, they were refused entry. Sergeant Patrick McAvinia and Superintendant John Byrne, both former RIC men arrived at the gates to gain access. When the mutineers saw these two ex-RIC men weapons were drawn and Superintendent Byrne was narrowly missed by a shot. (Perhaps Kildare might claim to have seen the first shots of the Civil War rather than those of a month later in Dublin's Four Courts.) The two ex-RIC men fled, and while being chased by a mob they entered the Railway Hotel where they tried to make a phone call. A crowd gathered outside and threatened to burn the place down. The RIC men escaped out the back door and hid in the house of the Carmelite friars before escaping back to Dublin the next day.

Tensions did not completely ease, as on 17 June, days before the seizure of the Four Courts in Dublin by anti-treaty forces, Daly met a force of anti-treaty men from Dublin outside the town who went with him to the barracks, tied up the guards on duty and commandeered the rifles and ammunition from the armoury with some more of the civic guards joining them and then returning to Dublin and to the Four Courts.

The matter was raised in Dáil Éireann where it was reported that:

> We have positive evidence that on Sunday, 18th June, Rory O'Connor, Ernest O'Malley, and Thomas Barry, with an armoured Lancia car, and a force of Irregulars from the Four Courts, held up members of the Civic Guard, disarmed them, and took possession of their arms, at the Cross at Kildare. The disarmed civic guards were there and then informed by the O'Connor-O'Malley-Barry

party 'that they had declared war on England, that they had issued an ultimatum for Monday morning, and that they did not want to be fighting with Irishmen,' and they asked the civic guards 'to come along with them'.

The Civic Guard did not remain in Kildare much longer and had vacated the barracks by late September 1922. The overall impact of the Civic Guard's short stay in Kildare and the mutiny was that the new police force was reconstituted as an unarmed one which aimed to have closer links to the wider community and be much less like a colonial police force in the way the RIC was perceived. The nature and pace of events also highlighted the tension in the country between pro and anti-treaty forces in the build-up to the civil war and showed that the animosities of the war of independence were not to be easily quelled.

An argument over the payment of a bill by the Civic Guard ended up being discussed in the Dáil when Deputy Aodh Ó Culachain enquired about an account owed by the Civic Guard at Kildare Barracks to Mr Laurence Berns, poulterer, Kildare. Berns had furnished bills several times to the commandant's office, Civic Guard Depot, for £15 for provisions supplied in December 1922, but was not paid.[2]

> The Minister, Kevin O'Higgins, stated that he was informed that Mr. Berns supplied eggs to the guards' mess at their depot in Kildare. Provisions so supplied are not chargeable to public funds, and consequently payment in such cases is a matter for settlement between the trader concerned and the officer in charge of the messing account. I understand that Mr. Berns has been repeatedly informed that not more than fifty dozen eggs were supplied by him, and payment for that quantity amounting to £7 10 shillings has been repeatedly offered to him in settlement of his account. Liability for any greater quantity is denied.

Another Kildare resident, Brigid Doyle, of Hospital Street had an issue with the military and sought compensation from the military authorities after her horse was commandeered by Captain O'Donoghue and Private Michael Dillon, a native of Kildare town on 1 July 1922 for a period of eight weeks.[3]

A Civic Guard pipe band was formed in Kildare Barracks shortly after their arrival in April 1922 when pipe master Daniel J. Delaney gathered six other recruits, including John Meighan who had played in a pipe band in County Kilkenny These men were some of the first to receive new uniforms.[4] The pipe band would often lead up to 1,000 men on route marches to Monasterevin and Newbridge. The band also played the reveille at 6.30 a.m. each morning and remained at Kildare until they were transferred to Dublin in August 1922.

Civic Guard Sports

The Civic Guard engaged in a number of sporting pursuits while stationed at Kildare. A boxing tournament was organised for August 1922 but was postponed following the death of Arthur Griffith but were eventually held in the riding school of the barracks.[5] The first Civic Guard national sports day was held in September 1922 in the barrack field shortly before the barracks was vacated. General Eoin O'Duffy, recently appointed Commissioner of the Civic Guard travelled from Dublin for the sports. The Civic Guard Pipe Band was on hand to entertain the crowd. The manager of the local Hibernian Bank assisted in judging the cycling events, while the Southwell Challenge Cup was presented by J.J. Murphy of Kildare for the best performing individual guard.[6]

Civil War

The civil war impacted directly on Kildare town. Despite the strong national army presence at Kildare, The Curragh and Newbridge, anti-treaty forces remained active in the area. The first local casualty, however, was a Free State soldier named Sean Nolan who was killed in action on 5 July 1922 at Kells, County Meath. He ran from cover to throw a grenade at anti-treaty forces surrounded in a building. Sean Nolan was 24 years old and the son of Jeremiah and Annie Nolan who had lived at Poundgreen, Kildare town. He was interred at Grey Abbey, Kildare.

IN LOVING MEMORY OF
VICE-COMMANDANT SEAN NOLAN, KILDARE.
WHO FELL IN ACTION 6TH JULY 1922,
AT CURRAGHTOWN HOUSE, KELLS. AGED 24 YEARS.

OF DUTY MINDFUL TO HIS LAST DRAWN BREATH
HE TO HIS COUNTRY HIS YOUNG MANHOOD GAVE
ALONE HE WALKED TO DANGER AND TO DEATH
AND WON WHAT HE HAD CRAVED A PATRIOT'S
GRAVE.

A few metres away in the same graveyard lie seven men who fought on the other side:

TO THE MEMORY OF
COMDT BRYAN MOORE   I.R.A. AGE 37
SECTION COMM. JAMES CONNOR   "   "   24
VOLUNTEER PATRICK MANGAN   "   "   24
VOLUNTEER PATRICK NOLAN   ,,   ,,   24
VOLUNTEER JACKIE JOHNSON   ,,   ,,   18
VOLUNTEER STEPHEN WHITE   ,,   ,,   19
VOLUNTEER PATRICK BAGNALL   ,,   ,,   19
EXECUTED AT CURRAGH CAMP
DEC. 18TH 1922

Their deaths were far more controversial. An IRA column engaged in sabotaging trains passing Kildare who were members of the Rathbride IRA were captured in a dugout about two miles outside the town, brought to the Curragh Camp and seven were executed within a few days. One of those killed, Patrick Bagnall wrote to his uncle on the night before he was executed:[7]

Hare Park Prison,
18 XII 22
Dear Jimmie,
I hope you and Nellie are well. Tell all the boys and girls I was asking for them. I am writing to my sister and father. I am to be shot in the morning, 19th Dec. at 8.15. Mind Mary, and do what you can for her. I know this will nearly kill her. We are all here – seven of us – Johnston, Mangan, White, Moore, Nolan, Connor and I. We are all to go West together, so don't forget to pray for us. I know you and Willie will be sorry, but it is all for the best, and I hope it sets old Ireland free. Tell them all in Kildare I was asking for them. Don't forget Harry Moore. We are dying happy anyway, so good-bye old Kildare. Good-bye Jimmie and God bless you. I will meet you in Heaven. Tell Tom Byrne I was asking for him.
Your loving nephew
Paddy Bagnall.
The priest's name and address is Father --- Curragh Camp. A very nice man. You can write him if you want to. He said we will die like men anyway.

This small graveyard also contains a gravestone erected by the Commonwealth War Graves Commission to 3439 Private W.H. Honour, Inniskilling Dragoons, who died on 7 September 1914 at 38 years old. Represented in this small part of Kildare is the complex history that was early twentieth-century Ireland.

Works Corps
After the departure of the Civic Guard from Kildare, the barracks came under the control of the Works Corps, who would later form part of the Army Corps of Engineers and they held their annual sports at Kildare in August 1923.[8] There are few surviving records relating to this period, but the following were the senior military officers in Kildare in 1923:[9]

Officer Commanding:	Captain J. Flanagan
Quartermaster:	Lieutenant P. O'Rourke

A soldier stationed at the barracks at this time, Volunteer Thomas Clements was accidentally shot by a colleague in the barracks on 31 March 1923. Clements lived at Waverley Cottages on the edge of the Curragh and lost the use of his right arm as a result of the incident.[10] Clements was originally from Buncrana, County Donegal and had enlisted in the army in September 1922.[11] In late 1923, the works Corps, Salvage Corps and Engineers amalgamated into the Engineering Corps and Kildare was made ready for a significant development in the history of the army.

Army School of Instruction

The Army School of Instruction was established at the Military Barracks, Kildare by General Staff Organisation memorandum No. 8 dated 14 November 1923.[12] The School was responsible for 'giving all officers in the army a general course of training' and 'Training officers who have secured 75 per cent of the total marks allotted for merit in the general course of training and who have been specially recommended by their Commanding Officers, in the next higher rank to that which they hold or entering the School.'

The School intended to give one month's training to officers who had not completed the Officers' Training Course previously held at the Curragh and qualified officers would form a class composed of twenty cadets, thirty second-lieutenants, thirty lieutenants, twenty captains, ten commandants and five majors. The memorandum expands on the organisation of the school as follows:

> The School will be commanded by a Colonel, who will be responsible for the administration and interior economy and for supervising the training in the School. He will be assisted by the Chief Instructor, who will actively superintend all training within the School and who will be the Principal Lecturer. The Chief Instructor will be assisted by 9 Instructional Officers and 17 Non-Commissioned Officer Instructors, whose duties will be detailed by the Chief Instructor. The officer and N.C.O. Instructors will not be detailed for any duty other than that of training.[13]

The first transfers to the school, referred to as the Kildare Military College[14] in February 1924 and Officers' School of Instruction[15] in August 1924, were as follows:

Transfers

Major General Sean Quinn, Corps and Services to Kildare Military College
Colonel Francis Martin, Corps and Services to Kildare Military College
Captain John Chisholm, Corps and Services to Kildare Military College

By the middle of 1924, the Officers' School of Instruction at Kildare had the capacity for training 200 officers and had a staff of 164 officers, NCOs and men.[16] A separate NCOs School of Instruction with a capacity for training 280 students appears to have been in operation in the Curragh at the same time.[17] There was some minor disgruntlement about conditions at Kildare as the matter of troops being forced to remain in the barracks until 6 pm in the evening was raised in Dáil Éireann in April 1924. It was claimed that soldiers had to remain in barracks on Saturdays and Sundays, whereas the normal practice in other barracks was to allow men out at 2 p.m. and return by 10.30 p.m. at the weekend without passes.[18] In October 1924 three NCOs stationed at the barracks at this time fell foul of the licensing laws. Sergeant-Majors Thomas Connors, Hugh Peacock and John Murphy, all stationed at Kildare Barracks were charged by Guard Haverty for being in Michael Cunningham's public house at a prohibited hour. When Guard Haverty knocked on the door of Cunningham's Public House at 9.50 p.m. he did not gain access until 9.55 p.m. When he did get in, there were empty bottles in the yard and he discovered the three NCOs hiding there. [19]

Local representatives sought the use of military property to ease some of the housing shortages in the town. Hugh Colohan TD enquired of the Minister for Defence 'whether the four houses (Married Quarters) recently built by the British War Department at the rear of Kildare Military Barracks, on the road leading from the Railway Hotel to the Standhouse, could be transferred to the local authority, and on what terms, so that they may be able to ease, even in a small way, the housing problem which exists in an acute form in the town of Kildare'. The Minister for Defence, General Mulcahy, replied that 'the houses referred to may be required in the near future for occupation by troops. A decision cannot, therefore, be taken at present on the question of making them available for civilian tenants.'[20]

CHAPTER 13

THE ARTILLERY CORPS 1925–1939

On Friday last [20 February] 370 artillery arrived from Dublin to quarter at Kildare. The barracks is ideal for them as it was the old artillery quarters and every accommodation is available for these regiments.

KILDARE OBSERVER, 28 FEBRUARY 1925

No. 1 Battery, Artillery Corps at Kildare, 1931. (Courtesy of Brendan Culleton)

The Artillery Corps was formed at Islandbridge Barracks, Dublin (later called Clancy Barracks) on 23 March 1923 under the command of Major Patrick A. Mulcahy with the assistance of Commandant Paddy Maher, Commandant Edward O'Leary and Captain Tim Finlay, when they took over nine 18-pounder guns. The first official appointments to the Artillery Corps, in April 1923, were:[1]

Commanding Officer:	Major Patrick A. Mulcahy
Second-in-Command:	Commandant Patrick Griffin
Adjutant:	Commandant Edward O'Leary
Quartermaster:	Commandant Dominic Mackey
Training Staff:	Captain Harry Frowd St. George Caulfeild
Remounts:	Captain Tim Finlay
	Second-Lieutenant M. Delaney
Staff:	Second-Lieutenant E. Treacy
	Second-Lieutenant M. Buckley

These, however, were not the first to serve in artillery in the new Free State army: There were a number of gunners who served prior to March 1923 who continued in service into the new Corps. At the onset of civil war in June 1922, the Free State Army fired a number of 18-pounder field guns at the Four Courts in an attempt to oust anti-treaty forces who had occupied the building. The first gun was manned by Sergeant William Copley and Corporal Michael McLoughlin and a number of other unidentified gunners, under the command of Captain Tommy Doyle. It is well known that the gun crews were not trained for the task and were issued with the wrong type of ammunition. One of these guns was subsequently fired at an engagement at Millmount, Drogheda and at Passage West, Cork after the landing of Free State troops in August 1922. The military census of November 1922 reveals that a sizeable number of men throughout the army were designated as artillery, concentrated at the Curragh, Victoria Barracks, Cork; Portobello, Dublin and at Tralee, County Kerry. These gunners were involved in a number of actions during the course of the civil war.[2]

William Copley (1888–1952) had more experience than most. He was born in Limerick and enlisted in the Connaught Rangers in 1902 at 14 years of age. On completion of five years' service, he re-enlisted on 16 July 1907 with the Royal Dublin Fusiliers. He was stationed at Gravesend in England with the Second Battalion when the war broke out, went to France in August 1914 with the British Expeditionary Force and was injured in the fighting at Le Cateau. He was captured by the Germans and sent to Limburg as a prisoner for the remainder of the war and was demobilised in March 1919. He married Winnifred Doherty in 1919 and enlisted in Dublin in the new army on 17 July 1922. Copley was one of those who manned the 18-pounder guns in the shelling of the Four Courts. He spent much of the civil war at the Curragh before transferring on its formation to the Artillery Corps, and was subsequently one of the first to be transferred to the anti-aircraft battery on its formation in 1931. Having been a prisoner of the Germans at Limburg for over four years, it is somewhat ironic that he spent a period during the Emergency years in the Curragh guarding German prisoners who had crash-landed in Ireland. He continued to serve in the Artillery Corps at Kildare until 1946 when he retired as a company-sergeant.

Many of these original gunners continued in the Artillery Corps at Kildare, such as Patrick Webb who was originally from New Row in Athy, County Kildare who was the eldest son of William and Maria Webb. He continued in the service with a stint in the anti-aircraft battery in the 1930s. Sergeant Hugh Bryan, who had an address in Scotland, enlisted in Dublin in April 1922 and was stationed in Victoria Barracks, had served previously with the Royal Field Artillery having joined at Athlone in September 1915, served in Salonika from November 1915 to May 1917 and in France from July 1917 to April 1918.[3] Another gunner with a Scottish address was Louis O'Carroll who enlisted on 1 July 1922 when he was 19 years old and remained with the corps until the 1950s.

Major Patrick Anthony Mulcahy (1897–1987) the first commanding officer of the Artillery Corps was from Waterford and served with the British Army during the war. He had worked in Ennis post office as a telegraphist and joined the Royal Engineers on 26 April 1916 as a specialist telegraphist, the same week his brother, the future Minister for Defence Richard Mulcahy was participating in the rising in Dublin, an event that delayed Patrick's journey to England for enlistment in the Royal Engineers. He served in France from February 1917 as a sapper in the telegraph system and left the British army in February 1919. He joined the mid-Clare brigade of the IRA as an intelligence officer and commanded the North Tipperary flying column until the truce. He joined the National Army in 1922 as a colonel-commandant and served with the Signal Corps in the Third Southern Division. He commanded the Artillery Corps from its foundation in 1923 and served as Director of Artillery from 1931–35 and 1942–49, as Quartermaster-General from 1949 and as Chief of Staff of the Defence Forces from 1955–59 before taking up a career in the horseracing industry.[4]

Patrick Maher (1895–1986) was a native of Cloughjordan, County Tipperary. He served with Tipperary No. 1 Brigade IRA during the War of Independence and joined the national army in 1922, serving with the Third Southern Division in the Signal Corps at Portlaoise. He served as Director of Artillery from 1935–42 before taking up an appointment to manage Shannon Airport from 1942 until his retirement in 1960.[5]

No. 1 Battery was formed on 10 July 1923 with an establishment strength of five officers, eighteen NCOs and ninety-three gunners and its first task was a display at the army championships meeting in July 1923.[6] The actual strength was eleven officers, sixty-two other ranks and ten horses. In 1924 the Artillery Corps moved to Marlborough Barracks (later renamed McKee Barracks). Under the reorganisation of the army in February 1924 and the demobilisations and demotions during the same period, the Artillery Corps was commanded by the following:

Officer Commanding:	Colonel Patrick A. Mulcahy
Adjutant:	Commandant Patrick Maher
Quartermaster:	Commandant Dominic Mackey

The Corps set about creating a professional force and the task of selecting suitable officers, NCOs and men was carried during the summer of 1923 as some of the original gunners were replaced by more suitable candidates. The first training officer in the corps was Major Harry Frowd St George Caulfeild, (1881–1961) who was commissioned into the Royal Field Artillery in 1900 serving until 1907. He was recalled into service in February 1915 as an Acting Captain, serving in the United Kingdom with 3A Reserve Brigade, Royal Field Artillery and during the war as an Acting Major. Major Caulfeild had also served with Q Section of the Auxiliary Division Royal Irish Constabulary (ADRIC) or 'the Auxiliaries' as they were known during the War of Independence. Ultimately, he may have served as little as three months as training officer of the Artillery Corps. He was replaced by Garrett Brenan in November 1923,[7] another former gunner with the Royal Garrison Artillery. During this period after the initial establishment of the corps examinations were held in 1924 to remove unsuitable officers and introduce more suitably qualified ones.

Mulcahy found an ex-British army gunner to command No. 1 battery: A report on potential artillery gunners recorded that: 'Captain McLoughlin did a good exam and I am anxious to retain him in the Corps.'[8] Captain James McLoughlin (1895–1966) was transferred from the General Headquarters Inspection Staff to the Artillery Corps on 1 October 1924 and was appointed officer commanding No. 1 Battery. He was born at Kilcorney, Enfield, County Meath in May 1895. He enlisted in the Royal Garrison Artillery in November 1915 serving with a siege battery in France from 1916–18 and being wounded in action in March 1917. After the war he served in the Sudan and was posted to Cork in 1919 as a sergeant where he married Margaret Molloy in Kinsale in October 1921. He enlisted in the army on 25 August 1922 in Kinsale, serving with the 59 Infantry Battalion and as officer in command of Innishannon Barracks. He served as adjutant at Portobello Barracks before being posted to the Artillery Corps as battery commander of No. 1 Battery in October 1924. He served in the Military College from 1931 as the artillery instructor and, during the Emergency, commanded the V Brigade at Kilkenny and from 1942, the III Brigade. He served as Director of Artillery from 1949 to 1955.

No. 2 Battery was formed in Dublin on 2 January 1925 under the command of Captain William Tierney prior to the move to Kildare. The experience of senior staff of the new Artillery Corps – which included Irish Republican Army, British and Canadian Army backgrounds – was crucial in creating an experienced army corps. Also crucial to this development were the non-commissioned officers who carried out the day-to-day running of the corps, training and instilling the culture of the organisation. The NCO class were almost exclusively ex-British army.

To Kildare

The entire Artillery Corps moved by train to Kildare town in February 1925, a major undertaking as the horses and limbers had to be loaded onto the train, unloaded in Kildare and brought through the town to the new barracks. The *Kildare Observer* reported that:

> On Friday last [20 February] 370 artillery arrived from Dublin to quarter at Kildare. The barracks is ideal for them as it was the old artillery quarters and every accommodation is available for these regiments.[9]

Sergeant Bill Bonar recalled the horses and guns being unloaded from the railway station in Kildare and brought to the barracks.

> We came from the railway station with increasing speed and came around Graham's corner (into Market Square) at full tilt with outriders on the lead horses urging them on, drivers shouting, whips cracking, horses galloping and gun and limber wheels crashing on metalled road.[10]

Sergeant William Bonar (1902–80) was born in Tullygordan, County Donegal in 1902 and enlisted in the British Army in May 1918 at 16 years of age and served in Mesopotamia (Iraq) during the Arab rebellion of 1920–21 with 2 Battery, XIII Brigade, Royal Field Artillery in operations in the Euphrates area south-west of Baghdad. He enlisted in the Free State Army on 6 June 1924 and was posted to the Artillery Corps. He was a career soldier and typical of the experienced NCOs that the new Artillery Corps relied on to train the gunners, and he would serve during the corps' formative years. He was one of the first men posted to the anti-aircraft battery on its foundation, serving during the Emergency with the IV Field Artillery Regiment in Mullingar and retiring in February 1947 with the rank of company sergeant.

The impact of the army's arrival on the population level of Kildare was immediate. While there was no census in Ireland in 1921 for a comparison, the 1926 census recorded the following occupations at Kildare:

	Male	Female
Producers and Repairers	211	16
Transport and Communication	76	3
Commerce, Finance and Insurance	61	39
Public Administration and Defence	384	3
Professional Occupations (Teachers etc.)	15	32
Personal Service	29	127
Clerks and typists	9	8
Other Gainful occupations	102	-
Total Employed	887	228
Total Unoccupied	110	434
Total Population	**1,244**	**872**

The military published an army directory in 1926 that recorded the following staff of the Artillery Corps at Kildare in 1926:[11]

Headquarters Staff

Officer in Command:	Colonel Patrick A. Mulcahy
Adjutant:	Commandant Patrick Maher
Quartermaster:	Captain Richard Callanan
Assistant Quartermaster:	Lieutenant Thomas J. Lambert
Horsemaster:	Captain Thomas P. Finlay
Instructional Officer:	Captain Garrett Brenan

No. 1 Battery, Artillery Barracks, Kildare

Officer Commanding:	Acting Captain James McLoughlin
Second in Command:	Lieutenant Denis J. Cody
Right Section Officer:	Second-Lieutenant Michael J. Kelly
Left Section Officer:	Second-Lieutenant Peter P O'Farrell

No. 2 Battery, Artillery Barracks, Kildare

Officer Commanding:	Captain William Tierney[12]
Second in Command:	Acting Lieutenant Michael P. Buckley
Right Section Officer:	Second-Lieutenant Charles Trodden
Left Section Officer:	Second-Lieutenant Eugene Kilkenny

Garrett Brenan (1884–1966) was born in Kilkenny and served with the Antrim Royal Garrison Artillery (Special Reserve) as an officer from 1906. He was promoted to Captain on 9 May 1909. In 1911 he was living in Dublin. He was posted to France with the rank of Captain on 29 April 1916 and was promoted Acting Major in command of a battery on 9 December 1916. He served with 79 Siege Battery, LXVII Brigade. He was awarded the Croix de Guerre on 23 July 1918 and was mentioned in dispatches on 18 May 1918 and 23 December 1918.[13] He reverted to Captain from 1 November 1919 on ceasing to command a battery. He was transferred to the Artillery Corps in November 1923.[14] He was appointed Instructional Officer with the Artillery Corps in 1926 but did not remain at Kildare very long. He retired to Ballyragget, County Kilkenny and died on 11 May 1966.

Richard J. Callanan (1901–1986) was born in Kilree, County Kilkenny and served with the Longford Brigade IRA during the War of Independence commanding D Company and joined the National Army on its foundation. He became Officer Commanding Eastern Command in 1958 and served as Assistant Chief of Staff from 1961–62. He was a brother-in-law of Patrick Maher.

Denis J. Cody was a native of Thomastown, County Kilkenny. He enlisted in the army in 1922. He was transferred from 11 Battalion to the Artillery Corps on 11 November 1924.[15] He subsequently commanded Columb Barracks Mullingar, retiring in November 1953. Thomas Lambert, a native of Blackrock, County Dublin served with E Company, 6 Battalion IRA during the War of Independence having joined in 1917. He joined the National Army in 1922 and served at Kildare until his retirement in 1946. He died in Donnycarney, Dublin on 14 June 1959.[16]

The strength of the Artillery Corps at Kildare was based on similar lines to that of the British Army units that were stationed there a few years earlier. Each battery contained the following:

1 Battery Sergeant Major, 1 Battery Quartermaster Sergeant, 1 Farrier, 5 Signallers, 1 Artificer, 1 Wheel Builder, 2 Saddlers, 3 Clerks, 3 Cooks, 1 Wagon Line Corporal, 2 Clerks (Pencillers), 2 Shoeing Smiths, 1 Battery Office Orderly, 1 Storeman, 5 Batmen-Groom-Horseholders, 2 Trumpeters, 4 Coverers, 4 Sergeants (No. 1), 40 Gunners, 29 Drivers.

The army calculated that Kildare Barracks was capable of accommodating twenty-three officers and 924 other ranks in 1928 although the number actually accommodated was less than 400.[17] Discipline in the Artillery Corps was stricter than in other army units. John 'Pal' Byrne who enlisted in the Corps in 1928 recalled:

> Discipline had become strict, very strict, and strictest of all in the artillery. Only the highest standards of training, drill and dress were tolerated and woe-betide he who was lax or sloppy. But we soon became accustomed to this new army style as we felt that it made us better soldiers and a better unit, and in our knee britches, long leggings and leather bandoliers we felt that we were the pride of the army.[18]

The Artillery Corps were immediately involved in ceremonial duties with No. 1 Battery, travelling by road to participate in the St Patrick's Day parade in Dublin on 17 March resting at Kill and Rathcoole on the way before spending the night at the Hibernian Schools in the Phoenix Park.[19] In respect of the annual Wolfe Tone commemoration at Bodenstown, County Kildare on 21 July 1925, it was noted that:

> The main body of the troops participating did not move until the Sunday morning. On that date a Battery of Artillery, under the command of Captain J. McLoughlin left Kildare Barracks, Curragh at 05.00 hours, proceeding by road to Bodenstown, and was followed along the same route three hours later by a Troop of Mounted Infantry under the command of Instructional Officer T. Clancy.[20] On 6 August 1925, No. 2 Battery participated in

the annual Griffiths-Collins anniversary parade as 7,000 troops marched through the centre of Dublin.[21]

The First Shoot

Training in the 1920s and 1930s was an arduous task for the Artillery Corps. As in the days of the British army, there was no live firing carried out at Kildare so every summer, the batteries travelled to camp in the Glen of Imaal in County Wicklow. Although artillery had been fired during the Civil War, there was no chance for the Artillery Corps to fire live shells. Major Bryan Cooper spoke at length in Dáil Éireann in May 1925, during a debate on the army estimates, on the need for artillery officers to experience the effects of live fire in the Glen of Imaal and the necessity to open the artillery ranges. The Minister for Defence, Mr Hughes, replied that 'the artillery will get an opportunity in the Glen of Imaal this season of seeing whether they can shoot straight or not'.[22] In the same debate, on a discussion about the cost of maintaining horses in the army, he was asked as to whether the horses used by artillery officers were of any use or just ornamental. Hughes replied 'For use, undoubtedly. You cannot have an artillery officer walking after his gun. I am sure it would look undignified.'[23]

Finally, the opportunity had arrived. The Artillery Corps carried out their first shoot in the Glen of Imaal on 1 September 1925 when they had received enough ammunition to fire the 18-pounder guns. It was reported in *An-t-Oglach* that 'on the 1st September was fired by No. 1 Battery the first shell in the first firing practice of the first Irish artillery'. The commanding officer Patrick Mulcahy recalled that:

> 'We had guns and we had knowledge but we couldn't start shooting until the ammunition arrived – eventually it did. I remember the morning the first shoot was carried out. The first round was fired at 10 o'clock by myself to ceremoniously open it up.'[24]

The guns were under the control of the training officer Captain Garrett Brenan and a surviving gun record sheet records six rounds fired on 1 September 1925 and further firing during the remainder of the week. This was the same gun that fired 375 rounds during the Battle of the Four Courts from 28 June 1922 under the command of Captain Johnny Doyle and was fired at Passage West, Cork on 8 August 1922. [25]

The next day, while the camp continued in the Glen of Imaal, No. 1 Battery under the command of Captain McLoughlin marched to Dublin to participate in a review in the Phoenix Park of troops of the Eastern Command comprising of 2,500 troops.[26] Following the review, the Battery returned to the Glen of Imaal, most likely after being on the move since before dawn. Someone involved in the events asked in *An-t-Oglach*: 'When No. 1 Battery was half way on the road from Dublin who spread a rumour that the canteen in camp was closed down? A joke's a joke, but cruelty is another matter.'[27]

An-t-Oglach reported that the first practice was carried out on Friday 11 [sic] September 1925 although all other contemporary reports refer to the 1 September 1925:

> No. 1 Battery, consisting of 4 guns and wagons, paraded in drill order at Coolmoney Camp at 10.30 hours, and moving off without delay reached a point close to the selected firing position at 11.15 hours.
>
> The Minister of Defence, accompanied by the Minister of Finance, the Chief of Staff, D.A.A.G., Q.M.G., Major-General Hogan, G.O.C. Eastern Command; Major-General MacEoin, G.O.C. Curragh Camp; Major-General Brennan, G.O.C. Southern Command, and Col. Dunphy arrived at 12 noon, and were received by Major Mulcahy, O.C. Artillery, with whom they proceeded to inspect the Battery on the roadside. After the inspection, the Battery proceeded to occupy the selected position. The target consisted of two lines of figures representing infantry entrenched at a range of about 5,000 yards, and the Ministers and General Officers having taken up a position from which to observe the shooting, the O.C. Artillery directed the Battery Commander to open fire.
>
> The range was quickly found and effective fire was brought to bear on the target, firing continuing for about an hour.
>
> Subsequently the Ministers and General Officers inspected the targets and were highly pleased with the results of the shooting.

The party returned to Coolmoney, and after lunch the Artillery Camp was inspected.[28]

On their return from the Glen of Imaal, No. 1 Battery were entertained by No. 2 Battery Dramatic Class to a concert and play which was held in the Recreation Hall, Kildare Barracks on Wednesday, 16 September 1925. Participants from No. 2 Battery were Corporal C. Griffen, Drivers P. Ryan, J. Roe, D. Quinn, M. Quinn and J. Purdue, Gunners R. McAnespie, T. O'Toole, T. Smith and T. Rice.[29]

Annual Camp

Following this first successful shoot, the Artillery Corps's long relationship with the Glen of Imaal began. Annual training for the army was organised on a large-scale basis from this time, with units sent to Kilbride Camp, County Wicklow, Finner Camp, County Donegal and Kilworth Camp, County Cork. In 1926, the Artillery Corps were under canvas at Coolmoney Camp in the Glen of Imaal from 14 to 31 July 1926.[30] It was reported that they carried out a demonstration shoot on 29 July 1926:

> Nos. 1 and Nos. 2 Batteries carried out a demonstration shoot in the presence of the President, the Minister for Defence, the Chief of Staff, several other Ministers, and a number of senior officers. The shoot was highly successful.[31]

The weather was not good at that particular camp and it was reported that 'Before the end of the present week we hope to be back in our galvanised huts in Kildare. Rain sounds much nicer off galvanised than off canvas. The number of swimmers has dwindled a lot in the past week or two. There is no need to get into the river when you can get just as wet on the bank.'[32] This shoot was filmed by British Pathé News and shown under the title 'In the Wicklow Mountains President Cosgrave and Mr. Hughes, Minister for Defence, watch Irish Artillery Practice.' The film camera caused some excitement which was remarked upon by the *An-t-Oglach* correspondent who reported that: 'No. 1 Battery made "some rush" to see the Pathé Gazette.'[33] Getting the guns from Kildare to the glen was a major exercise for both horses and men. One of the hills on the road from Kildare to Wicklow became known as 'Sub-section Hill' as it was on this point of the journey that the horses pulling the guns were changed on the way to the glen.[34] There were attempts in the 1920s to examine a replacement to the horse with tests carried out with a Fordson tractor to see whether a tractor or horse was better for artillery in Ireland.

> A very difficult route was laid down, which included rocky paths, steep slopes, fords – in fact, all classes of obstructions likely to be met with by a gun during warfare.
>
> The horse-drawn gun and limber first travelled the route and succeeded in leaving the tractor behind. In spite of expert driving, the tractor failed to overcome some of the obstacles. The horses completed the course to the delight, needless to say, of the drivers and gunners.[35]

There was, of course, routine training to be attended at the Curragh. For example, a musketry course was held in the Army School of Instruction at the Curragh from October to December 1926. Second-Lieutenant Peter P. O'Farrell, Left Section commander; No. 1 Battery; Second-Lieutenant Eugene Kilkenny, Left Section commander, No. 2 Battery; and 54038 Sergeant J. Boles attended.[36]

Gunners and Drivers

The Artillery Corps referred to soldiers as drivers and gunners unlike infantry units where a soldier holds the rank of private. The Artillery Corps outlined in two short articles in *An-t-Oglach* in June and August 1926 the roles of gunners and drivers.

> When a man joins the Artillery it is first decided whether he will become a Gunner or Driver. As far as possible a man is given his own choice, but certain qualifications must be considered. For instance a man 6 feet tall would not be very suitable as a Driver.
>
> The Gunner receives instruction in a variety of subjects, namely, foot-drill, gun-drill, laying-drill, musketry, rifle-drill, knotting and lashing, semaphore, range-finding, shells and fuse setting, topography, director work and gunnery, as well as receiving a

course of physical training.

When in the recruit stage he will first of all go through the foot-drill and find himself gravel crushing for about one month or maybe six weeks on the square, after which he receives lectures on elementary gunnery and the parts of the 18 pdr Field Guns. He is then instructed in standing gun-drill, which the average Gunner takes at least six months to become efficient in. He next learns a little about knotting and lashing, which is very useful in Artillery work, and his knowledge of this subject is put to the test in camp life for the transportation of guns, etc.

Having completed the more or less elementary stage the Gunner is then taught gun-laying – embracing the use of the dial sight, field and sight clinometers, which are very interesting instruments in themselves. From this point onwards the Gunner becomes really keen in his work – which reaches the culminating point during the annual field firing practice in camp, when live ammunition is fired from the guns, which echo and re-echo along the mountain ranges for miles around.[37]

The writer noted that the driver is the one who counts to get the gun into position and that the gunner comes into his own at that stage. He noted that the driver, above all else must have an interest in and liking of horses which is more than 'two bob each way at the Curragh or Baldoyle'. The writer states:

> Like his brother soldier, the gunner, he has to go through his paces on the square, and does his rifle and marching drill for some weeks until he is 'passed out.'
>
> Then he is introduced to stables and here soon becomes proficient in the art (and it is an art) of grooming a horse. He is getting along famously now, although he is not told so. Then, one never-to-be-forgotten day the orderly sergeant approaches and, in his most mournful note, tells him: 'You're for riding school tomorrow, 9 o'clock.' He looks as sympathetic as only an orderly sergeant can look.
>
> However, our bold recruit turns up, in every sense of the word,

next morning, and every morning for a couple of months, until he is finally discharged as an efficient horseman. In the meantime he has been taught all there is to know about the care and cleaning of harness and how to harness his horses, and has received numerous lectures on driving and the care of his horses. He also goes through his course of dismounted driving drill, and eventually turns out in a team for driving drill proper.[38]

Many of those who joined the Artillery Corps at Kildare had previous service in other Irish army units. Lawrence Newman (1907–99) was from Blackhorse Avenue in Dublin and had enlisted in 1925. He completed two years service in February 1927 and left the army. Like many others, work was hard to get and he worked at odd jobs for eight months before deciding to re-enlist. He recorded that:

> There was still no sign of permanent work turning up, so I decided to return to the Army on 10 October of that year. There were only 4, all ex-soldiers, put on the train and drafted to the Curragh Camp. They did not lose much time getting us dressed and formed into a platoon, of about 25 men. Our instructors were Sergeants Warne and Goddard. Little did I realise that one day I would become their brother-in-law.[39]

Coincidentally Warne and Goddard had both served in the Royal Field Artillery during the war and were stationed at Kildare after the war where they fell for two sisters. Percy Warne (1896–1944) married Brigid Byrne in 1919 and Ernest Goddard (1899–1988) married Molly Byrne in 1920 but both had to return to England for demobilisation and then came back to Ireland in 1923 to enlist in the Free State army. Warne, from Ipswich, ended up in 3 Battalion in the Curragh and Goddard in the Army School of Physical Instruction. Lawrence Newman married a third sister, Rose Byrne, in 1933. He was posted to the Artillery Corps and recorded his early memories of going to Kildare:

> We finished our training and were paraded on the square by the CO inspections. He informed us that some artillery officers were

arriving to look us over and select 30 for the Artillery Corps in Kildare Barracks. We collected our kits and marched down to Kildare Barracks. We were well received by all the artillery lads and were billeted in one of the old tin huts. The food was not so hot. You had to parade with your mug and plate and march to the dining hall seven days a week. Friday you got boiled fish. Very few of the lads would eat it. They went to the canteen and got tea and cakes. I remember Frank Donnelly complaining one day to the Orderly Officer about the quality of the food. We all backed him up but it did us no good and poor Donnelly was the bad guy after that. They were always on his house after that even though he was a good horseman.[40]

After initial training at Kildare, gunners were assigned to a battery. Lawrence Newman was posted to No. 2 Battery under the command of Bertie Thomson. He was there for less than a month when Lawrence and a colleague decided to take a trip home to their families in Dublin during the weekend. They got a bus on the Curragh Road to Dublin but on their return they were taken at the barracks gate to see the Commanding Officer and were sentenced to fourteen days CB (confined to barracks). CB generally consisted of peeling potatoes and fatigues. Sergeant Crowley, a Corkman, oversaw the punishment and stayed with them at all times, walking stick under his arm. Gunners were then required to undergo live fire training.

> After our training, we were all paraded for the Glen of Imaal to do fire exercises. Myself and two others were appointed to the barracks policemen under a Sergeant Crowley. He did not remain long with us and was replaced by Corporal Corcoran. Our job was to patrol the camp during day and night and mainly to stop the lads from going down to the river Slaney to catch trout. When the Glen finished we returned to Kildare and took over duties from the Red Caps who were returned to the Curragh.

The presence of military policemen at the gates of Kildare seems to have been an oversight by the military in the Curragh who eventually realised that the artillery should be guarding its own barracks. Lawrence Newman was promoted as follows:[41]

Corporal:	12 May 1933
Temporary Sergeant:	14 July 1943
Sergeant:	31 January 1947

He served with the following units:

No. 2 Battery, Artillery:	March 1928
Depot Artillery:	September 1931
I AA Regiment:	January 1960

Lawrence married Rose Byrne at Kildare in 1933 and they had five children, Lawrence, Elizabeth, Patrick, Francis and Philomena. As is the army way, he was not taken onto the married establishment until 1935. He remained in the Artillery Corps until he retired in 1967. He got a civilian job in the Curragh with the Corps of Engineers, later getting a transfer back to Kildare with the Engineers.

The Artillery Corps gained another experienced gunner in 1927 when Bertie Stuart Campbell Thomson (1884–1952) was transferred from the School of Instruction at the Curragh. The military career of Bertie Stuart Campbell Thomson is a fascinating story. He was born into a military family at Chatham, England on 4 November 1883 where his father James Thomson was serving with the Sixth Regiment of Foot (Warwickshire Regiment). In November 1897 at the age of 14, B.S.C. Thomson enlisted in the Royal Artillery at Woolwich as a trumpeter. He served in South Africa from 1899 to 1905, which included service during the Boer War and transferred to India until January 1908. He fought at the Relief of Ladysmith and the Tugala Heights.

He was discharged from the British army from 55 Battery (XXXVII Brigade) at Fethard, County Tipperary in March 1911 with the rank of corporal, having completed thirteen years service. He married Caroline Sayers in 1911, emigrating to Canada in the same year. When war broke out in 1914 he enlisted in the Canadian army on 8 January 1915 and served with the Royal Canadian Artillery. His brother Duncan enlisted in the Warwickshire Regiment for the duration of the war. Thomson was posted overseas with the VI Howitzer

Brigade Ammunition Column, Royal Canadian Field Artillery. This Brigade was sent to England in September 1915 prior to service in France. On 10 October 1916 Regimental-Sergeant-Major B.S.C. Thomson was granted a temporary commission in the Canadian Field Artillery, posted to 2 Canadian Division Ammunition Column attached to VI Brigade Canadian Field Artillery for duty.[42] On 21 October 1916 he was posted to VII Brigade Canadian Field Artillery and on 25 October at Courcelette he was posted to D 21 (Howitzer) Battery and was involved in heavy fighting in November and December 1916 when his battery suffered many casualties.

Following his service in the British army, he moved to Ireland and enlisted in the new Free State Army. As well as having served previously in Fethard, Thomson's mother Frances was Irish, which goes some way towards explaining his reason for serving in Ireland. He served in the Army School of Instruction in the Curragh as an instructional officer with the rank of Captain, prior to returning to artillery following their transfer to Kildare in 1925.

He served as commander of the I Field Artillery Brigade in the 1930s and was involved in musical societies and the arts in Kildare. B.S.C. Thomson was well known for his artistic talents. He contributed regular cartoons to the army journal *An-t-Oglach* and contributed line drawings of many of the features in St Brigid's Cathedral, Kildare for publication in a short history of the Cathedral published in 1930. His caricatures were well known in Kildare. On one occasion after spotting a gunner taking a break while working in the stables, a caricature of the man, leaning on a pitchfork, appeared on the mess noticeboard for all to see.[43] Another gunner recalled a time he spent in hospital: 'One day Captain B.S.C. Thomson arrived at my bedside to see how I was. He took a pad out of his pocket and a black crayon pencil. While maintaining a pleasant chat he pencilled away and handed me the finished drawing. That drawing showed me resting with one elbow on the pillow and the other hand on my head. I recognised it as a work of art and thanked him.'[44] Two of Thomson's original images adorn the walls of Reggie Darling's barbers in the Curragh. He was still at Kildare during the Emergency and was posted to Cork. He was one of the very few, therefore, who could claim service in the Boer War, The First World War and the Emergency. After his retirement, he died in Salisbury, Southern Rhodesia (Harare, Zimbabwe) in March 1952.

Military Mission to America

Another crucial development in the corps at this time was the military mission to America. The fledgling Free State army looked abroad for assistance in many aspects of its development and the military mission of 1926 was a crucial part of this initiative. While much expertise had been gained from, primarily ex-British soldiers, the army looked further afield, partly as a way of distinguishing itself from the British army but also to get the best expertise in areas of development. The Army School of Music was commanded by Commandant Saurzweig from Germany while the Army Equitation School called upon a Russian national Paul Rodzianko. The new army had to develop its own expertise. Charles Trodden (1904–47), born in Belfast, was selected, in July 1926, on behalf of the Artillery Corps to travel to America with the Military Mission. His father Ned Trodden, a barber, was murdered in his home in Belfast in September 1920 in an official reprisal by a group known as the 'Murder Gang' during the troubles of that time.[45] Trodden attended the Battery Officers' Course at Fort Sill, Oklahoma from 15 September 1926 to 10 June 1927. Eighty-three officers, including two from Cuba, participated in this course: eleven of them failed. On his return, Trodden was prominent in establishing the Artillery School at Kildare. He also participated in a coastal artillery course in Shoeburyness in England in 1930. He married Eileen Collin-Powell in Cork in 1931 and died in Dublin in December 1947. The main training room in Kildare Barracks was named Trodden Hall in his honour.

The Gunners

The Artillery Corps was only as good as those who served, and only the brightest and best generally went to Artillery. The gunners who served at Kildare came from a variety of backgrounds with many officers and NCOs having wide and varying degrees of military experience.

Henry (1904–80) and Eugene Brannigan (1911–2006), two brothers from Tullybrian, County Monaghan were amongst the earliest members of the corps. Henry Brannigan enlisted at Ballybay Barracks on 1 July 1922 and was posted to 58 Infantry Battalion at Dundalk during the Civil War. He was only 17 years old and was a company-sergeant at this time. Henry was injured in an accident in Dundalk in November 1922 when he shot himself in the ankle while cleaning his revolver. He was discharged on 28 April 1924 during the reduction in size of the army but re-enlisted again on 27 October 1924 being posted to the Artillery Corps in Dublin and transferring to Kildare in 1925. The following are the units in which he served:

58 Infantry Battalion, Dundalk:	1 July 1922 – 28 April 1924
Artillery Corps, Kildare:	27 October 1924 – 9 October 1929
Artillery School of Instruction:	10 October 1929–15 September 1931
Field Artillery Brigade:	16 September 1931–14 February 1934

He was promoted to corporal in June 1925 and to sergeant on 30 November 1931. Brannigan was a Monaghan inter-county footballer and was prominent on the artillery teams of the time.

His younger brother Eugene Brannigan was born at Old Cross Square, Monaghan in September 1911 and enlisted on 30 October 1930 at 19 years of age. He was a cabinetmaker before enlisting. His service record with the Artillery Corps gives an indication of the experience of many as they progressed through their careers:

Unit	Date	Location
Regimental Training Depot	21 October 1930	Curragh
Field Artillery Brigade, Kildare	31 January 1931	Kildare
1 Field Battery	12 Ocober 1931	Kildare
Field Artillery Brigade	11 April 1932	Kildare
Field Artillery Brigade, 1 Battery	12 October 1933	Kildare
Field Artillery Brigade	9 March 1934	Kildare
Coastal Artillery, Cork	1946	Cork
Retired	29 May 1957	

Eugene retired with the rank of BQMS. The Brannigans had a third brother Joseph who also served in the army as an officer and retired with the rank of lieutenant-colonel.

Patrick Culleton (1901–66) was born in Mountmellick, County Laois in 1901. He enlisted in the army together with his brother Jerry at Mountmellick on 15 April 1922. Patrick was given the number 16713. On enlistment his name was written as 'Cullerton' and his entire service was under this name. He served during the civil war and was stationed at Tommevara, County Tipperary. He transferred to the Artillery Corps on its foundation where he was a trumpeter. He served with 1 Field Battery during the 1920s and was a member of the 1 Reserve Battery on its foundation in 1931. He remained in the Artillery Corps until September 1939. After military life he went on to work as a salesman.[46]

Another gunner was James Cummins who was from Cork city. He enlisted in the National Army in 1922 and was posted to the Artillery Corps. His brother Joseph was an officer in the army. Cummins served at Kildare until the 1940s when he was posted to the coastal defences at Spike Island. When he died in 1957, he was the most senior Sergeant Major in the army. As a Corkman, he had the pleasure of playing for Kildare against Kerry in the All-Ireland football final of 1926.[47]

One recruit to the army was David Scott (1903–62) from Boardsmill, County Down who had served as an underage soldier with the Royal Irish Rifles, in the British army. He was not on the face of it a likely recruit, coming from a northern Protestant background. His son, David Scott who also served in the army recalled that: 'During the Civil War, General Michael Collins made a call for ex-British soldiers to enlist and my father enlisted out of a sense of loyalty to Collins.'[48] Two other northerners who joined with Scott were Bernard McCourt and Louis O'Carroll who would, like Scott, serve as NCOs until after the Emergency. Scott would ultimately serve as regimental sergeant major retiring on 27 March 1958. His son, also David Scott served in the Defence Forces with the Army School of Music retiring in 1990 with the rank of instructional sergeant-major.

Other early recruits who would see service into the 1950s included William Downey, who served with K Battery of the Royal Horse Artillery at Vimy Ridge. He went on to be a company sergeant-major with the 3 Field Battery in 1937 and regimental sergeant-major from 1943–46. Laurence O'Reilly, born in County Wexford in 1903, who had been interned at the Curragh during the War of Independence, and enlisted on 4 May 1927 (No. 68308). Other recruits to serve into the 1950s were:

Patrick Egan, born 13 April 1902 enlisted on 12 April 1927 (No. 68131)

James O'Donnell, born 20 July 1899 enlisted on 13 June 1924 (No. 58859)

Richard Duggan, born 4 November 1903, enlisted on 5 October 1925 (No. 66990)

Joseph Barlow, born 18 January 1907, enlisted on 29 January 1925 (No. 64204)

John Brabston, born 11 May 1906, enlisted 10 May 1925 (No. 65534)

James Sheridan, born 12 October 1907, enlisted 3 November 1924 (No. 62787)

Thomas Taylor, born 13 August 1907, enlisted 5 February 1923 (No. 54000)

Louis O'Carroll, born 10 November 1903, enlisted 1 July 1922 (No. 53408)

Bernard McCourt, born 9 August 1903, enlisted 28 July 1924 (No. 60175)

CHAPTER 14

THE COOLMONEY CAMP DIARY – 1936

'The 13th Field Battery gave a display of indiscipline during breakfast hour by throwing eggs round the dining marquee. The matter is at present under investigation...'

COOLMONEY CAMP DIARY– FRIDAY, 19 JUNE 1936

Artillery shoot with 18-pounder field guns in the Glen of Imaal, 1930s. (Courtesy of Mary D'Arcy)

A surviving handwritten camp diary for Coolmoney Camp gives a full account of the annual training camp held in the Glen of Imaal in May and June 1936.[1] The diary contains fascinating details of the parties coming and going to camp and is reminiscent of war diaries kept by British units during the First World War. It records the arrival of regular and volunteer batteries, the number of rounds fired, the numerous inspections, visiting dignitaries and a number of unusual and even amusing incidents, which no doubt, were not seen as amusing at the time. To most gunners, the basics of the shoot and camp were no different to those carried out by the British since 1899 in the Glen of Imaal and not much different to those carried out until the 1990s. The batteries undergoing training reported to Kildare before moving to Coolmoney Camp. The camp opened on 16 May when the advance party of 1 Field Battery arrived at the camp and continued until 17 July when 4 Field Battery left camp for Kildare and returned possession to the camp caretaker. The scale of units trained and dates of occupation of the camp were as follows:

1 Field Battery (Regular)	18 May – 2 June
1 Light Battery (Volunteer)	26 May – 2 June
3 Light Battery (Volunteer)	26 May – 2 June
9, 10, 11, 12 Field Batteries (Volunteer)	27 May – 2 June
3 Field Battery (Regular)	3 June – 23 June
13, 14, 15 16 Field Batteries and 4 Light Battery	12 June – 23 June
4 Field Battery (Regular)	23 June – 17 July
5, 6, 7, 8 Field Batteries, 2 Light Battery (Volunteer)	4 July – 14 July

The 1, 3 and 4 Field Batteries were regular batteries of the I Field Artillery Brigade and they took it in turns to act as depot battery during the course of the

1936 annual practice camp with the Artillery School and Depot staff remaining in camp for the duration. The camp was occupied by four volunteer field batteries and one volunteer trench mortar battery, working in three separate rotations. There were also first-line reservists in the camp undergoing their annual training. Every unit of the corps attended except the anti-aircraft battery, which commenced separate training at Gormanston range, County Meath from 1936. The diary is a remarkable document recording the arrival and departure of officers and men and their batteries and the various dignitaries who came to witness the shoots. The annual camp was a serious business with regular officers, volunteer and potential officers put through their paces acting in the different tasks they might be presented with, firing the different charges and weapons. It also records a number of incidents of note such as missing targets, a complaint about food, hikers on the range and an unhappy farmer – a diary that could just as easily have recorded any annual camp held in the Glen of Imaal throughout the twentieth century.

Monday 18/5/36

On Monday the 18th of May 1936 the 1Field Battery under 2/Lieut. G. Heffernan proceeded by road from Kildare to Coolmoney Camp, Glen of Imaal, Co.Wicklow.

Battery strength: 3 officers, 85 other ranks, 60 horses.

An advance party under 2/Lieut. C.E. Shortall occupied Coolmoney Camp on 16/5/36. This party which consisted of 1 officer and 26 other ranks erected tents and marquees on site and had the camp in a fit state for occupation by the battery. The camp commandant Captain H.E. MacNally and the camp adjutant and quartermaster 2/Lieut. W. Donagh arrived on the 18/5/1936. One medical orderly, 2 transport drivers and 2 signallers (radio operators) were attached to the camp staff as from Monday 18/5/36.

Tuesday 19/5/36

Sergeant Scanlon reported his arrival in camp. Thirteen (13) other ranks departed to carry out duties in Kildare Barracks during the absence of the captain's escort. The medical officer, Capt. P. Fahy accompanied by the camp commandant and adjutant carried out an inspection of the camp. Observations were made. The 1st Field Battery were employed on camp fatigues and light testing.

<u>Wednesday 20/5/36</u>

The A/Brigade commander, Capt. D.J. Collins inspected the 1 Battery lines. 2/Lieut. P. Hally proceeded to the Curragh Camp with escort to draw the following ammunition:

100 rounds H.E. 106 E

100 rounds H.E. 101 E

The 1st Battery was employed on camp fatigues and light testing.

<u>Thursday 21/5/36</u>

Divine service was celebrated in camp at 10.30 hours by the Rev. Fr. Lawrence Brophy, Donard. At 11.30 hours, a party under Sergeant Redmond proceeded to the ranges to complete arrangements for the anti-tank shoot on Saturday 23/5/36. The camp commandant inspected the 1st Battery lines at 12.00 hours. Laying drill was carried out in the forenoon and battery gun drill in the afternoon. 150 rounds of ammunition were loaded by 2/Lieut. W. Rea in preparation for Friday's shoot.

50 rounds H.E. 106

50 rounds H.E. 101 E

50 rounds shrapnel

100 rounds of shrapnel arrived from the Curragh. The horses were on grazing.

<u>Friday 22/5/36</u>

Comdt. P. Maher and Capt. D. Cody arrived in camp and proceeded to the ranges to take control of the shooting. Capt. P. Fahy, Medical Officer was in attendance at the gun positions during the firing. 2/Lieut. G. Heffernan acted as B.C. [battery commander] and 2/Lieut. P. Hally as G.P.O. [gun position officer]. 2/Lieuts. Rea and Shortall as section officer. All officers were exercised. Capt. H.E. MacNally performed the duties of range safety officer.

Battery position: Leitrim

Target area: Crissadaun to Hart O.P. [observation post]

97 rounds of H.E. were expended (50 rounds x 106 and 47 rounds x 101E). Another 50 rounds of shrapnel were loaded by 2/Lieut. C.E. Shortall in preparation for Saturday's anti-tank shooting. A convoy of five lorries under 2/Lieut. J. Murray arrived with the following ammunition

at 17.30 hours:

   380 rounds H.E. 106

   270 rounds H.E. 101E

   150 rounds shrapnel 80

   100 rounds H.E. 106 for 4.5 Howitzer

Gunner C. Grabdon, barber, reported his arrival in camp.

Saturday 23/5/36

Capt. D.J. Collins and Capt. D. Cody arrived in Camp from Kildare to control and inspect the anti-tank shooting carried out by the 1st Field Battery. 2/Lieut. C.E. Shortall acted as B.C. and 2/Lieut. P. Hally acted as G.P.O. Capt. H.E. MacNally performed the duties of safety officer.

   Battery Position and OP: East of Leitrim

   Target Area: White Rock to Hart OP

The following officers of the volunteer force reported their arrival in camp:

2/Lieut. D. Horgan, 2/Lieut. W. Murphy, 2/Lieut. D. Sullivan

2/Lieut. D. Horgan took over the duties of orderly officer at 11.00 hrs. The camp adjutant carried out an inspection of all building, tents etc. and found the camp to be in a very clean condition. 2/Lieut. J. Murray and escort arrived in camp at 12.30 hrs. with a convoy of ammunition.

160 rounds	H.E.	106	18-pounder
328 rounds	H.E.	101 E	18-pounder
160 rounds	H.E.	106	4.5-inch howitzer
228 rounds	H.E.	101 E	4.5-inch howitzer

20 rounds of shrapnel were expended by the battery during the day's anti-tank shooting.

Sunday 24/5/36

Divine service was celebrated in camp at 10.30 hours by the Rev. Fr. Lawrence Brophy, Donard.

Monday 25/5/36

Capt. D.J. Collins, A/Brig Commander and Capt. D. Cody, OC Artillery School arrived in camp in connection with the anti-tank range and the making of suitable targets in areas that were practically featureless.

2/Lieut. G. Heffernan and a fatigue party assisted in this work.

2/Lieut. P. Hally was instructed to carry out a 100% check of all ordnance on charge of the 1st Field Battery and to submit a certificate to this effect showing deficiencies (if any) to this officer before 16.00 hrs. on 26/5/36. The following ammunition was loaded by the 1 Battery:

20 rounds	shrapnel	
50 rounds	H.E.	101E
100 rounds	H.E.	106

The following ammunition arrived under escort commanded by Capt. J.K. Ryan and was taken on charge:

70 rounds	smoke 4.5-inch Howitzer
30 rounds	star shell 4.5-inch Howitzer
400 rounds	Stokes Brandt ammunition
260 rounds	smoke 18-pounders

The horses were on grazing.

<u>Tuesday 26/5/36</u>

The 1st Field Battery proceeded to the ranges at 08.00 hrs. Capt. D. Collins and Capt. D. Cody arrived in camp at 09.00 hrs. and immediately left for the ranges. Engagement of target was carried out during the forenoon and engagement of tanks in the afternoon.

In the forenoon, 2/Lieut. P. Hally acted as B.C. and 2/Lieut. W. Rea as G.P.O. 2/Lieuts. D. Horgan and D. O'Sullivan acted as section commanders. Capt. H.E. MacNally performed the duties of range safety officer.

Battery Position: East of Leitrim House

Target Area: White Rock to Hart

The following officers were also exercised 2/Lieuts. G. Heffernan, C.E. Shortall and W. Murphy. For the anti-tank shooting 2/Lieut. P. Hally acted as B.C., 2/Lieut. C.E. Shortall as G.P.O. and 2/Lieuts. Heffernan and Rea as section officers. The 1 Light Battery Cadre and the 3 Light Battery arrived from Kildare under the command of Captain F. Slater at 10.30hrs. The 1Light Battery Cadre was comprised of one officer, one C/S, one battery quartermaster sergeant, 3 corporals and 2 gunners. The 3 Light Battery strength was 4 officers, 1 acting sergeant, 2 corporals, 1 acting corporal and 65 volunteers. The following officers of the 3 Light Battery reported their arrival.

2/Lieuts. M. Somers, J. Long, J. Murphy, R. Neary

The Battery was employed in the forenoon erecting tents etc. 100 rounds of mortar ammunition was issued to Capt. Slater in preparation for shooting on Wednesday. Training on the Stokes Brandt was carried out prior to the loading of the above ammunition. The camp adjutant carried out an inspection of the camp.

It was now time for the first volunteer batteries to commence their training. The first batteries were based in the Southern Command area. 9 Battery was based in Cork, 10 Battery at Tralee, 11 Battery at Waterford and 12 (Howitzer) Battery at Clonmel. The 3 Light Battery which fired the Stokes trench mortar was based in Kilkenny and the regular battery, 1 Field Battery, that acted as depot battery, although based at Kildare was assigned to the Southern Command in Cork. Two men of the second line reserve also reported from 23 and 24 Field Batteries.

Wednesday 27/5/36

The 3 Light Battery proceeded to the ranges at 08.00 hours to carry out firing practices with the Stokes Brandt. Capt. D.J. Collins and Capt. D. Cody directed the shooting and Major McGrath, Comdt. P. Maher and Capt. M. Delaney were present during the firing.

The 1 Field Battery was employed on camp fatigues. The advance party for the 9, 10, 11 and 12 Field Batteries under 2/Lieut. Kerins arrived in camp at 10.30 hours and proceeded to make arrangements for occupation by the batteries. The 9, 10, 11 and 12 Field Batteries under Capt. C. Trodden arrived in camp at 16.30 hours. 200 rounds of ammunition (i.e. 50 shrapnel, 50 101E and 100 106E) were loaded by Capt. Trodden in preparation for the Thursday's shooting. Sight testing was also carried out.

Battery Strength:

9 Field Battery: 3 officers, 2 Sergeants, 2 corporals and 26 volunteers (21 gunners, 5 drivers)

10 Field Battery: 1 officer, 6 corporals and 33 volunteers (22 gunners, 11 drivers)

11 Field Battery: 2 officers, 1 sergeant, 5 corporals and 36 volunteers (28 gunners, 8 drivers)

12 Field Battery: 1 officer, 4 sergeants, 1 corporal, 18 volunteers (14 gunners, 4 drivers)

One man of the 23 Battery and 3 of the 24 Battery also reported (2 line) 2/Lieut. P. Curran arrived at 16.00 hours with pay. Work on the anti-tank range was carried out in the afternoon under the direction of Capts. D.J. Collins and D. Cody.

The following second lieutenants reported their arrival in camp:

2/Lieut. T. Brick A.D.C. 9 V.F. Battery

2/Lieut. T. Kerins ADC 10 V.F. Battery

2/Lieut. M. Power A.D.C. 11 V.F. Battery

2/Lieut. J. Foran A.D.C. 12 V. F. Battery

Thursday 28 /5/36

The 9, 10 and 11 Batteries departed for the ranges at 08.00 hrs. under the command of Capt. C. Trodden and returned at 14.00 hours. The 12 Field Battery under the command of 2/Lieut. Foran left for the ranges at 12.30 hours.

Battery Position:	Leitrim
Target Area:	White Rock to Hart

Capt. C. Trodden performed the duties of B.C. at G.P.O. 2/Lieuts. J. Brick and Power acted as section officers and 2/Lieut. G. Heffernan as range safety officer. The following officers were exercised: 2/Lieuts. D. O'Sullivan, W. Murphy, T. Kerins, D. Horgan and 108002 Cpl. J. McCarthy. 29 rounds of shrapnel, 12 rounds of H.E. 101E and 100 rounds of H.E. 106 were expended during the day's shooting.

The following ammunition was loaded by the 9, 10 and 11 Batteries:

62 rounds	H.E. 101E
39 rounds	H.E. 106
40 rounds	smoke

In the afternoon the 12 (Howitzer) Battery fired from the position at Seskin Schools into the area at White Rock and Camara. Capt. Trodden was B.C. and 2/Lieut. W. Rea G.P.O. 2/Lieut. Foran and Kerins acted as section commanders, Capt. H.E. MacNally as safety officer.

60 rounds of H.E. 106 were expended.

The 1 Field Battery was employed on camp fatigues. The camp commandant and adjutant carried out an inspection of the camp. 2/

Lieut. C.E. Shortall proceeded to the Curragh with a load of empty cartridge cases, 52 horse and 26 men proceeded to Kildare by road. These horse and 18 of the men were 3 and 4 Battery personnel.

Friday 29/5/36

Col. O'Higgins, Comdt. P. Maher and Capt. Keenan arrived in camp and witnessed the shooting of the Volunteer Field Batteries and the 3 Light Battery. The 9, 10 and 11 Batteries proceeded to the ranges at 08.00 hours. Capt. C. Trodden acted as B.C. and G.P.O. 2/Lieuts. T. Kerins and Horgan as section officers and 2/Lieut. P. Hally as safety officer. The batteries fired from the position east of Leitrim House into the area White Rock–Hart. The following officers were also exercised:

2/Lieut. Brick, Power, W. Murphy, D. O'Sullivan, 108002 Cpl. McCarthy, 10 Bty.

21 rounds of shrapnel; 97 rounds HE 101E; 39 rounds HE 106 and 40 rounds smoke.

The above batteries were issued with 150 rounds of shrapnel in preparation for Saturday's anti-tank shooting.

In the afternoon, the 3 Light Battery fired the Stokes Brandt from a position in the vicinity of Ballyvaughan into the area Military Road – Camara.

2/Lieut. J. Long was B.C. 2/Lieut. M. Somers, second in command and 2/Lieuts. Neary and Murphy section commanders. The 1 Field Battery was employed on camp fatigues and range fatigues. 2/Lieut C.E. Shortall proceeded to the Curragh with a load of empty cartridge cases. 52 horses and 26 men proceeded to Kildare by road. These horse and 18 of the men were 3 and 4 Battery personnel.

A wireless message was received from O.C. Kildare stating that the lorry required to return the empty cartridge cases was not available.

Saturday 30th May 1936

The 9, 10 and 11 Field Batteries proceeded to the ranges at 08.00 hours to carry out anti-tank practice. All volunteer officers were exercised in the duties of B.C.; G.P.O.; and section commander. Capt. D.J. Collins and Capt. D. Cody conducted the shooting. Capt. C. Trodden was in charge of the batteries. 50 rounds of shrapnel were expended. The afternoon was spent in cleaning the guns and cartridge cases. The 1 Field Battery was employed on camp fatigues and in preparation for their march back to Kildare. One lorry load of 1 Battery stores was dispatched to Kildare 15.30 hours. The 3 Light Battery was also employed in cleaning their equipment and stores. Capt. D. Collins and D. Cody returned to Kildare at 14.00 hours. The cadets from the Military College under Capt. McLoughlin witnessed the shooting.

Captain McLoughlin, formerly battery commander of 1 Field Battery and later the I Field Artillery Brigade was attached to the Military College during the 1930s. One of the young cadets who travelled to the Glen of Imaal on that day was Cyril Mattimoe, a future artillery officer and Director of Artillery. Mattimoe recalled the lectures given by Captain McLoughlin in the College. On one occasion McLoughlin was discussing the devastation caused by artillery during the battle of Passchendaele. He told the class that he wasn't there for the initial attack but arrived in time to see what the artillery had done. He continued to talk into lunchtime when one of the cadets put his hand up: 'Sir, it's past one o'clock, it's our lunchtime!' Mattimoe recalled that for the young cadets of the 1930s, they were very much removed from the previous generation and World War One was not a priority.[2]

After two weeks of training the 9, 10, 11, 12 volunteer batteries headed south to Cork, the 3 Light Battery to Kilkenny and the 1 Field Battery left for Kildare. The 3 Field Battery with Athlone as its nominal headquarters now took over work as the depot battery in preparation for the next set of volunteer batteries scheduled to arrive from the Western Command. The 3 Field Battery arrived in a number of parties with ten NCOs and 48 gunners in addition to a number of reservists under Second-Lieutenants Rea and Murray and commenced their own training, preparation of ranges and ammunition. Preparations were interrupted by Army Week, which occurred during annual camp so that 9 horses, 1 NCO and 40 other ranks had to return to Kildare on 9 June. Later in the week Second-Lieutenant J. Murray, Company-Sergeant Downey, Sergeants Sexton and McGough, Corporals Duffy and Haughney, Drivers Slevin, Somers, MacCawley and Farrell returned to Kildare for tent-pegging and jumping competitions, while Captain Wall left to participate in the All-Army Tennis Championships.

With the camp prepared, next up, on 12 June were the batteries of the Western Command. The 13 Field Battery, based in Mullingar, 14 Battery at Longford, 15 at Letterkenny, 16 at Ballinasloe and 4 Light (Mortar) Battery at Castlebar arrived. The strength of the batteries was considerably lower than the Southern Command units exercised the previous week. The volunteer officers were recorded as follows: Second-Lieutenants T. Lyons, M. Touhy and S. Gibbons, 4 Light Battery; J. McDermott, 13 Field Battery; J. Kiernan, 14 Field Battery; J. Campbell, 15 Field Battery; J. Sweeney, N. Monaghan, J. McEvoy, 16 Field Battery. The battery strengths were as follows:

4 Light Battery: 3 officers, 2 sergeants, 2 corporals, 22 men
13 Field Battery: 1 officer, 1 sergeant, 1 corporal, 52 men
14 Field Battery: 2 officers, 3 corporals, 39 men
15 Field Battery: 1 officer, 1 sergeant, 2 corporals, 1 acting corporal, 66 men
16 Field Battery: 3 officers, 3 corporals, 2 acting corporals, 6 men

These batteries received instruction in driving drill and equitation, while the volunteer signallers were instructed by Sergeant Redmond. Capt. Donnelly took over the 3 Field Battery guns from Captain Wall and eight light guns for laying and battery gun drill. Due to poor weather, the batteries were confined initially to anti-tank and various other lectures. By Thursday 18 June, the weather had improved enough to carry out range practice.

Thursday 18/6/36
2/Lieut. W. Mahoney went to Kildare to purchase the necessary requirements for the dinner on the occasion of the minister's visit on 22/6/36. 2/Lieuts. J. Murray and W. Rea returned from Kildare at 17.00 hours. The 15 Field Battery proceeded to the ranges at 08.00 hours under the command of 2/Lieut. J. Campbell. Capt. W. Donnelly acted as G.P.O. and 2/Lieuts. McEvoy and Monaghan section commanders. Capt. H.E. MacNally was range safety officer.

Battery Position: Vicinity of Camara Cross
Target Area: Military Road to Crissadaun
The following officers were also exercised:

2/Lieut. J. Kiernan

2/Lieut. J. Sweeney

2/Lieut. J. McDermott

The 4ᵗʰ Light Battery (trench mortars) left for the ranges under the command of 2/Lieut. T. Lyons at 13.00 hours. 2/Lieut. S. Gibbons and 2/Lieut. M. Touhy were section commanders. Capt. S. Slater acted as range safety officer.

| Battery position: | Vicinity of Ballyvaughan |
| Target area: | White Rock – Hart O.P. |

Comdt. P. Maher and Capt. Flanagan witnessed the shooting of both batteries. Capt. J. McLoughlin and Capt. C. McGoohan were present during the trench mortar shooting.

2/Lieut. W. Donagh went to the anti-tank range with the range maintenance party at 15.30 hours and carried out repairs. During dinner hour the 13, 14 and 16 batteries complained that the stew was unfit for consumption. The medical officer examined the meat and reported that it was in perfect condition but that too much 'herbs' were put in the stew. An alternative ration was issued. 2/Lieut. W. Donagh inspected the camp at 11.30 hours and found all correct. 100 rounds of H.E. were expended by the Field Battery.

40 rounds of trench mortar ammunition was expended by the light battery.

Friday 19/6/36

The following officers arrived in camp: Major P. Mulcahy, Comdt. P. Maher and 2/Lieut. W. Mahoney. The 15ᵗʰ Field Battery left for the ranges at 08.00 hours under the command of 2/Lieut. J. McEvoy. Capt. W. Donnelly was G.P.O. 2/Lieuts. J. Campbell and B. Reilly were section commanders. 2/Lieut. J. Murray was range safety officer.

| Battery position: | Seskin School |
| Target area: | White Rock to Camara |

The 13, 14 and 16 Batteries went to the White Rock range at 12.30 hours. 2/Lieut. B. Reilly was B.C. and G.P.O. 2/Lieut. M. Monaghan and Sweeney section officers and 2/Lieut. W. Rea range officer. The 3 Field Battery was employed on camp fatigues and the 4 Light Battery carried out their full programme of training. The 13 Field Battery gave a display of indiscipline during breakfast hour by throwing eggs round the dining marquee. The matter is at present under investigation. Capt. H.E. MacNally inspected the camp at 11.30 hours. A party under the command of 2/Lieut. J. Murray went to the ranges at 15.30 hours to paint objects that could be used as targets. 180 rounds of ammunition was expended.

Saturday 20/6/36

The 13, 14 and 16 Field Batteries proceeded to the ranges at 08.00 hours under the command of 2/Lieut. J. Kiernan. 2/Lieut. M. Monaghan was G.P.O. and 2/Lieuts. McEvoy and Campbell section commanders. 2/Lieut. J. Murray was range safety officer.

Battery position: Camara cross

Target area: Military Road to Crissadaun

The 4 Light Battery carried out training on the trench mortars and the 3 Field Battery was employed on camp fatigues. Capt. H.E. MacNally inspected the camp at 11.30 hours and found all correct. 121 rounds of ammunition were expended. Capt. D.J. Collins and Capt. D. Cody left for Kildare at 14.30 hours.

All weekend leave was cancelled by orders received from the Brigade adjutant.

On Sunday 21 June, the men attended service and there was difficulty in operating the wireless to contact Athlone, Curragh or Dublin. The following day, a number of dignitaries, the Minister for Defence Frank Aiken, TD and Oscar Traynor, TD Parliamentary Secretary; the Assistant Chief of Staff Major-General McNeill, the Quartermaster-General Colonel E.V. O'Carroll and the officer commanding the Eastern Command Colonel S. O'Higgins witnessed the volunteer batteries in action. This completed the training for the 13, 14, 15 and 16 batteries who left by mechanised transport for Athlone on 23 June while the 3 Battery departed for Kildare under Captain Wall leaving Second-Lieutenant Rea to take over the camp on behalf of the 4 Field Battery who were due to arrive for their training and depot duties.

Wednesday 24/6/36

The 4 Battery arrived in camp at 16.00 hours having come by road from Kildare. The battery strength was: 2 officers, 7 N.C.O.s, 37 men and 38 horses. Capt. B.S.C. Thomson and 2/Lieut. A.O'Byrne reported their arrival. Some difficulty was experienced in the final evacuation of the 3 Field Battery on this date due to the fact that lorries with 4 Battery advance party and stores did not report to camp headquarters. 2/Lieut. W. Rea had made all preparations for the occupation by the 4 Battery. The anti-tank range was again put in working order by 2/Lieut. W. Rea. The camp commandant carried out an inspection of the camp.

Thursday 25/6/36

The 4 Field Battery were employed on gun drill, laying and battery gun drill. 2/Lieut. W. Mahoney and 2/Lieut. A. O'Byrne supervised training. Capt. B.S.C. Thomson went to Kildare at 13.30 hours to check sports equipment. 2/Lieut. A. O'Byrne tested the fire safety appliances and found that the amount of hose at present in camp was totally insufficient to deal with outbreaks of fire in the forage barn or the magazine. Extra hose was applied for and the engineers were asked to fix one F.H. [fire hydrant] in the vicinity of the magazine – forage barn. Capt. H.E. MacNally inspected the camp at 11.30 hours and observations made by him were later attended to by the camp sergeant major.

Friday 26 and Saturday 27 June were spent on gun drill and laying and camp fatigues while Second-Lieutenant Rea brought a party to the anti-tank range to carry out repairs. There was an unusual and potentially dangerous occurrence on 29 June:

Monday 29/6/36

The camp commandant and camp adjutant went to the anti-tank battery position and served a warning notice on hikers who had pitched camp in the area near Ford 'B'. The actual campsite was inside the danger area for all battery positions.

The 4 Field Battery commenced its own shoot on Tuesday 3 June from Camara gun position under the command of Captain B.S.C. Thomson with Second-

Lieutenant P. Curran as gun position officer, Second-Lieutenants A. O'Byrne and W. Rea were section officers and Second-Lieutenant D. Mahoney was range safety officer. Following on from the fire inspection of 25 June an extra fire-fighting appliance arrived from the Curragh. The 4 Field Battery carried out its range practice on 1 and 2 June, once at Seskin gun position and then at Leitrim gun position.

The remaining two weeks of camp were for the batteries of the Eastern Command who arrived on Friday 4 July. The 4 Field Battery was assigned to Dublin and the 5 and 6 Field Batteries were Dublin-based while 2 Light Battery was based at Kildare. The 7 Field Battery came from Monaghan while 8 Battery was based in Dundalk thereby, excepting the anti-aircraft battery, ensuring that the entire Artillery Corps attended camp in 1936.

The officers who arrived were: Capt. M. O'Carroll, officer commanding eastern volunteer training cadre; Second-Lieutenants P. Brennan and R. Rowan, 2 Light Battery; Second-Lieutenants F. Connaughton, J. Nolan, and [?] Reddin, 5 Field Battery; Second-Lieutenant M. Doyle, 6 Field Battery; Second-Lieutenant P. McKenna, 7 Field Battery; Second-Lieutenant S. Smyth, 7 Field Battery; Second-Lieutenant C. O'Sullivan, 8 Field Battery; Second-Lieutenant P. Quinlan, 10 Field Battery.

The Battery Strength were as follows:
5 *Field Battery:* 2 officers, 2 corporals, 2 a/corporals, 23 gunners, 11 drivers. Total: 40
6 *Field Battery*: 1 officer, 1 sergeant, 1 corporal, 1 a/corporal, 10 gunners, 13 drivers. Total: 27
7 *Field Battery:* 2 officers, 2 corporals, 1 a/corporal, 16 gunners, 7 drivers. Total: 28
8 *Field Battery:* 1 corporal, 3 a/corporals, 13 gunners, 3 drivers. Total: 20
2 *Light Battery:* 2 officers, 1 sergeant, 2 corporals, 63 gunners. Total: 68

On Sunday 5 July, the camp commandant received a complaint from Mr Finlay of Ballytoole, Knocknarrigan, stating that the troops had caused considerable damage by going through his meadows and crops and breaking down his fences and leaving gates open. The troops were paraded and instructed that

Mr Finlay's lands were out of bounds and a notice to this effect was published in orders. Mr Finlay was still not satisfied and sought compensation for the damage to his crops. On Monday 6 July the 4 Field Battery were employed in camp fatigues and training in preparation for the night firing. The 5, 6, 7 and 8 Batteries carried out gun drill, laying, battery gun drill and fuse setting under the supervision of Capt. M. O'Driscoll. The 2 Light Battery were in training under the supervision and instructions of Capt. F. Slater. Capt. M. O'Carroll took over the battery from the camp quartermaster and the camp commandant inspected the gun parks, stables and lines. Capt. D. Collins and Capt. D. Cody arrived from Kildare and inspected the training, which was in progress at 11.30 hours. 2/Lieut. W. O'Mahoney proceeded to the range with a fatigue party to erect targets for the night firing.

Tuesday 7/7/36
All batteries carried out training as per programme. 2/Lieut. W. Mahoney went to the ranges at 09.00 hours to complete the erection of targets. 2/Lieut. P. Hally and 21 other ranks arrived from Kildare to take part in the night firing on Wednesday.

The 21 other ranks who arrived with 2/Lieut. P. Hally appear to have been with the 1 Field Battery.

Capt. D. Collins and Capt. D. Cody arrived from Kildare at 19.00 hours. Capt. H.E. MacNally and 2/Lieut. W. Donagh went to Ballytoole to interview Mr. J.W. Finlay. The 2 Light (Mortar) Battery carried out their full training programme for the day and loaded and prepared ammunition for Thursday's shooting. It was noticed at 18.00 hours that one of the two targets that had been erected for the night firing had disappeared. 2/Lieut. W. Mahoney was instructed to investigate the matter. Comdt. P. Maher and Capt. R. Callanan arrived from Dublin at 19.00 hours and later witnessed the night firing.
100 rounds of ammunition were expended by the 5, 6 7 and 8 Batteries.7 rounds of star and 5 rounds of H.E. were expended by the 4 Field Battery. 4 rounds of smoke and 36 rounds of H.E. were expended by the 1 Field Battery.

Thursday 9/7/36

The 5, 6, 7 and 8 Batteries went to the ranges (anti-tank) at 09.15 hours under the command of Capt. M. O'Carroll. Weather conditions were responsible for the late hour of leaving camp.

B.C. and G.P.O.:   Capt. M. O'Carroll
Section commander: 2/Lieut. V. Smith and 2/Lieut. J. Nolan
Range safety officer: 2/Lieut. W. Rea
Battery position: East of Leitrim
Target area: White Rock to Hart O.P.

All officers were exercised as G.P.O. and section commanders in the engagement of tanks. 2/Lieut. W. Mahoney went to the ranges to investigate the disappearance of the target erected for the night shooting. He went at 06.30 hours and returned at 10.00 hours. He reported that no trace or portion of the target was left and that it had obviously been willingly taken away by some person or persons unknown. Capt. H.E. MacNally carried out an inspection of the camp at 10.30 hours. The 4 and 1 Field Batteries carried out training in preparation for the night firing on Friday. Capt. F. Slater went to the ranges at 12.00 hours by tractor and A.C.E. trailer.

Mortar position: Ballyvaughan Hill
Target area: White Rock to Camara O.P.

2/Lieut. R. Rowan and P. Brennan were exercised as battery commanders.

Friday 10/7/36

The 5, 6, 7 and 8 Field Batteries proceeded to the ranges at 08.00 hours under the command of Capt. M. O'Carroll. 2/Lieut. P. McKenna was B.C., 2/Lieut. F. Connaughton G.P.O. and 2/Lieuts. W. Reddin and C. O'Sullivan section commanders. 2/Lieut. W. Rea acted as range safety officer.

Battery Position: Camara Cross
Target area: Military Road – Crissadaun

100 rounds of H.E. were expended. 2/Lieut. W. Mahoney went to the ranges to erect targets for the night firing. The 1 and 4 Field Batteries went to the ranges at 18.00 hours to carry out night firing practices by the aid of star shells. Shooting finished at 24.00 hours.

The following officers witnessed the shooting: Major Gen. H. MacNeill,

Major Gen. J. Sweeney, Col. O'Higgins, Major Mulcahy, Comdt. P. Maher, Col. McCorley.

A tea ration was served on the ranges at 21.00 hours. The 4 Field Battery expended 28 rounds (20 star, 8 H.E.). The 1 Field Battery expended 70 rounds (50 smoke, 20 shrapnel). All volunteer batteries were marched to the ranges to see the shooting.

The 11 and 12 July were spent in preparation for the President's visit on Monday 13 July.

Monday 13/7/36
The 5, 6, 7 and 8 Field Batteries proceeded to the ranges at 08.00 hours to carry out observed shooting in the forenoon and anti-tank practices in the afternoon. A dinner ration was served to the above on the ranges. The 2 Light Battery went to the ranges at 08.00 hours and returned at 13.00 hours.

Battery position for field batteries: East of Leitrim
Target area: White Rock – Camara
Battery position for 2 Light Battery: Ballyvaughan

The 4 Field Battery was employed on camp fatigues in preparation for the President's visit. Capt. H.E. MacNally and 2/Lieut. W. Donagh inspected the camp at 12.00 hours.

The following arrived in company with President De Valera: Mr. F. Aiken Minister of Defence; Mr. O. Traynor, Parliamentary Secretary; Mr. Patrick MacMahon; Mr. J. Irwin; 2/Lieut. Vivion De Valera; Master Ruaidhri De Valera; Master O. O'Ryan; Master Tairdhealbhac De Valera; Major General McSweeney; Major General McNeill; Col. Hayes; Col. O'Higgins; Major P. Mulcahy; Comdt. P. Maher; Capt. R. Callanan; Capt. J. Flanagan; Capt. J. Budd; Capt. E. Prendergast; Comdt. E. Hegarty.

The President accompanied by the Minister for Defence and Parliamentary Secretary inspected the camp at 14.00 hours and then proceeded to the anti-tank range to witness the shooting.

The appearance of dignitaries at annual shoots was not unusual and President De Valera attended a number of training camps to witness shoots, particularly during the Emergency Years. It is noteworthy that the Camp Diary mentions the attendance of three of his sons, Vivion, Ruaidhri and Tairdhealbhac at the shoot, together with the Minister for Defence who was making his second summer visit to the camp. Vivion De Valera was himself a volunteer officer. Amongst the other attendees, Major-General Hugo McNeill was assistant chief of staff and Major-General Sweeney, J.A. Sweeney was officer in command of the Curragh Command.

After this visit, the Eastern Command batteries were finished their annual camp and the 5, 6 7 and 8 Batteries evacuated camp on Tuesday 14 July, proceeding to McKee Barracks, Dublin by mechanical transport under the command of Capt. M. O'Carroll. The 2 Light Battery left for Kildare at 13.00 hours by M.T. under the command of Capt. F. Slater, followed by two 18-pounder field guns sent by tractor, the rest following to Kildare the next day with 23 reservists of the 4 Field Battery under Second-Lieutenant Curran and CQMS O'Mahoney. On Thursday 16 July, three lorries transferred the remaining ammunition from Coolmoney Camp back to the Magazine at the Curragh while Company-Sergeant Rogers remained with a fatigue party in striking marquees and store tents.

The last entry in the Coolmoney Camp diary was on Friday 17 July as another successful annual training camp came to an end:

Friday 17/7/36

The 4 Field Battery under Capt. B.S.C. Thomson left for Kildare by road at 08.00 hours, accompanied by medical orderly and ambulance. All tentage on charge to the battery was inspected by Capt. M. Kelly, ordnance and assessments made in respect of damages noted. The work of striking tents was proceeded with and the camping ground was cleared by 16.00 hours. The canteen staff left camp at 15.00 hours with stocks of goods etc. The camp and Coolmoney House was inspected at 16.30 hours by the camp commandant and camp quartermaster and handed over to the caretaker Mr. Keogh at 19.30 hours. All camp staff details left camp at 18.30 hours. All barrack services were handed over to Capt. Ryan on Thursday 23rd July and the following amounts represent the deficiencies and breakages:

Sergeants Mess   £1=16=8
Officers Mess   £2=13=11
General deficiency   5=0

CHAPTER 15

EXPANSION OF ARTILLERY CORPS: 1930s

Two officers with clip boards stood at the edge of the square. Tests seemed to be of driving drill, dropping the guns into action stations and so on. The square was alive as three more subsections were tested. During the lecture the scene grabbed attentive glances. Not one of us had seen the like before. We agreed we now felt we belonged to something real and exciting. 'Did you never see a horse before', the corporal said sharply. 'Now pay attention if you want to pretend to be soldiers.'

MEMOIRS OF TOM MAHER

Volunteer gunners at Kildare. (Military Archives, Dublin)

The Anti-Aircraft Battery: 1931

The 1 Anti-Aircraft battery of the Artillery Corps was established at Kildare on foot of an order dated 16 September 1931. The corps had purchased four 30-cwt guns from England, which arrived in October 1928, and Lieutenant M.P. McCarthy was sent on a training course to Larkhill, England in October 1929. There was a great interest in the corps in working with the anti-aircraft guns and many experienced N.C.O.s jumped at the chance, but the guns remained in Dublin unused for over two years. The formation of the battery caused some stir at the highest level in Kildare, as the corps was already 50 men short on its establishment.

The records of Dáil Éireann show that the Minister for Defence was asked in March 1931 'whether there is an anti-aircraft gunnery unit attached to the Artillery Corps of the army, and if so, will he state its strength in personnel and pieces'. The minister replied: ' The answer to the first part of the question is in the affirmative. It is not considered in the public interest to give information asked for in the second part of the question.'[1] Major Patrick Mulcahy received a call from Government Buildings and between the time that the question was asked in Dáil Éireann and responded to a few days later, Mulcahy had appointed Lieutenant McCarthy to command the battery and Lieutenant Dolan as his second in command. They were sent to Dublin to collect the two 3-inch 20 cwt and two 3-inch 30 cwt anti-aircraft guns that were lying in Islandbridge Barracks. They were transported to Plunkett Barracks, Curragh as there were no buildings large enough at Kildare to hold them. Unlike other units of the Artillery Corps, the original members of the anti-aircraft battery at Kildare are recorded:

Officer in Command: Lieutenant Maurice P. McCarthy
Second in Command: Lieutenant James J. Dolan

Second-Lieutenant K.T. Curran (*addition from 14 January 1932*)
Non Commissioned Officers
24519 C/S Dickson, R.
33050 Sergeant Hurley, J.
9256 Corporal Harpur, J.
367 A/CQMS Copley, W.
67035 A/Sergeant Carroll, C.
16584 Corporal O'Brien, W.
3775 Corporal Webb, P.
57787 A/Corporal Bonar, W.
Gunners

Section A	Section B
70690 Gunner Byrne, P	71207 Gunner Brennan, J.
71519 Gunner Campbell, M.	71663 Gunner Byrne, T.
71224 Gunner Carey, J.	71225 Gunner Carey, D.
68200 Gunner Cooney, D.	71259 Gunner Cleary, T.
71206 Gunner Conway, J.	71265 Gunner Condon, J.
71268 Gunner Dowling, W.	71187 Gunner Currie, P.
71217 Gunner Greaney, D.	71196 Gunner Fitzpatrick, J.
71184 Gunner Guilfoyle, G.	71269 Gunner Griffin, J.
71226 Gunner Jackson, P.	71181 Gunner Hogan, J.
71139 Gunner Joyce, M.	71374 Gunner Hoyce, (Joyce??) J.
71276 Gunner Kinsley, T.	71248 Gunner Kearney, J.
71171 Gunner Kerley, D.	71154 Gunner Keogh, J.
71057 Gunner Lee, P.	71270 Gunner Larkin, J.
71258 Gunner Mathews, M.	71360 Gunner Lennon, R.
71362 Gunner McArdle, G.	71353 Gunner Murray, T.
70817 Gunner McMahon, M.	71505 Gunner McBride, A.
71357 Gunner Sherry, A.	71390 Gunner Nolan, M.
71277 Gunner Swain, G.	71252 Gunner Surman, G.
71242 Gunner Ward, E.	71143 Gunner Walsh, R.

John Condon (1911–2000) recalled his early days in the Artillery Corps and the anti-aircraft battery following his enlistment with about 700 other men and nine weeks training at McDonagh Barracks.[2]

The big day for us was in December 1930 when all 700 of us were mustered on the square not knowing where we might be posted. We paraded in full kit, our personal belongings, including a few bikes on the verges. Officers from various corps selected men they thought suited their particular units. Lieutenant Jimmy Dolan, (who had been in the army since its inception and who had risen through the ranks) accompanied by Captain Maurice McCarthy from Artillery selected 42 of us to form the first anti-aircraft battery and without delay we climbed onto two lorries with all our belongings and were brought to Dun MhicAoidh in Kildare town. Lodged in two wooden huts under Sergeant Joe Hurley who became company sergeant, later Sergeant Major in McKee Barracks and then in Baldonnel. Also waiting for us there was Sergeant Christy Carroll who remained with us until his untimely death in St. Mary's Hospital beside the Hibernian Schools complex in the Phoenix Park during the war years.

Condon was a Kilkenny man from the townland of Skeagh, which was the name he was referred to by all during his time in the army.

The Volunteer Reserve: 1931

The military was at a numerical low in the late 1920s and supplemented itself with the creation of a volunteer reserve. Training of the Artillery Volunteer Reserve was divided between the various batteries. The 1 Field Battery took responsibility for training volunteers from the Southern Command area, the 2 Field Battery trained volunteers from the Eastern Command and the 3 Field Battery was responsible for training volunteers from the Western Command. The first drafts began to arrive on 17 April 1934 for their twenty-eight days initial training. Potential NCOs were selected from the volunteers for a further period of three months training. Some of these NCOs were then selected for potential-officer courses so that by spring 1935, each volunteer battery had a number of trained officers and NCOs. The training of volunteer batteries continued until April 1939.

Tom Maher joined the Volunteer Reserve at Kilkenny in 1935. He was sent to Kildare for training and arrived a few days after Christmas 1935 for twenty-eight day volunteer training, with snow on the ground in the town. Maher recalled that:

> In hut No. 11 we met our new hut mates, some from Derry but mostly from other parts near home. The day of arrival was devoted to preliminaries like talks on daily routine, bed making-down and making-up, falling-in, saluting, bounds and so on.

Next morning all volunteers on initial training were divided between four 4.5-inch Howitzers placed on the edge of the parade ground and two 18-pounders. We had our first introduction to parts, workings, ammunition and firepower. As a volunteer was about to ask a question all heads turned in the direction of the sound of hooves. Trotting on to the dirt square was a team of six horses hauling a gun followed by a team of four horses hauling an ammunition wagon. Each team had an outrider. This was a subsection and was followed by three more subsections. The soldiers riding the left-hand horses and the same with the ammo limbers were, to us, brilliant in their shining appearance. Two officers with clip boards stood at the edge of the square. Tests seemed to be of driving drill, dropping the guns into action stations and so on. The square was alive as three more subsections were tested. During the lecture the scene grabbed attentive glances. Not one of us had seen the like before. We agreed we now felt we belonged to something real and exciting. 'Did you never see a horse before', the corporal said sharply. 'Now pay attention if you want to pretend to be soldiers.'[3]

Lawrence Newman was orderly room clerk when the volunteer force was formed. He recalled that 'It was some job dressing these lads – often 20 or 30 would arrive from different parts of the country and had to be dressed and on the square in 24 hours.'[4] Many local men also took the opportunity for part-time soldiering.

> A great crowd of lads from Kildare town joined up, Davy, Reggie, Tom, Joe Judge and lots of others too numerous to mention. At that time they were called up every summer – two weeks training in the Glen of Imaal. This procedure was carried out every year until October 1939 when they were called into permanent service

and drafted to various parts of the country. Some were camped in More-O'Farrell's at Kildangan, Tipperary, Waterford, Wexford and in every county in Ireland. There was no shortage of armaments. There were 50,000 or 60,000 rifles, machine-guns, and the British flooded the country with 4.5 inch howitzers, 2-pounder anti-tank guns, 17 pounders etc. About 1943 we were issued with a new rifle, the mark IV .303 which was a great improvement on the old mark 3 rifle.

Competition was key to morale and training in the volunteer reserve. The Chief of Staff, Michael Brennan, on a visit to Kildare Barracks in September 1936 said that employers should encourage their employees to join the volunteer reserve. His speech was reported in the *Irish Independent*:

In this country there were several serious problems, such as unemployment, housing, education: in which most people were interested, and which they talked about, but hardly anybody discussed the most important problem of all – national defence. One most important thing was to encourage young people to join the volunteers.

Employers could assist in facilitating and encouraging employees, and giving them preference in employment, particularly when they were prepared to learn to defend their country, and in doing so to defend their employers' business.

If people could only understand how serious the position was they might think of this aspect of it.

Employers would think themselves mad if they had not insurance policies, but insurance policies would be of little use without protection if trouble came, and he feared it would come. He hoped trouble never would come, but they should be prepared. If the public understood that housing and other matters were only secondary problems they might be more anxious to assist, because the best and least expensive way of defending the country was through a volunteer force.[5]

The best battery of 1936 turned out to be the Kildare-based one. At a ceremony at Kildare Barracks, the Chief of Staff awarded the 2 Light Battery a trophy for the most efficient battery. The award was accepted by Lieutenant Raymond Rowan and Lieutenant Patrick Brennan of the volunteer reserve. [6]

The highlight of the year for the volunteer force was annual training and Chapter 14 on Coolmoney Camp Diary gives a good account of what that was like. The volunteer officers and those who were potential officers were well drilled and examined at these annual camps with their performances tested as in the 1936 camp: [7]

3 Light Battery (Mortars)
2/Lieut. J. Long
Neutralisation
Corrected for obvious mistakes made by detachments instead of checking, Prov. Bracketing. Effective Shoot.
2/Lieut. L. Neary
Accuracy
Initial order correct, Estimate of range good, jumped his Bracket, went into fire for effect at the wrong elevation, made necessary corrections. Effective shoot eventually.
2/Lieut. M. Somers
Accuracy
Procedure correct. Excellent shoot.
In addition to the officers, the batteries were also tested. The following were on the anti-tank range:
9 Battery (Cork)
Preparation good. Tactical control poor. Bad teamwork between Nos I and layers. Detachments very slow to get on to targets.
10 Battery (Kerry)
All volunteer officers were exercised as gun position officers and section commanders.
Preparation good. Detachments were slow to get on to target. Poor team work between Nos I and layers. Section commanders were slow in giving out orders and tactical control was not good.

Preparation good. Tactical control poor. Detachments very slow to get on to target. Moving targets not effectively dealt with.

Lt. G. Heffernan – shooting
Orders and procedures correct. General conduct good. Z.P. suitable, satisfactory.

Lt. O'Sullivan – neutralisation
Orders and procedure correct. Incorrect A/S on No. 1 gun. Never checked even though range was checked. Fire for effect fairly effective.

2/Lieut. Brick – Neutralisation
Procedure correct. Slow to observe and correct. Fire for effect. Satisfactory.

Lt. T. Kerins
G.F. Target
Orders and procedure correct. Opening range faulty. Fairly satisfactory.

Ceremonial Role – The Mounted Escort (The 'Blue Hussars')

The army decided to establish a ceremonial unit in 1931 in advance of the Eucharistic Congress being held in 1932. The unit was to be called the Mounted Escort but was informally and more commonly known as the 'Blue Hussars'. The Artillery Corps with the majority of army horses became the home of this unit and it provided the vast majority of the hussars. Their uniforms were designed in spring 1932 and seventy were made at a cost of £2,165.[8] The unit first appeared in public at the Eucharistic Congress in 1932. The officer-in-command was Lieutenant Dan Collins with second lieutenants P.J. Hally and William Donnelly:

> I remember one rehearsal, they had to pull up in the grounds of a hotel in Dun Laoghaire where they were to wait for some people to come. Bill Donnelly was one of the group. They naturally attracted a lot of attention and Bill in particular. There was a group of priests looking on and suddenly one of them exclaimed 'By God, 'tis Bill Donnelly,' everything became natural then. The atmosphere of awe and splendour was lost for it was only Bill

Donnelly from Birr![9]

Rehearsals for the ceremonies involved the unit travelling to Dun Laoghaire. Mulcahy recalled that:

> We used to practise at 3 or 4 o'clock in the morning and were coming back from Dun Laoghaire and had arrived at Merrion Square. It was a slippy morning and I should have had more sense. I was riding 'Big Tom'; I reined him and he fell. Fortunately, he knew me as I knew him. When he fell he felt my leg under him; he momentarily lifted himself to enable me to get my leg out. Horse sensitivity was often very touching.[10]

Another gunner, Sergeant 'Pal' Byrne recorded his memories of the Hussars:

> The highlight of my time in Kildare was the formation of the Blue Hussars and such a body of men has never been seen since in the Irish Army, with their light blue breeches and tunic with gold facings and dark busbies with orange plumes. We rehearsed day and night and were given the stamp of approval by President De Valera when he inspected McKee Barracks. After our first public appearance as escorts for Papal Nuncio Cardinal Lauri we provided escorts for many distinguished dignitaries.[11]

Larry Newman, who was serving with the depot artillery at this time, had responsibility for minding the uniforms in the early years:

> Some 10 officers and 40 other ranks were selected to form the ceremonial guard of honour. When the uniforms arrived, there was great excitement in the Barracks when there was a general parade on the barracks square – a full dress rehearsal was held and everything was 100%. After two years we handed the uniforms over to the equitation school in McKee Barracks, Dublin.

The Mounted Escort was also in attendance at a number of shows at the RDS in Ballsbridge, Dublin. P.J. Hally recalled the circumstances of one such event:

A number of horses and men were selected from the Mounted Escort squadron and trained as a musical ride entertainment. We were invited to give displays at the Spring Show by the RDS committee. I was put in charge of the musical ride. It was a similar performance to the one given by the Royal Canadian Mounted Police at the RDS this year [1988]. The troops lined up and Donnelly came forward to the front. He whispered into his horse's ear and the horse lay flat on the ground. Donnelly having dismounted lay on his back on his horse's belly and pretended to go asleep to soft bed-time music from No. 1 Army band. It was always a great hit with the public.[12]

The unit did not appear during the Emergency Years 1939–49. An attempt was made after the war to re-instigate it, but with the mechanisation of the army it was found that there were not enough horsemen or horses, and the motorcyclists of the cavalry corps took over the ceremonial role. There were many different members of the Artillery Corps involved in the Blue Hussars but a surviving group photo records the following members:

Gunners Meade, O'Neill, Nobby Clarke, Lennon, Keogh, Eugene Cronin, Michael Hagens, Driscoll, Brabazon, Tom Byrne, Bill Sheridan, Nugent, David Scott, Scully Barlow, Joe Moore, Cooney, Edward Caffrey, Sergeant McGough, CS Tom McGrath, Lieutenant P.J. Hally, C.S. Rogers, Gunners Winters, Frank Donnelly, Cassells.

The Artillery Corps was also involved in numerous other ceremonial occasions: and it is not always the case that such events go according to plan. On the inauguration of Douglas Hyde as first President of Ireland in June 1938, a twenty-one gun salute was prepared for when he was passing by. The observer spotted a horse-drawn carriage approaching and the order was given to commence firing. As the carriage drew nearer, it became apparent that it was a horse-drawn hearse and a different citizen of Dublin had been given full military honours on his way to his final resting place!

The Volunteer Force, on occasion, also provided a number of men to assist in the Mounted Escort.

> Training began to fill a gap in the Captain's Escort, better known as the Blue Hussars. Drills and evolutions took place on the Curragh Plains, watched with interest by many people including schools of riders from the many racing stables.
>
> An exercise in horse control was to field 40 horses in line, each a horse width apart. A lance was issued to each of us leaving one with one hand on the reins. Sergeant Sexton ordered the line to advance with other NCOs behind, warning to keep the line straight. When 'left wheel' was ordered the left horse so turned in its own ground as to be hardly noticeable. The right hand horse cantered. The rest conformed suitably. It was, we were told, quite a sight to see as there was no bulge in the line.
>
> We learned about the role of the front and rear troops vis-à-vis the position of 'Personage's Carriage' (VIP had not been invented) and what would happen if the Personage was in danger. Also, we were exercised in 'tent pegging' with the lances – well just once anyway. This consisted of pieces of wood stuck at a slant in the ground to which we cantered and endeavoured to stick the lance in one.[13]

Increased Strength

By 1936, the Artillery Corps had undergone a significant transformation. The full extent of artillery being managed from Kildare was as follows:

1 Field Battery (Cork)	Permanent
2 Field Battery (Kildare)	Volunteer
3 Field Battery (Athlone)	Permanent
4 Field Battery (Dublin)	Permanent
1 Anti-aircraft (Kildare) – cadre	Permanent
5 Field Battery (Dublin)	Volunteer

6 Field Battery (Dublin)	Volunteer
7 Field Battery (Monaghan)	Volunteer
8 Field Battery (Drogheda)	Volunteer
9 Field Battery (Cork)	Volunteer
10 Field Battery (Tralee)	Volunteer
11 Field Battery (Waterford)	Volunteer
12 Field Battery (Clonmel)	Volunteer
13 Field Battery (Mullingar)	Volunteer
14 Field Battery (Longford)	Volunteer
15 Field Battery (Letterkenny)	Volunteer
16 Field Battery (Ballinasloe)	Volunteer
1 Light Battery (Kildare) – cadre	Permanent
2 Light Battery (Kildare)	Volunteer
3 Light Battery (Kilkenny)	Volunteer
4 Light Battery (Castlebar)	Volunteer

The strength of the permanent force at this time was one major, one commandant, seventeen captains, twelve lieutenants, seventy-six non-commissioned officers and 342 men giving a total of 449 all ranks.

Training of the officers, NCOs and men of these batteries was the responsibility of Kildare Barracks and the focus of annual camps in the Glen of Imaal was to give the batteries a chance to demonstrate the result of many hours of training with live firing. Both regular and volunteer officers were trained in the different roles they might be called upon to carry out, including battery commander (BC), gun position officer (GPO) or section commander. Officers and men also had to be trained in the various types of shoots, i.e. neutralisation, destructive and anti-tank shooting. There were also the different types of ammunition, High Explosive with different charges i.e. 100E and 106E; shrapnel, as well as star shells and smoke.

The gunners also had to be familiar with the different positions on the guns and support such as gun layers, No. 1 and signallers. Training was very much integrated between regular and reserve units at camps. The surviving Coolmoney Camp diary records the gun layers trained during the 1936 camp:

4 Field Battery (Regulars)

74273 Gunner Harmon J.
73736 Gunner Collins C.
105122 Gunner Walsh G.
5 Field Battery (Volunteers)
100141 Gunner Keogh N.
113806 Gunner O'Callaghan J.
113804 Gunner Courtney B.
6 Field Battery (Volunteers)
106378 Gunner Darcey F.
106125 Gunner Hamilton R.
7 Field Battery (Volunteers)
115495 Gunner Coiley
101839 Gunner Duffy J.
3 Field Battery (Regulars)
68552 Gunner Flynn M.
101123 Gunner O'Brien W.
75366 Gunner Lawless M.
108281 Gunner Doyle J.
104431 Gunner Keane J.
111824 Gunner Bates C.
75369 Gunner Heffernan J.
13 Field Battery (Volunteers)
113766 Gunner Sealy P.
108524 Gunner Dalton M.
14 Field Battery (Volunteers)
105121 Gunner Kenny J.
115475 Gunner Nulty M.
101262 Gunner Farrell, T.
16 Field Battery (Volunteers)
105037 Gunner Stephenson J.
109304 Gunner Broderick M.

74381 Driver [illegible], J.
103410 Gunner Reidy J.

113835 Gunner O'Callaghan D.
113805 Gunner Wrigley H.
100241 Gunner Byrne M.

114965 Gunner O'Neill T.

105202 Gunner Corrigan J.

74353 Gunner Flynn W.
112517 Gunner Mullen R.
108423 Gunner Gleeson M.
110596 Gunner Callaghan W.
113065 Gunner Bonar W.
107242 Gunner Plunkett J.
75347 Gunner McHugh J.

107336 Gunner Hughes Thos.
101284 Gunner Reilly G.

105124 Gunner Nolan M.
106107 Gunner Monaghan A.

114509 Gunner Fahy F.
109379 Gunner Finnerty P.

Mechanisation of the Artillery Corps

The changeover from a corps relying on the horse to a mechanised force took place in 1938.

Mulcahy recalled the difference it made when he returned to artillery after a period with the Air Corps:

> We loved our horses and we hated parting with them. I never appreciated what a difference their going could make until I came back to the Corps in 1942 to take over from Colonel Paddy Maher, who had retired to run Shannon Airport. It was during this time as Director that full mechanisation came. I got a real surprise when we were arranging to go to the Glen for a practice shoot. I had Major-General Hally in command – he was probably a Commandant or a Major then – to make arrangements for the move. I said: 'I suppose we'll move on Friday as usual, rest Saturday and Sunday, shoot Monday.' 'Oh no, Sir, we leave at 9 o'clock Monday morning and we shoot at 11!' In my time the horses and men had to be rested. That really showed the huge change that had taken place during my sojourn with the Air Corps.[14]

Horses involved a lot of work and some of it was not too pleasant:[15]

> Rising at 6 a.m. to do up the horses and get their breakfast. The commanding officer would inspect the horses and drivers or gunners, whichever happened to be at hand and would know when a horse was out of sorts, colic being the main offender. The man in charge of the horse would inform the CO of this, and this man, with the help of a comrade, would have to see to the horse himself. This usually would mean he had to roll up his sleeve and put his arm up the back passage of the horse and claw down the hard dung. They used to turn out the horses very well by all accounts, including oiling the horses' hooves. Exercise would mean a rider on one horse leading two out the Frenchfurze road across by Strawhall towards Gibbet Rath and back along the road to Kildare Barracks. The drivers also had to be able to 'cold shoe'

a horse.

All gunners, because they were a mounted corps, wore spurs throughout the 1920s and 1930s. This also extended to the new anti-aircraft battery throughout the 1930s which did not use horses. As a result, despite the impracticality of the situation, these gunners wore spurs at all times. One driver, John Condon recounted to his son how the only dispensation he got was when driving the truck when he could remove his spurs but gunners had to put their spurs back on before getting out of the truck. When the Second World War, or the Emergency as it was referred to in neutral Ireland, began, the gunners were finally allowed to remove their spurs, much to the annoyance of the traditionalists.

The horses finally departed from the corps in 1939. Commandant Maher, in his memoirs recalled:

> The week or so before St. Patrick's Day in 1939 was a sad one. Many artillery horses were taken over by Horse Transport Section of S and T Corps. We brought the remainder to Dublin by road. The auction took place in McKee Barracks. I had some kind of job, standing near the stables as a pointsman for would-be purchasers, catalogue in hand. Experienced NCOs were available to answer queries and generally help. Most were sold in the most simple way. An abiding memory is of a lady with a slight limp in jodhpurs seeking 'Slievenamon', an artillery horse of the Army Jumping Team that won renown for Ireland in Toronto, New York, London and other great cities. It was a favourite in the stables but seen as on 'light duty' and much petted.[16]

Coastal Artillery

The handover of the treaty ports to the Irish Free State in 1938 presented a whole new set of problems for the Artillery Corps at Kildare. There were no trained personnel to man the forts. Coastal artillery was a very different discipline to field gunnery. Major McLoughlin had served with coastal artillery after the war but he had gone to the Military College in the Curragh. In May 1938, a military mission was sent to London to prepare for the transfer of the coastal defence forts. Major Maher, Director of Artillery, headed the delegation with the intention of organising training for twelve Irish officers and training in Cobh by the Royal Artillery. Training was subsequently organised, in June 1938, for a number of officers:

The British War Office has agreed to reserve (a) twelve vacancies for artillery officers on the first part of Course No. 338 (Coast Artillery – regular) which will commence at Shoeburyness, Essex, on the 19th June, 1938, and terminate on the 9th July, 1938, and (b) three vacancies on the second part of this course (Counter Bombardment and Fortress System of Range Finding) which will last for a period of two weeks. The War Office further agreed that the officers who attend the second part of the course should remain on until the completion of a gunnery staff course which is at present in progress at the Military College of Science, Woolwich, and which will terminate on the 30th September, 1938. Verbal sanction had been received from the Department of Finance.

The following Officers have been detailed to attend the first part of Course No. 338: Captains D.J. Collins, C. Trodden, M.P. MacCarthy, D.J. Farrell, Second Lieutenants A. Dalton, W. Donagh, P.J. Hally, J. Murray, J.H. Byrne, W. Rea, P.J. O'Callaghan.

Of these, Captains Trodden, Farrell and MacCarthy will undergo the second part of the course and Captains Trodden and Farrell will remain on for the gunnery staff course terminating on the 30th September next.

I am, accordingly, to request that you will be good enough to inform the British War Office without delay of the acceptance of the vacancies and to intimate that it would be appreciated if an early indication could be given of the fees chargeable; the time and date on which the officers should report and whether public quarters will be available on a repayment basis.[17]

A number of British army gunnery instructors remained on at the forts to facilitate the proper training and operation of the forts.

By the late 1930s, the Artillery Corps at Kildare ran its own School and

Depot, provided Artillery support to the Military College at the Curragh, had expertise in anti-aircraft and coastal defence as well as both regular and reserve field batteries in a mechanised corps, meaning that the core expertise and units were in place by the time the Second World War commenced and the threat of invasion was a very real prospect.

Image 20: Officers of the Artillery Corps, Kildare 1931.

Third Row: 2/Lt. A. Dalton, Lt. P.P. Farrell, Lt. C.F. Byrne, Lt. P. Doyle, Lt. M. Buckley, 2/Lt. P. Curran, 2/Lt. W.A. O'Maloney, 2/Lt. K. Curran.

Second Row: 2/Lt P.J. Hally, Lt. D.J. Farrell, Lt. J.J. Dolan, Capt. D.J. Cody, Lt. T.J. Lambert, 2/Lt. J.L. O'Brien, Lt. W.P. Donnelly, Lt. M.P. McCarthy.

Front: Capt. C. Trodden, Capt. J. McLoughlin, Comdt. P. Maher, Major P.A. Mulcahy, Capt. R.J. Callanan, Capt. B.S.C. Thomson, Capt. M. O'Carroll. (Courtesy of Artillery School, Curragh)

Image 21: Gunners at Kildare enjoying a lighter moment. (Courtesy of Mary D'Arcy)

Image 22: D Sub-section No. 1 Battery 1929 Rear: Corporal P. Canny, Gunner A. Watters.

Third Row: Driver J. O'Grady, Gunner D. Walsh, Gunner L. O'Leary.

Second Row: Corporal W. McNamara. Gunner M. Hannon, Gunner C. O'Connell, Driver P. Crawley, Gunner Lawlor, Gunner T. Curtis, Gunner C. Carroll, Driver H. Byrne, Gunner M. Walsh

Front Row: Gunner J. McGowan, Driver W. Farrell, Gunner L. Murray, Driver T. Kavanagh, Sergeant T. Shanahan, Gunner P. McDermott, Driver D. Kavanagh, Gunner T. Hillick, Gunner W. Bonar. (Courtesy of Mary D'Arcy)

Image 23: A drawing by Captain Bertie Stuart Campbell Thomson. (Courtesy of Reggie Darling)

Image 24: No. 1 Battery, Artillery Corps, 1931 (Courtesy of Brendan Culleton)

Image 25: Sergeant Patrick McGough overseeing the instruction of members of the Volunteer Reserve on a 3.7-inch howitzer. The gunner on the left is David Wilson of Hospital Street, Kildare suggesting that these are members of the Kildare based 2 Light Battery circa 1935. (Courtesy of Paddy Newman)

Image 26: The Mounted Escort, more commonly known as the Blue Hussars, was formed from Kildare gunners and made their first appearance in 1932. (Courtesy of Military Archives, Dublin)

Image 27: The first Anti-Aircraft Battery, 1932. The officers are: Lt. J. Dolan, Capt. Maurice McCarthy and Lt. Kevin Curran. Gunner John Conlan is in the third row, third from left and William Copley is in the front row fourth from left. (Courtesy of Conor Copley)

Image 28: Colonel James McLoughlin, Director of Artillery demonstrates a 25-pounder High Explosive shell to Colonel James Flynn, Assistant Chief of Staff; Lieutenant-Colonel Ronald Miers, DSO, British Military Attache; Colonel H.B. Waddell, US Military Attache and Colonel Patrick A. Mulcahy, Quartermaster General; Glen of Imaal, County Wicklow 1950. (Courtesy of Colonel Michael Moriarty (Retd))

Image 29: Major Charles Trodden (1904–47) who participated in the Military Mission to the USA in 1926 and attended Fort Sill, Oklahoma. Trodden Hall at Kildare was named in his memory. (Courtesy of Eibhir Mulqueen)

Image 30: Commandant Thomas Wickham was killed in Syria on 5 June 1967 while serving with the United Nations Truce Supervision Organisation. Wickham Hall at Kildare was named in his memory. (Courtesy of Colonel Ray Quinn (Retd))

Image 31: Standing: Lieutenants Kevin Duffy and William Phillips, Seated: Lieutenants Padraic O'Farrell, Noel Bergin, Michael McMahon training on an L70 Bofor anti-aircraft gun at Gormanston Camp, 1955. (Courtesy of Lieutenant-General Noel Bergin (Retd))

Image 32: Heavy Mortar Troop, 19 Infantry Group, Cyprus 1970–71.

Front: Sergeant J. Kenny, Gunners P. Confrey, T.Ryan, T. Cunningham, P. Hughes, T. Larkin, P. Matthews.

Centre: Corporal S. Fortune, Gunner G. Dunne, Sergeant P. Keyes, Gunner T. Carroll, Sergeant S. Mullins, Corporal K. Herron.

Rear: Lieutenant G. Boyle, Sergeants M. Murray, D. Finn, Gunners P. Webb, I. Langford, Corporal J. Kelly, Battery-Sergeant N. Fahy, Captain J. H. Murphy. (Courtesy of Lieutenant-Colonel J.H. Murphy (Retd))

Image 33: A combined shoot by members of the 5 and 6 Field Batteries of the VI Field Artillery Regiment in 1984 on the occasion of the twentieth-fifth anniversary of the foundation of the unit in 1959. (Courtesy of Commandant Paddy Walshe (Retd))

Image 34: Gunners of the 3 Field Battery shortly after the arrival of the 105 mm light gun in 1981 which they fired for the first time on 12 March 1981 in the Glen of Imaal. Left to right: Sergeant Peter Webb, Sergeant Butch Halpin, Corporal John Kelly, Sergeant Martin Page, Battery Sergeant-Major Donnie Finn, Sergeant Martin Kelly, Corporal Brian Murphy. (Courtesy of RSM Donnie Finn (Retd))

Image 35: Brigadier-General P.D. Hogan plants a tree with senior officers, 1985. Captain Bill Gibson, Lieutenant Dave Brown, Lieutenant-Colonel Ciaran O'Halloran, Lieutenant-Colonel Tom O'Boyle, Lieutenant-Colonel Dermot McLoughlin, Unidentified Cavalry Officer, Colonel P.J. O'Cathain, Lieutenant-Colonel Patrick Monahan, Commandant Gerry McCutcheon, Lieutenant-Colonel Tom McDunphy. (Courtesy of Commandant Paddy Walshe (Retd))

Image 36: Captain Pat Graham and Sergeant Joe Foley perform the ceremonial lowering of the tricolour for the last time on 24 September 1998 saluted by the Commanding Officer Lieutenant-Colonel Gerry Swan. (Courtesy of Commandant Paddy Walshe (Retd))

CHAPTER 16

TRAGEDIES, CRIMES AND ENTERTAINMENT

In regard to deficiency of 1 blanket single soldier it
is pointed out that out of a consignment of 1,000 new
blankets received from DBO Curragh on 16/2/30 only 999
can be accounted for on the date of the inspection.

INSPECTION REPORT, 10 JANUARY 1934 CRIMES

Gunners enjoying a light moment at Kildare. (Courtesy of Mary D'Arcy)

As with the British occupation, soldiers in the new army also found themselves before the courts on numerous occasions. A young man named Joseph McGaley was arrested for stealing two pairs of military breeches and military leggings from Kildare Barracks in August 1927. McGaley had a pass to enter the barracks to deal with soldiers' bicycles and was accused of stealing the items although he testified that a soldier sold them to him. The prospect of a soldier selling a uniform to McGaley was dismissed by Lieutenant Lambert of the Artillery Corps who testified that when a man was discharged from the military he had to surrender his military clothing before receiving civilian clothing back in return. McGaley was sentenced to three months with hard labour. [1]

There was an attempted robbery of the safe from the commanding officer's office in April 1932 when an ex-gunner Denis O'Regan, aged 25, and two other men set about in an audacious robbery attempt.[2] William Wakefield acted as a chauffeur and they stole a car in Dublin and arrived at the gates of the barracks where they knocked at the gate and were let in with the assistance of a Private O'Hanlon who was stationed at Kildare. They drove to the COs office and unlocked the door, taking the safe and put it in the rear seat of the car. They broke open the safe and removed £25 and dumped the safe in the canal at Blanchardstown, County Dublin. When O'Regan's room was searched, Detective Gordan found a receipt for a pair of boots bought the day after the robbery. There were two postcards under his pillow. The first postcard contained the message: 'If key fails, auger as large as possible. Will see you No. 3 straight in gate.' On the second postcard was written: 'Drive to O.C.'s house. Will time Orderly Officer. Arrive about 10 or near. Work alone if possible. Lay in Barracks.'

On 29 May, 1932, James Dempsey was charged with larceny from the wet canteen at the barracks.[3] At a court case held at Naas circuit court, Gunner

Phelan and Gunner Scully testified that they had arrived at the canteen at five minutes to six for a drink and discovered that the door was broken open. There was no one in the canteen so they called the barrack orderly sergeant. Lieutenant William O'Mahoney, Orderly Officer was called and went with Dempsey to inspect the premises. Dempsey checked a tin box where the money was held and said that there was about £13 missing. Dempsey was acquitted on the grounds that there was no evidence that he carried out the crime.

One volunteer force gunner who had an apparent difficulty with the military was Gunner O'Donoghue who was dismissed after only two weeks training. The matter came before Dáil Éireann:

> The O'Mahony asked the Minister for Defence whether he will state the period of service given (a) in the Army, and (b) in the Army Reserve by Gunner J. O'Donoghue, of Ballinstruer, Stratford-on-Slaney, and No. 72994, Artillery Barracks, Kildare; his character in the Army; and the date upon which he would normally be due for discharge from the Reserve; and if he is aware that he was recently called up for a month's training, but dismissed after two weeks of the training period and discharged from the Reserve; and if he will state the reasons for such discharge; and if he will also state for what reason his pay has been withheld from him.
>
> Mr. Aiken: Thomas O'Donoghue had one year 51 days Army and 254 days Reserve service; his character in the Army was 'Very Good'. He was normally due for discharge on the 6th July, 1944. He was called up for training as stated and discharged from the Reserve on the 17th May, 1934, for the reason that his services were no longer required. All reserve pay due in this case has been issued.
>
> The O'Mahony: Am I correct in assuming that the real reason he was discharged from the Reserve was because he happened to be a member of the League of Youth?[4]

Tragedies

There were also a number of tragedies in the 1930s. A young officer, 24-year-old Lieutenant Daniel Davis of Lackahane, Creagh, County Cork, who was posted to the Artillery Corps from the Military College after completing his cadet training in November 1933, was killed on 17 February 1934 when exercising a horse near the racecourse and the animal apparently reared up and fell on him.[5] Another gunner, Driver Bernard Rall, aged 35, died on 7 February 1932. He was taking part in a display in the barrack field when a noise startled the horse. He was thrown from the horse but his foot got caught in the stirrup and he broke his neck. He was interred at the Grey Abbey cemetery. His gravestone bears the inscription 'erected by his comrades in the Artillery Corps'.

Entertainment

The artillery barracks was the location of many social nights in the 1920s and 1930s. In their first year at Kildare the Artillery Corp's Dramatic Class staged the well-known comedy 'The Lord Mayor'. *An-t-Oglach* reported that 'It would be impossible to make distinction between any one of the artists, but "Mrs Murphy" and "Mrs Maloney" charwomen, kept the house in roars of laughter. The parts of the "Lord Mayor" and "Gaffney" the solicitor, were excellently played. In fact the whole play was produced in a most perfect manner and left nothing to be desired.'[6] The cast were Drivers Roe Ryan and Quinn, Corporals Griffen and Byrne, Drivers Purdue, Smith, Phelan, Rice, Hand and McAnespie. The *Kildare Observer* reported a 'Cinderella Dance' in October 1928 in which close to 150 couples participated. Music was provided by the Bailey Brothers Orchestra Kildare, and the couples had the facility of a newly-laid dance floor.[7] The barracks had a long tradition of children's parties and over 100 attended a Christmas party on 21 December 1933 where they were given handsome and seasonable presents by Commandant Maher, Officer in Command. The hall was decorated by Sergeant White, Gunner Fanning and Gunner Sweeney. The MC for the occasion was Sergeant-Major James Cummins.[8] Pursuits involving horses were always a favourite of the artillery and the barracks also hosted numerous gymkhanas in the barracks field under the auspices of the Naas Harriers Hunt Club. These usually involved children's activities and musical entertainment. The officers of the corps generally participated in the events and in their organisation.[9]

Barrack life at Kildare was reported in a short article in the army journal *An-t-Oglach* in January 1926 by an Artillery Corps correspondent under the pseudonym 'Trail Eye':

I will try to explain what we have done and hope to do, in the way of barrack amusements and comfort for the troops here in Kildare. The holding of whist drives, Irish classes, concerts, etc., in barracks is only right and proper.

Field sports: A glance through the back numbers of *An-t-Oglach* will prove that the Artillery Corps have always been in the front line at sports. Our football and hurling teams are well known to the readers of *An-t-Oglach* and throughout the army. Our tug-o-war team has made its name. Every branch of sport has its supporters here, and its supporters are useful, as can be proved by our collection of cups and medals. Our recent Corps sports were the first in this army at which all classes of events both mounted and dismounted were catered for. We hope to make our sports a big event next year.

Whist Drives have been going strong for some time past, and are proving a huge success.

Dramatic class: The reports which appeared in *An-t-Oglach*, of the entertainments provided by our Dramatic Class should be sufficient proof of the talent we have here. Irish items predominate at these productions. The Billiards Table, which was recently installed in the Men's Recreation Room is providing the means of passing many a pleasant hour. When the new Recreation Hall is fully completed, with Library and Reading Room, we hope to have it as good as any at present going.

Boxing: The fact that our boxers recently won the Novices' Cup at the Curragh Tournament, speaks for itself.

Suppers have been supplied to the troops in Kildare since last May, and have now become a 'standing order'.

The Corps Band, while not recognised by the School of Music, still helps to liven up many a dreary evening in barracks.

Last, but not last, I mention Irish classes. Here in Kildare we have plenty of men – officers and other ranks – only too anxious to study Irish and attend classes. Unfortunately, we have not got anyone proficient enough to teach the language.[10]

There were several families living in the married quarters in the barracks. Following the arrival of the Artillery Corps, the barracks were occupied by the married men and their families in June 1925 as follows:

No. 1	367	Sergeant W. Copley (Artillery)
No. 2	42859	Company-Sergeant M. Kelly (Artillery)
No. 3	55570	Private J. Monohan (ATC)
No. 4	55712	Gunner M. Walsh (Artillery)
No. 5	1035	Sergeant Albert White (Artillery)
No. 6	47129	Company-Sergeant J. Hill (Artillery)
No. 7	47134	Sergeant J. Redmond (Artillery)
No. 8	1899	Sergeant Edward Keogh (Artillery)
No. 9	41405	Sergeant M. Quinn (Artillery)
No. 10	53976	Driver B. Rall (Artillery)
No. 11	21734	Gunner J. Daly (Artillery)
No. 12	52880	Driver Clarke (Artillery)
No. 13	56797	Gunner T. McCormack (Artillery)
No. 14	5758	Driver T. Curley (Artillery)
No. 15	42412	Gunner P. Kirwan (Artillery)
No. 16	4869	Driver C. Jordan (Artillery)
No. 17	51986	Sergeant J. Carroll (Artillery)
No. 18	40168	CQMS C. Clancy (Artillery)
No. 19	48178	Gunner J. Cullon (Artillery)
No. 20	47227	Company-Sergeant T. McGrath (Artillery)

Major Mulcahy Commandant and Commandant Maher also lived in the barracks with their families from January 1926.

The case of the missing blanket!

Inspections formed an enormous part in military life. An inspection of the stores carried out in January 1934 turned up an anomaly.[11]

Inspection report
Visited on 10/1/1934
In regard to deficiency of 1 blanket single soldier it is pointed out
that out of a consignment of 1,000 new blankets received from DBO
Curragh on 16/2/30 only 999 can be accounted for on the date of
the inspection.

Despite four years having passed since the blankets were issued, the issue did
not rest there. The quartermaster of the Curragh Military District, Major T.
McNally was asked to investigate the discrepancy. He wrote to the Quartermaster
General's Department:

15 May 1934
Deficiency of 1 Blanket, Single Soldier
Of 100 bundles (10 each) received from District Barrack Officer, a
few bundles were broke, and a few days after the inspection by Mr.
Whelan, the blanket shown as deficient was found concealed behind
a number of intact bundles.

If the loss of one blanket caused such a stir, the next case was bound to cause
a national crisis – not one, but three missing blankets! The quartermaster of
the I Field Artillery Brigade was not very impressed to find that three blankets
could not be accounted for and requested that Captain Pierce Wall explain the
discrepancy. Captain Wall advised the Quartermaster that:[12]

...Comdt Fleming HQ Southern Command entered billets occupied
by men of the Artillery Corps in the Agricultural showgrounds, Cork
and gave instruction that 3 blankets were to be removed.

Captain Wall advised that Sergeant Maxwell and Corporal Brannigan were
present when the blankets were taken. A national crisis was averted!

CHAPTER 17

SPORT

All the officers of the Corps worked in whole-hearted fashion
for the success of the meeting, and visitors were entertained
in a manner quite equal to anything that the garrisons of
Newbridge and Kildare had known in the past.

KILDARE OBSERVER, 4 AUGUST 1928

Artillery Corps – Winners of the GHQ Football League 1925 Rear: Driver A. Coleman, Driver P. Quinn,
Driver P. Winter, Gunner J. Ryan Third Row: BSM J. Cummins, Driver C. O'Neill, SS J. O'Connell,
Gunner T. Henry, Gunner A. Hall Second Row: Gunner M. Walsh, Commandant D. Mackey (Capt.),
Major P. A. Mulcahy, Lieutenant, C. Trodden. Front: Gunner T. McCormack Front: Corporal E. Brannigan,
Gnr M. Davis. (Courtesy of Artillery School)

A s with the British Army, sport played an important part in the training and recreation of the Free State army and each command held their own sports. In addition to athletic events, the artillery competed in mounted events and competitions between the Headquarters Company and two batteries. The first annual Artillery Corps sports were held at Kildare on 31 October 1925 with the alarm race being the most exciting event.[1] It was reported that:

> The race was started by three blasts on a whistle, which represented the alarm. Immediately, the whistle sounded the teams galloped to their guns, hooked in, and proceeded at the gallop to a position allotted to them, where they came into action. Although D sub-section No. 1 Battery, were the quickest to get away, C sub-section, No. 1 Battery, were the first into action, and fired their round by a short lead from D Sub. C Sub were accordingly declared the winners.

The winners were as follows: One mile flat: 1st Gunner T. McCormack, No. 2 Battery; 2nd Gunner J. Redmond, No. 2 Battery. 880 yards: 1st Gunner T. McCormack, No. 2 Battery; 2nd Sergeant T. Shanahan, No. 1 Battery. 440 yards: 1st Gunner T. McCormack, No. 2 Battery; 2nd Driver J. Kelly, No. 2 Battery. 220 yards: 1st Driver J. Kelly, No. 2 Battery; 2nd Gunner P. Murphy, No. 2 Battery. 100 yards: 1st Driver J. Kelly, No. 2 Battery; 2nd Gunner P. Murphy, No. 2 Battery. 120 yards hurdles: 1st Gunner Cody, No. 2 Battery; 2nd Lieutenant Lambert, HQ Company. Relay race: won by B sub-section, No. 2 Battery. Obstacle race: 1st Driver J. Ward, No. 2 Battery; 2nd Driver P. Hogan, No. 2 Battery. Sack race: 1st Gunner McNamara, No. 2 Battery; 2nd Gunner T. Rice, No. 2 Battery. Veteran's Race: 1st Gunner F. Collins, No 1 Battery, Gunner P. Kirwan, No. 1 Battery. Tilting the bucket: Won by Gunners Sloan and Dunne, No. 1 Battery. High jump: 1st Lieutenant Lambert, HQ Company; 2nd Gunner

McNamara, No. 2 Battery. Long jump: 1st Gunner Cody, No. 2 Battery; 2nd Corporal Canny, No. 1 Battery. Hop, step and jump: 1st Gunner Cody, No. 2 Battery; 2nd Corporal Canny, No. 1 Battery. Putting 16 lbs shot: 1st Gunner Harris, No. 1 Battery; 2nd Corporal McGrath, No. 1 Battery. Flinging 56 lb weight: 1st Corporal Sheeran, No. 2 Battery; 2nd Gunner O'Gorman, No. 1 Battery. Hurling puck: 1st Gunner Kelly, No. 1 Battery; 2nd Sergeant-Major Cummins, HQ Company. Tug-of-war: B sub-section, No. 2 Battery. Best clown: Gunner J. Cahill, No. 2 Battery. Sergeants' Jumping: 1st Sergeant Boles, No. 1 Battery; 2nd Sergeant Shanahan, No. Battery. Corporals' Jumping: 1st Corporal White, No. 2 Battery; 2nd Corporal Canny, No. 1 Battery. Sub-section Jumping: 1st A sub-section, No.1 Battery; 2nd A sub-section, No. 2 Battery. Peg-driving: 1st A sub-section, No. 1 Battery; 2nd D sub-section, No. 1 Battery. Best turned out GS Wagon and Team: Driver J. Coleman, HQ Company; Driver W. Mitchell, No. 2 Battery. Prizes were presented by Commandant Patrick Maher.

While no record survives for the 1926 annual sports, the 1927 were given considerable coverage with the programme, which was an extensive one, taking place over two days.[2] The main military events were won by the following batteries or sections as follows:

Inter Battery Cup – horse jumping: No. 1 Battery
Sub-Section Cup: B sub-section No. 2 Battery
Elvery Cup: A sub-section No. 2 Battery.

Individual winners were listed as follows: Hop, Step and Jump: Corporal Brannigan; 56 lbs: Gunner O'Brien; Javelin: Gunner Leahy; Long Jump: Driver Kelly; High Jump: Gunner Leahy; Discuss: Sergeant Shearan; 16lb shot: Gunner O'Brien; Tug-o-war: A sub-section No. 2 Battery; 120 yards hurdles: Gunner Cody; 100 yards: Sergeant Shanahan; 220 yards: Sergeant Shanahan; 440 yards: Sergeant Shanahan; 880 yards: Gunner McCormack; Obstacle Race: Gunner Murphy; Veterans' race: Corporal McNamara; Best Mounted Man: Trumpeter Cullerton; Sergeants' Jumping: Sergeant T. Shanahan; Corporals' Jumping: Corporal P. O'Neill; Officers Jumping (confined): Captain J. McLoughlin; Officers' Jumping (open): Second-Lieutenant D.G. Leonard. Officers Tent Pegging: Major P.A. Mulcahy; Gunners and Drivers' Jumping: Driver J. Daly.

The 1928 annual sports give a good indication of the individual events, with events such as tent-pegging and jumping events being particular to the Artillery Corps and other mounted units:

120 yards hurdles: 1st Corporal Brannigan; 2nd Gunner Rafferty; 3rd Lieutenant Lambert. Hop, step and Jump: 1st Gunner Rafferty; 2nd Corporal Brannigan; 3rd Corporal Rice. Slinging 56lb: 1st Sergeant Sheeran; 2nd Gunner O'Brien; 3rd Gunner Lyons. 100 Yards Flat: 1st Sergeant Shanahan; 2nd Gunner Rafferty; 3rd Lieutenant Lambert. One mile flat: 1st Sergeant Shanahan; 2nd Gunner Ryan; 3rd Gunner Flynn. Throwing the Javelin: 1st Gunner Goddard; 2nd Sergeant Sheeran. Long Jump: 1st Corporal Brannigan; 2nd Driver Kavanagh; 3rd Gunner Rafferty. 880 Yards Flat: 1st Gunner Ryan; 2nd Corporal Brannigan; 3rd Gunner Lehane. Putting 16lb shot: 1st Gunner O'Brien; 2nd Sergeant Carroll; 3rd Driver Hughes. Sub-Section Tug of war: 1st A Sub. No. 2 Battery. Decathlon Race: 1st Gunner Mulraney; 2nd Driver Brown. Sub-Section Relay Race: 1st Gunner Flynn; 2nd Gunner O'Riordan. High Jump: 1st Sergeant Shanahan; 2nd Lieutenant Lambert; 3rd Corporal Sullivan. Veteran's Race: 1st Gunner Larkin; 2nd Corporal McNamara. 220 Yards Flat: 1st Sergeant Shanahan; 2nd Gunner Goddard. Throwing Discus: 1st Sergeant Sheeran; 2nd Gunner O'Brien; 3rd Driver Hughes. Youths' Race: 1st Jerry Walsh; 2nd Jim Walsh. Three Miles Flat: 1st Gunner McGowan; 2nd Gunner Ryan; 3rd Gunner Flynn. 440 Yards Flat: 1st Sergeant Shanahan. Ladies Race: 1st Mrs Kelly; 2nd Mrs Turner. Corporals' Jumping: 1st Corporal Phelan 2 Battery; 2nd Corporal Holden 2 Battery. Officers' Jumping (confined): 1st Lieutenant P. Doyle; Captain Finlay. Sergeants' Jumping: 1st Sergeant-Major O'Neill; 2nd Sergeant Bowes. Officers' Tent Pegging: 1st Major Mulcahy; 2nd Captain McLoughlin. Drivers' Half-Section Jumping: 1st D Sub section No. 1 Battery; 2nd B Sub-section No. 2 Battery. Officers' Jumping (Open): 1st Captain Finlay; 2nd Lieutenant Leonard. Wrestling on Horseback: 1st A Sub-Section No. 1 Battery; 2nd D Sub-section No. 2 Battery. Sergeants' Jumping (open): 1st Company-Sergeant Cousins; 2nd Sergeant Shanahan.

The *Kildare Observer*, known in the past for its Unionist sentiment, noted in its coverage of the 1928 sports that:

All the officers of the Corps worked in whole-hearted fashion for the success of the meeting, and visitors were entertained in a manner quite equal to anything that the garrisons of Newbridge and Kildare had known in the past.[3]

At the artillery sports in July 1933, the winners were[4]:

100 yards: Gnr Kerley; 220, 440, 880 and 1 mile: Lieutenant Banahan; 3 miles: Gunner Lacey; Long Jump: Gunner Bolter; High Jump: Gnr Byrne; Hop, Step and Jump: Corporal Maxwell; 16lbs Shot, 56lbs shot over bar: Gunner O'Brien; Javelin: Corporal Byrne; Discus: Gunner Hughes; Pole Vault: Lieutenant Murphy; Tug of War: 2nd Battery; Jumping: Driver Somers; Corporal Maxwell; Sergeant Kennedy; Captain Callanan.

The *Kildare Observer* noted the performance of the artillerymen in its sports column:

The athletics section of the Artillery Corps' annual sports brought several promising young athletes into action, of whom more will assuredly be heard in the near future. Purposely disregarding that splendid and youthful winner, Lieut. T.M. Banahan (3rd Field Battery), holder of the 1933 army 880 yards title; who has already made a name for himself, I select the following as distinctly promising – Gunner Kerley (Anti-Aircraft Battery) for the 100 yards and 220 yards. Lieut O'Connor (1st Field Battery) for the 440 yards; Gunner Dowling (Anti-Aircraft Battery), for the 880 yards and one mile flat; Gunner Lacy (1st Field Battery) for the one mile flat; Gunner Christie (3rd Field Battery) for the three mile flat; Gunner P O'Brien (2nd Field Battery) for the 16lbs shot and 56lbs without follow; Cpl. Byrne (Anti-Aircraft Battery), for the javelin, and Sergt R. Kennedy (2nd Field Battery) for the javelin.[5]

The Minister for Defence attended the artillery sports in 1937:

Mr. Frank Aiken, Minister for Defence, was an interested spectator at the annual mounted sports of the Artillery Corps at the Curragh yesterday. He presented the prizes to the winners and congratulated them on the skill which they had shown.

A large crowd was thrilled by the contests. The uncanny accuracy of Corporal White in the tent pegging competition for N.C.O.s won him round upon round of applause, and another popular winner was Lieut. Banahan, the well-known army runner, who carried off the officers' open jumping in excellent style.[6]

Officers' Jumping (open) 1. Lt. T. Banahan 2. Lt. W. Rea 3. Lt. W. Shortall

Sergeants' Jumping: 1. Sgt J. Keogh (1stBty), 2. CQMS Boles (1stBty), 3. C.S. Downey (3rdBty).

Corporals' Jumping: 1. Cpl Haughey (3rdBty), 2. Cpl White (1stBty), 3. Cpl Brophy (4thBty).

Drivers' Jumping: 1. Driver Senior (3rdBty), 2. Driver Gorman (1stBty), 3. Driver Brabston (4thBty).

Officers' Tent Pegging: 1. Lt. J. Doan, 2. Lt. J.H. Byrne (4thBty), 3. Lt. W. Rea (4thBty).

N.C.O.s Tent Pegging: 1. Cpl White (3rdBty), 2. Sgt Sexton (3rdBty), 3. C.S. Rogers (1st Light Bty).

Drivers' Tent Pegging: 1. Driver Brabston (4thBty), 2. Driver Moans (4thBty), 3. Driver Cronin (4thBty).

Rescue Race: 1. Driver Gorman (1stBty), 2. Driver Donnelly (4thBty), 3. Driver Flynn (4thBty).

Wrestling on horseback: 1. 3rd Battery, 2. 3rd Battery.

Musical Chairs: 1. Driver Donnelly (4thBty), 2. Driver Brabston (4thBty), Dvr Moans (4thBty).

Best Sub-Section Turn-Out: 1. 3rd Battery (c).

Best Turn-Out (Man and Horse): 1. Dvr O'Keefe (4thBty), 2. Dvr McSweeney (3rdBty), 3. Trooper Lennon (1stBty).

Novelty Race: 1. Dvr Delaney (1stBty), 2. Dvr Brabston (4thBty), 3. Dvr Dunne (1stBy).

Inter-Battery Cup: Best all-round performance and Sub-Section Cup won by 4th Battery.

The men in the barracks also enjoyed billiards. At the Army Billiards Championships the Artillery Corps beat Supply and Transport at a tournament in Islandbridge, Dublin. The artillery team consisted of Sergeant Maxwell, Sergeant Scanlon, Sergeant Keogh and Corporal Brannigan.[7]

Boxing

Boxing played a major part in military life and the Artillery Corps's first foray into army boxing was at a tournament at the Curragh in December 1925 when they won the Novices Boxing Tournament with Driver H. Byrne, Gunner T. Curtis and Driver Moans all recording victories. The victorious artillery team bore the trophy back to Kildare and 'even the fact of their lorry breaking down three miles from home could not damp their rejoicing'.[8] At a tournament held in the Curragh Gymnasium in February 1926, Drivers Moans and Fenlon represented the Artillery Corps.[9] The reporter for *An-t-Óglach*, the army journal, reported on the bout between Private Joynt (15 Btn) and Driver Moans (artillery) in the bantamweight that:

> Joynt's experience gained him victory. Fit, he made the pace so hot that the unfit Artilleryman could barely stay. But Moans was game. He fought back, stabbed Joynt with a neat left and sought often to cross a wicked right; failing to do so he surprised everybody by retiring in the fourth round.
>
> In the cruiserweight Private Kidley (Curragh) was up against Driver Fenlon (Artillery). It was reported that: 'Kidley jabbed his inexperienced opponent with a strong left then crossed a neat right which floored Fenlon, who pluckily arose, but so staggered and dazed that in seconds he threw in the towel. The fight lasted about thirty seconds'.

At a boxing tournament held at the Curragh Gymnasium in February 1928, a number of artillerymen participated.[10] Private Chase (Reception and Training Depot) beat Deans (Artillery) on points. McGuinness (1 Brigade) beat Uzell

(Artillery Corps) in the second round. Kelly (Islandbridge) knocked out Driver Curtis (artillery) in the first round while Ryan (1 Brigade) knocked out Gunner Moans (Artillery) in the first round.

The Artillery Corps team for the All-Army Junior Boxing Championships, to be held on February 21st and 22nd, is as follows:- Featherweight, Gnr Ryan (1st Field Bty); light-weight, Gnr Hayes (Arty Depot), Cpl E. Brannigan (1st Field Bty), Cpl. Loftus (3rd Field Bty); welterweight, Dvr. Moloney (1st Field Bty, Gr. De Courcey (Depot of Arty); middleweight, Gnr. Fleming (3rd Field Bty).

Both Cpl Loftus and Dvr Moloney competed in last year's championships. Loftus beat Pte O'Brien (Ordnance Corps, Dublin) in the first series and Pte Folinn (1stBatt, Galway) in the second series, but was himself defeated in the third series by Pte Donnelly (2nd Battn, Dublin), who subsequently went out in the final to Pte Curtis (4thBattn, Cork). Moloney fought his way to the semi-final of the welter-weight by beating Pte McDonnaca (1stBattn., Galway), Pte Ryan (4thBattn., Cork), and Pte O'Hegarty (1stBattn., Galway) only to be ousted by Pte Flynn (recruit Training Depot) who in turn gave way to Pte O'Keeffe (5thBattn., Dublin) in the final.[11]

Cross-Country Running

The Artillery Corps also featured strongly in athletics in particular with Lieutenant Tommy M. Banahan representing them. Lieutenant Banahan (2 Field Battery) finished third in the District Cross-Country Championship in December 1933 with Gunner Murphy (2 Field Battery) finishing in fifteenth place and Gunner Scullion (2 Field Battery) in twentieth place.[12] The first All-Army Junior Cross-Country Championships were held in January 1934 and the Artillery Corps won the team competition. The Artillery Corps team was as follows:

1st Field Battery: Lt. T O'Brien, Gnr Lacy, Gnr McCabe, Gnr Lane, Gnr F. Flynn, Dvr Nugent.

2nd Field Battery: Gnr Fanning, Gnr Murphy, Gnr Molloy, Gnr O'Neill, Gnr McQuaid.
3rd Field Battery: Lt T.M. Banahan, Gnr Cullagh, Gnr Dooley, Dvr Christie, Gnr Fleming.
Artillery Depot: Gnr Murphy, Gnr Scullion, Gnr McLoughlin, Gnr Arnold, Gnr Gorman.[13]

The individual placings were as follows:
1. Cpl M Sheedy (Recruit Training Depot), 2nd Lieut. T.M. Banahan (Artillery Corps), 3rd Gnr Murphy (Artillery Corps), 4th Gnr Scullion (Artillery Corps), 5th Pte Byrne (Dept of Defence), 6th Lieut O'Brien (Artillery Corps), 7th Pte O'Gorman (Recruit Training Depot), 8th Gnr Fanning (Artillery Corps), 9th Gnr Dooley (Artillery Corps).[14]

Basketball
The Artillery Corps also ran a strong basketball league. Players reported in 1933 were as follows:[15]

Left Section (1st Field Battery): Donagh, Flynn, Fulton, Brannigan.
Right Section (1st Field Battery): Maloney, Creavey, Byrne, Delaney, Bready, O'Shea, McCabe.
Left Section (2nd Field Battery): Kennedy, Brabston, Karney, Kavanagh, Cassen, Byrne.
Right Section (2nd Field Battery): Curran, Moran, Meade, Phelan, Carney, O'Neill, O'Driscoll.
Left Section (3rd Field Battery): Loftus, Moran, Pearce, Doyle, Dunne.
Right Section: (3rd Field Battery): Murray, O'Donnell, O'Meara, Cotter, Egan.
Brigade Headquarters: Dalton, Mooney, Walsh, Lynch, Mullen.
Depot Artillery: Ryan, De Courcey, Flynn, Byrne, Ryan.

The Artillery Corps appointed a welfare board similar to those constituted by order units in the army to deal with sporting matters. The Artillery Welfare Board committee for 1934 was:[16]

Presiding: Comdt. P. Maher, Officer Commanding Artillery Corps
Honorary Treasurer: Captain Callanan
Honorary Secretary: Lieut J. P. Kelly
Football and Hurling sub-committee: Capt Trodden, Lt. Donnelly, Sgt Kennedy, Cpl Nolan, Cpl Byrne, Gnr Duggan.
Athletics sub-committee: Lt O'Brien, Lt Curran, Lt Banahan, Cpl Cooney, Sgt Redmond, Cpl Nolan.
Basketball sub-committee: Lt Dalton, Lt Curran, Lt Donagh, Gnr Byrne, C/Sgt Hall, Gnr Walsh.
Boxing and Gymnastics sub-committee: Lt Hally, Sgt Kennedy, Sgt Carroll, Cpl Loftus, CQMS Prendergast, Gnr Mooney, Gnr Walsh.
Golf and Tennis sub-committee: Capt Wall, Lt Hally, Lt Slater, CS Cleary, Lt Solan, Lt Murray, Capt Lambert, Gnr Swayne.
Library sub-committee: Lt O'Mahoney, Cpl O'Carroll, Cpl Copley, Lt Keneany, Lt Slater.
Amusements sub-committee: Capt Thomson, Capt Lambert, Lt Hally, Sgt Hughes, CQMS Prendergast, Sgt Phelan, Sgt Scanlon, Gnr Tully, Dvr Donnelly, Cpl Egan, Cpl Cooney, Gnr MacAnespie.

Foreign Sports

In early 1920s Ireland, the Gaelic sports of Gaelic football and hurling were heavily promoted in the military. However, soccer and rugby, two games that were frowned upon in many circles, were openly played at military barracks despite not being sanctioned by the Army Athletic Association. The matter was raised at the athletic association's convention of 1923 where it was stated that 35per cent of the men were not catered for by a ban on soccer and rugby. Some delegates at the conference wanted to go further and ban golf and tennis.[17] Soccer and rugby remained banned but continued to be played on military pitches throughout the country. Kildare Barracks had its own soccer team in the 1920s and 1930s named Oakville and they put out a team against Curragh transport in April 1926.[18] The match was noted in the army journal *An -t-Oglach* demonstrating the reality of the time.

There are few other references to Oakville other than a match in the fourth round of the Leinster Shield 1932, when the team met Arbour Celtic of Dublin at Kildare Barracks.[19] The team was: Kennedy (goal), M. Walsh, H. Moran, J. Fulton, Lennon, Geary, Delaney, Turley, Lambert, Moans and O'Shea. Kennedy put in a fine performance in goal while Martin Walsh was a former County Kildare Gaelic football player. The game ended in a draw after extra time with the replay in Dublin.

The Artillery Corps had a rugby team from at least the 1930s. A barracks team played a match at the Curragh against the Special Services, Curragh. Kildare won the match by three points to nil, their best players being Coram, Banahan and Trodden.[20] The Artillery Corps hosted a rugby team from the Honourable Artillery Company of the Royal Artillery at Kildare in the 1960s, the same unit with which Erskine Childers (Snr) had served during the Boer War. The players were billeted in the barracks during their stay and one unfortunate gunner found himself and his bunk sitting on the barracks square when he awoke the next morning! Golf was also popular and the local golf club's main prize dating from the 1920s is known as the Artillery Cup.

Gaelic Games

Gaelic games were an intrinsic part of military life from the 1920s and Kildare was prominent in Gaelic sports. The Artillery Corps was in the unusual position of being part of the General Headquarters Command for sports, having originally being based in Dublin. This continued throughout 1925 and 1926, despite objections from the Artillery Corps who would have preferred to play in the Curragh Command area. Indeed, it was noted in 1925 that 'it was an act of true sportsmanship on the part of GHQ to travel to Artillery's ground, and a fitting climax to the many amenities displayed by both teams during a busy and strenuous season of both hurling and football fixtures'.[21] The artillery hurling team which lost in the final were Captain T. Finlay, Captain W. Tierney, Sergeant-Major J. Cummins, Corporal W. Lynch, Gunners J. Lyons, J. Leahy, M. Murphy, A. Larkin, J. O'Connell, Drivers T. Finn, W. Mitchell, J. Kelly, M. Kelly, J. Hayes, D. Quinn. Artillery won the 1925 football final with the following team: Commandant Dominic Mackey, Lieutenant Thomas Lambert, Sergeant-Major J. Cummins, Corporal Henry Brannigan, Trumpeter Michael Davis, Gunners Arthur Hall, Thomas Heavy, John O'Connell, Thomas McCormack, Thomas Rice, John Ryan and Martin Walsh, Drivers Cyril O'Neill, David Quinn and Patrick Winters. Substitutes were Gunners J. Mulvanny and P. McGough. Sergeant-Major James Cummins had the distinction of representing the Artillery Corps in both matches which were played on the same afternoon. He was a native of Cork, who served with the Artillery Corps from the beginning and was the goalkeeper on the Kildare team that played Kerry in the 1926 All-Ireland football final.

Kildare Barracks had its own Gaelic Football Team in the 1930s: it was called Kildare Sarsfields and played in the Kildare Junior championships. They met Kildare Town rivals, Round Towers, in the 1932 junior championship. Brannigan was outstanding for Sarsfields and O'Shea, Keogh, McInerney and Stanley for Round Towers.[22] Members of the First Field Battery team in the 1930s were as follows: H. Brannigan, E. Brannigan, P. McGough, J. Lynch, M. Walsh, D. Kavanagh, W. Moans, W. Lacy, M. Flynn, J. Curran, J. Hughes, J. Connell, J. Leonard, J. Fulton, H. Quirke.[23] Eugene Brannigan was an inter-county footballer who won the Ulster Senior Championship with Monaghan in 1926.

CHAPTER 18

THE NEW BARRACKS

I am of the opinion that the decision to rebuild Kildare Barracks involves unnecessary expenditure because we already have quarters in the Curragh Camp capable of accommodating 4,500 men and about 1,500 horses. We do not use all this accommodation for men and horses at the present time and I cannot foresee my associates calling for additional accommodation.

COLONEL M.J. COSTELLO

The new Officers' Mess, Kildare. (Courtesy of Michael Moriarty)

The late 1930s was a time of expansion and prosperity for the town. Kildare County Council built a new housing estate, Rowanville, named after Dr Lawrence Rowan, to the east of the barracks with eighty-three houses which were allocated to tenants (many of them former soldiers) in July and December 1939. A wallpaper factory opened the same year, and a beef boning factory, the Kildare Chilling Company, was also opened, greatly benefitting the local economy. The town had huge unemployment difficulties somewhat attributable to the barracks as explained in detail by a Dáil deputy at the time:

> What is said of the Curragh can be equally applied to Kildare Town. It is suffering from what produced unemployment in the vicinity of Curragh Camp. It is suffering from the fact that many people from other parts of the country join the Army, serve in the local barracks, are demobilised, and try to find employment in the area. That again means that the Curragh Camp and Kildare are suffering from a disability not associated with any local conditions, but associated, in the main, with the fact that the State attracts people to the Army, takes them to a barracks in the vicinity of Kildare or the Curragh, demobilises them from the Army, and these people often drift into the local town looking for work or for any kind of assistance they can get.
>
> As a matter of fact, proof of my statement in that connection will be found by reference to the census of 1926. I think it will be shown that 53 per cent of the people resident in the Kildare County Council electoral area were people not born in that area. If you examine the census I think you will not find any other place in the country where 53 per cent of the local residents were not born in the place. I hope in this case the Parliamentary Secretary

will, for these reasons, and because of the unemployment position which exists in the vicinity of the Curragh Camp and Kildare, have these matters attended to especially during the year. If he does, not only will he be providing for necessary military requirements, but, at the same time, he will be employing many unemployed people at work which is necessary and which will give them some definite means of livelihood.[1]

The 1936 census outlines the employment situation at Kildare and the other main towns in County Kildare. The census indicates that of the 849 persons in employment, 305 (including 4 women) of these were employed in public administration and defence, suggesting a much higher reliance on the barracks as a source of employment in comparison to other towns in the county.

1936	Kildare	Newbridge	Naas	Athy
Gainfully Employed	849	1,011	1,155	1,416
(*Admin/Defence:*	305	61	77	*28*)
Unemployed:	435	694	993	1,204
Under 14s	584	670	894	1,008
Population:	1,868	2,375	3,042	3,628

The issue of the state of the barracks and the reconstruction was raised at Dáil Éireann on a number of occasions from 1935 to 1938.[2] A barracks in a very poor state of repair was portrayed in 1935:

I think that if the Parliamentary Secretary had been able to visit there, he would see that it looks more like a ruined workhouse than an up-to-date military barracks. It has been grossly neglected in recent years and it does not seem to have seen a painter for a long time. It would be a difficult job, I think, to get the barrack to recognise any kind of a craftsman. In this case also, I hope that the Parliamentary Secretary will have this work carried out during the present year and that we will not have a substantial re-Vote next year in respect of this work.[3]

The Minister reported in October 1937 that 'definite plans for the reconstruction of Kildare military barracks have been settled, and the contract, drawings and specifications for the first section of the work are approaching completion. It is not yet possible to indicate when tenders will be invited or the work commenced.'[4]

The transfer of the Artillery Corps from Kildare to the Curragh was a matter of some concern to local business as reported in the *Leinster Leader* in November 1936:

> Our representative learns that the Ministry for Defence has decided to remove the Artillery Corps, up to now stationed at Kildare Barracks, to Plunkett Barracks, Curragh Camp. Portion of the transfer has already been effected. The removal of this considerable military force from Kildare is naturally a big loss to the tradespeople of the town, who are hopeful that the new wallpaper factory, when launched, will do something to offset this loss. Kildare Barracks, of course, lacks the modern conveniences of the new home of the Artillery Corps.
>
> A deputation of Kildare traders waited on Mr. Norton last week in connection with the rumoured transfer of the personnel at the Military Barracks, Kildare, to the Curragh Camp.[5]

Joseph A. Hennessey of the Kildare Town Development Association wrote to the Minister for Defence Frank Aiken TD on 3 September 1937:

> We find that you will appreciate the fact that the evacuation of the Military from the Barracks is an irreparable loss to the town of Kildare, first of all the business of the town is greatly affected, as for water there is a loss of £200 per annum in addition the local rates are affected.[6]

Mr Norton had an interview with the Minister for Defence in connection with the matter and was informed that the barracks at Kildare were structurally defective in certain respects, and that it was necessary to transfer the personnel to the Curragh Camp pending the reconstruction and renovation of the Kildare Military Barracks. The Minister for Defence advised Norton that it was not intended to close the Kildare Barracks permanently.[7]

Plans for the barracks hit another major stumbling block, not from the Department of Defence but from the military themselves. Major-General Michael J. Costello, a respected and influential Officer, wrote to the Assistant Chief of Staff on 11 March 1938[8]:

> I am of the opinion that the decision to rebuild Kildare Barracks involves unnecessary expenditure because we already have quarters in the Curragh Camp capable of accommodating 4,500 men and about 1,500 horses. We do not use all this accommodation for men and horses at the present time and I cannot foresee my associates calling for additional accommodation.

Costello had made a name for himself during the Civil War and became the youngest general in the army. He would later command one of the divisions during the Emergency years. Costello had a point because the anti-aircraft battery was already in the Curragh as there was no suitable accommodation at Kildare and with the removal of the horse from the Artillery Corps, the need for a barracks at Kildare was questionable.

Despite the reservations, the first tender was invited on 5 February 1938 for:

Contract 1:   Men's Quarters Block 3a and 3c
Contract 2:   Men's Quarters Block 3b and 3d
Contract 3:   Dining Hall, Building and Sanitary Block.

Blocks 9a and 4

The quantity surveyor, Francis D. Shortall, employed by the Office of Public Works to assess the project, estimated the costs of the first two contracts at £22,000 each and the cost of the third contract at £12,000.[9] The contracts for the four accommodation blocks were awarded to Mr A. Panton Watkinson, Dublin and contract three was awarded to Mr Samuel Phillips, Ormond

Road, Drumcondra Dublin.[10] A number of other military projects were also commenced at this time. Reconstruction work at Baldonnel Aerodrome and Collins Barracks Cork were commenced in 1938 with Panton Watkinson carrying out the former works, but the works at Kildare estimated at £300,000 were the largest undertaken by the Department of Defence. The scheme proposed an almost completely new barracks with quarters for officers and men, accommodation for guns, horses, field artillery, anti-aircraft gun teams, stores and a riding school. The men's accommodation blocks were each two storeys high and contained four billets to accommodate twenty-four men and two NCOs in each, giving enough accommodation to house ninety-six men and eight NCOs. With four blocks A, B, C and D, there was accommodation available for 384 men and thirty-two NCOs. Heating was provided by means of solid fuel furnaces situated under the officers' mess and a 'boiler house for turf-burning apparatus at sanitary block' was included in the plans prepared in June 1938.[11] The flooring of the new building was constructed from solid pine, the type of feature the Office of Public Works English-born architect William Henry Howard Clarke (1881–1977) was renowned for. He prepared the plans for Baldonnel Aerodrome and had worked on the reconstruction of the Four Courts and Custom House in the 1920s.[12] From 1934 he was entirely involved in new building work for the OPW and was particularly interested in 'wood carving, high class joinery and construction'.[13] He was assisted by another OPW architect named Thomas Byrne (1876–1939).

The next stage of the Kildare Barracks project, for battery command offices and workshops, was advertised in May 1939 with further development works in December 1940. The officers' mess, built of Wicklow granite by the contractor Sisk, was an imposing building befitting the new barracks, but it had one drawback. The main entrance faced the road and in practical terms was never used: consequently, everyone went in by the entrance facing the main square. When turf was delivered to fuel the heating system, it was unceremoniously dumped at the entrance to the mess before it could be put to use.

With the coming of the war and emergency in Ireland, entailing rapid expansion of the Artillery Corps, the barracks was still not fully completed. (The construction of the Artillery School block and lecture halls was tendered in 1940 and completed in 1942.) The barracks opened without ceremony or fanfare some time in late 1939 when the onset of war in Europe meant that the occasion was passed unrecorded. As Lieutenant-Colonel J.H. Murphy noted: 'It was built as an artillery barracks with gun parks, billets and messes of a very high standard. Kildare was also close to the rifle ranges at the Curragh and the artillery ranges at the Glen of Imaal. The Military College at the Curragh was close-by for demonstration and instruction, making the location ideal for efficiency and economy.'[14] It was the only purpose-built barracks constructed in the history of the Irish state and served its purpose well during its lifetime.

With the construction of the new barracks, many of the old hutments were put to good use. Some were sent to St Brigid's Park in Kildare and used by Round Towers Gaelic Football Club for clubrooms. A number of others were brought to the Curragh and used as officers' accommodation at K Lines near the golf course with a number still occupied in the late 1990s.

Some of the British army barracks was retained. The original gun and wagon lines were retained for storing the older guns and remained in use until the barracks closed in 1998. The Water Tower, albeit an unattractive structure, remained keeping good water pressure in the barracks for the rest of its existence. A former hay storage barn was converted into the radar training room.[15] The barracks never managed to get a gymnasium. The one for Kildare is reputed to have ended up in Ballincollig, County Cork. Some maintenance work was sanctioned at Kildare shortly after its construction. Internal and external renovation was carried out in 1946-47 at a cost of £2,150 and repainting carried out at an estimated cost of £1,120.[16]

One innovation introduced in the new barracks was the Raikes range, which would serve the corps well until the 1980s. The indoor range was based on the landscape around Kilworth, County Cork and used for training gunners in the art of proper target recognition and ranging. The smoke used to indicate where the simulated shells landed was simulated by a gunner smoking a cigarette under the ranges and exhaling the cigarette smoke at the relevant point where the shell landed.

CHAPTER 19

THE EMERGENCY YEARS 1939–1946

The general standard of gunnery showed a marked improvement during the 1943 practices and it was only necessary to bring one battery back to the school for further intensive training. The five batteries which had shown poor results in 1942 and which had been sent back to the school, all demonstrated the value of the additional training they had received there and one of them actually obtained first place in the 1943 inter-battery competition.

GENERAL REPORT ON THE DEFENCE FORCES, 1944[1]

A game of pitch and putt. (Courtesy of Martin P. Fleming)

Ciaran O'Halloran enlisted in the army on 2 September 1939 at Portobello Barracks, Dublin. His decision to join was prompted by seeing two large seaplanes land in Dublin bay. He was sent to McKee Barracks in Dublin for training with the 'Ack-Ack' (anti-aircraft) and was stationed at the anti-aircraft defences at Clontarf and Ringsend. The onset of the Second World War was a serious threat to Ireland and was referred as 'The Emergency'. The Irish Army handbook recorded the situation in its own unique way in 1940:

> As a first step the Defence Forces were mobilised and placed on a war footing. Seán Citizen then realised that he might have to depend upon his little-known Army to keep him out of the war. He sat up and began to take a live interest in it.[2]

The threat from the skies was the most real and the anti-aircraft batteries on the east coast kept a close vigil. On one occasion, Ciaran O'Halloran recalled that the gunners got the opportunity to bring their guns into action when a British Avro Fighter strayed too close to Dublin and the 'code red' was issued from control and they opened up their 3-inch guns. O'Halloran was selected for a potential officers' course and was dispatched to Kildare Barracks in 1942. There was no specific accommodation available so he was lodged in the administrative block with two men in each room. O'Halloran shared a room with J.D. Brereton for the duration of his training as they were trained as artillery officers.[3]

Emergency Expansion and Training

The Emergency years put an enormous pressure on the Defence Forces as the army underwent a rapid expansion and transformation. In 1940, the army comprised two brigades spread over the various commands throughout the country with a military strength of 19,136 – approximately 7,600 Regulars, 4,300 Reservists and 7,200 Volunteers.[4] It had been estimated in 1937 that Ireland required three divisions along with artillery, specialist, fixed defence, naval and air forces totalling over 100,000 men to defend the country but ultimately only two divisions and an additional brigade were created largely as a consequence of the lack of available equipment, particularly artillery, ammunition and manpower. Attempts were made to increase supplies of military equipment from England with varying degrees of success and some 18-pounder field guns, 4.5-inch howitzers and 3.7-inch anti-aircraft guns were received during 1940. The Defence Forces had 60 Bofor anti-aircraft guns and 31 anti-tank guns on order with the British, but these were in short supply and in demand for the British army, the bulk of their equipment having been lost following the evacuation of the expeditionary force at Dunkirk.[5] The threat from enemy aircraft action was very real, with a number of bombing incidents during 1940, eight of them occurring over three nights in January 1941 including bombs dropped on the Curragh on 2 January 1941.

The Chief of Staff's report for 1941–42 reflects the reality of the situation in respect of artillery:

> At the beginning of the period, sweeping alterations were made in the organisation in order to release personnel who were considered surplus in view of the improbability of obtaining further equipment. The number of field artillery battalions was reduced from four to three and the number of batteries in the AA battalion reduced from five and a training depot to one medium battery and one combined searchlight, Light Anti-Aircraft and training Depot Battery.[6]

However, during the period 1942–43, artillery was supplied by the British and the situation had improved dramatically. Five additional batteries were created to add to seventeen existing ones. By the summer of 1943, the corps was divided into seven artillery regiments, each containing three field artillery and one anti-tank battery, although the latter had only one anti-tank gun in each battery due to the lack of equipment.[7]

The lack of available ammunition greatly hindered the ability of the Artillery Corps to carry out proper training. There was limited range practice carried out in the summer of 1941, with the first three field artillery battalions exercised in the Glen of Imaal in June 1941 as detailed below. The corps was concerned about the lowering of standards due to the lack of range practice and in 1942 all of its batteries carried out practice in the Glen of Imaal. Each battery remained for a fortnight in Coolmoney Camp under the supervision of the artillery school at Kildare. Five batteries were deemed not up to standard and had to return to Kildare for a month in autumn 1942 followed by further range practice.[8] In 1943, training was up to such a standard that only one battery was sent back to Kildare for additional autumn training.[9] By the summer of 1945, the Corps had advanced to such a stage that the batteries were in a position to carry out regimental shoots with all batteries operating as a combined fire unit.[10] Once the war in Europe ended in May 1945, demobilisation and amalgamation of units commenced so that by the end of the year, the seven field artillery regiments were reduced to three[11] and down to two in 1947 with the anti-aircraft battalion also disbanded.[12] The consequence of the loss of personnel was that there were no range practices in the Glen of Imaal in 1946.[13]

Training Courses
The following courses are a sample of the training carried out at Kildare during the Emergency years:

April 1940 – March 1941	Potential officers courses	83 students
April 1941– March 1942	Potential officers courses	16 students
	Officers courses	20 students
	Potential NCOs courses	74 students
	Other NCO courses	56 students
April 1942 – March 1943	Officers courses	12 students
	Infantry officers trained	17 students

The end of the war also saw renewal of overseas training for artillery officers as follows: Lieutenant-Colonel P.J. Hally attended the seventeenth staff course at the Staff College in Camberley, Surrey in Britain from May to November 1946, followed by Lieutenant-Colonel Bill Donagh at the eighteenth staff course from

January to December 1947. Lieutenant-Colonel Patrick Curran attended the eighth intelligence course at the School of Military Intelligence at Wilton Park, Bucks in November and December 1946.[14]

The Artillery School also commissioned its own temporary officers during the Emergency years. The Minister for Defence, Oscar Traynor was at Kildare in April 1944 to present 14 cadets, under the command of Commandant Pierce Wall of the School of Artillery with their commissions as second lieutenants.[15] The new officers were:

> Philip Harrington, Templemore; Herbert Shortall, Dublin; William P.M. Murphy, Dungarvan; James D. Kavanagh, Dublin; James D. Murphy, Cork; Eoin C. Hogan, Borrisokane; Michael J. Whitty, Waterford; Gerald J. Kiernan, Dublin; Joseph G. Coleman, Athboy; Timothy J. Foley, Waterville; John J. Byrne, Mullingar; Michael F. O'Connor, Moyvane; Anthony Alvey, Clontarf and Henry K. McCracken, Baltinglass.

An *Irish Times* report from the time gives an example of artillery training, this time with the Local Defence Forces in the Glen of Imaal:

> Time after time, they heard the battery commander change the range and type of target to be aimed at, and just as rapidly did they see the gun crews probe them out with salvoes of accurately-aimed shells. Rarely did a projectile miss its mark, and when it did the inaccuracy was so slight as to warrant the target area still being regarded as within the danger-zone.
>
> For veteran artillerymen this was a standard of shooting to be reckoned with, but for mere amateurs it was little short of amazing. And that is just what they were – mere amateurs: men of the 41 Local Defence Force Field Artillery who for the first time were putting into practice months of theoretical work.

Commandant P.D. Kavanagh of the Artillery School recorded his memories of the School during the 1940s:

Being the School, the School staff were less than popular among the 'line' officers of the day, but there was no escape for anyone of any rank. A whole series of tests, written and oral, were carried out by the School staff. While the officers sat in Trodden Hall, sweating and grousing through written papers, lowly gun layers were being tested in fuse setting and sight setting and suchlike, and signallers were wrestling with messages, packed with pitfalls. The aim of all this was to produce professional and well trained 'Gunners' who were tested to the limit in the Glen of Imaal in shoots and exercises. To come last of the 22 competing batteries was to guarantee the frightful penalty of being dragged from one's home station and attached to the School for a period of several months' intensive training. The winning battery, of course, received the Magee Shield, the ultimate indescribable glory![16]

Coolmoney Camp, Glen of Imaal: June 1941

A report prepared by Commandant P.J. Hally, officer commanding the Depot and Artillery School, Kildare survives, with an account of training at Coolmoney Camp held from 5 to 14 June 1941. A surviving log sheet for one of the days, when the III Field Artillery Battalion consisting of 1 Battery firing 18-pounder field guns and 2 Battery armed with 4.5-inch howitzers was exercised, gives an indication of the type of shoot:

Date:	11 June 14.00 hrs
Observation Post:	Hart
Target Area:	Knocknamunnion Crissadaun.
	No shell to fall west or north of the Green Road.
1 Battery position:	Vicinity of house18-pounder80 rounds
	Instructional shoots chosen on ground
2 Battery position:	East of Camara X roads
	4.5-inch How.
	80 rounds

	Students of eighth potential officers course
	to be exercised in all firing duties.
Battery officers:	Second-Lieutenant K. Danaher (1 Field Battery),
	Captain W. Rea (2 Howitzer Battery)
Range Officer:	Second Lieutenant J. Fitzsimons
Signal Communications:	Each battery to arrange
	Ambulance and Medical Officer at Camara

Following completion of the camp, its commandant sent his report to the Director of Artillery in Dublin. The report shows the change from earlier times where the depot and school were finally in a position to prepare the ranges and manage the practice camp from their own resources rather than designating one of the batteries as a depot battery. It is also notable that the preoccupations of previous camps, transportation and horses, were no longer the issue that they had been, making for a shorter and more efficient shoot:

On Thursday 5 June 1941, practice camp was opened by the Depot and School, Artillery Corps. This unit looked after the Administration, Training and Range construction. Officers and Sergeants' Messes were established and controlled by Depot Officers. The camp from day-to-day had varying strengths.
On 12 June there was a total strength of 492.
The Depot and School staff, which is now up to strength, was capable of running this practice camp. It is suggested that this duty should be a normal one for the Depot and School unit.

The following units were exercised:

I Field Artillery Battalion.	4 FA Battery
	3.7-inch Howitzer Battery
II Field Artillery Battalion:	Right Section 5 Field Battery
	Right Section 8 Field Battery (Howitzers)
III Field Artillery Battalion	1 Field Battery
	2 Field Battery (Howitzers)

Students who had completed the eighth potential officers (emergency) course, fired for the first time as did recruit gunners in the batteries.

Right section 5 Field Battery	40 H.E.	51 shrapnel
Right section 8 Field Battery	84 H.E.	6 Star
1 F.A. Battery	58 H.E.	20 shrapnel
2 F.A. Battery (Hows)	77 H.E.	
4 F.A. Battery	62 H.E.	
3.7-in How. Battery	69 H.E.	16 smoke
Totals	390 H.E.	93 shrapnel
	6 Star	16 smoke

Gun Drill

The standard of gun drill was generally high except for the 3.7-in. Howitzer Battery and 2 Howitzer Battery. It is suggested that the N.C.O.s of these batteries be given local instruction in gun drill, fire discipline, engagement of targets and lectures in command and control.

Laying

Laying was generally of a high standard except for the 3.7-in. How. Battery. The laying here was of a very low standard, which might be due to the fact that layers were changed after every couple of rounds. It is suggested that layers be not changed during a series. It was fatal and not good instruction to change layers during a G.F. shoot.

G.P.O.A.s and B.C.A.s

Except in the case of the 5 and 8 Batteries and the B.C.A. of the 2 How. Bty., further instruction for these specialists is very necessary.

G.P.O.s

All G.P.O.s must learn to control and command their gun crews in action. Voice control must be practiced. All G.P.O.s must learn to appreciate the necessity of speed in G.F. shoots.

Recording targets and calculating or measuring switches and ranges for predicted shoots was not good and a higher standard of accuracy will have to be reached.

It is suggested that G.P.O.s boxes be provided to ensure that all necessary equipment is on hands for the G.P.O.

During practice camp it was noticed that G.P.O.s had not got full equipment in their command posts. In one case a G.P.O. had not got a range table Part I, a very necessary item of his equipment.

Officers and other ranks exercised as B.C.s

A high standard of shooting was obtained, but good shoots were often spoiled by bad work at the guns.

Instruments and Equipment

Directors, guns, equipment etc., were on hands and in good repair. The Howitzers of the 2 Howitzer Battery require an immediate wear test or a calibration shoot in order to adjust the muzzle velocities. The immediate replacement of some of the telephone sets is very necessary and should be attended to immediately.

Engagement of Targets

(a)   Ordinary artillery shoots such as neutralisation, Destruction, Gun Fire, Shrapnel, Smoke and Anti-Tank were understood by all. In the case of anti-tank shoots, it is found better to allow the layer to lay and fire the gun.

(b)   Single Gun. More and more training in the use of single gun is required. The Artillery School will publish a pamphlet describing the procedure for employing a single gun in support of Infantry and Cavalry. The contents of this pamphlet should be made known to all artillery personnel.

Co-operation

Firing practices were arranged to tie in with the Programme of the Military College and the Ordnance School. Artillery potential officers attended lectures and demonstrations given by infantry instructors of the Military College and in turn, Military College and Ordnance students received instruction in Artillery work.

Note: Individual reports on officers and potential officers have been sent to the Director of Artillery.

Tragedy at the Glen of Imaal – September 1941

The Artillery Corps incurred the greatest loss of life ever suffered by the Defence Forces in a tragic accident in the Glen of Imaal on 16 September 1941. During a demonstration by the Artillery School of a mine, it exploded killing fifteen members of the Artillery Corps and one from the Engineering Corps. The demonstration was attended by Commandant Kelly, officer commanding Kildare Barracks; Lieutenants Danaher, Fitzsimons, Keogh and Nolan of the Artillery School, Lieutenant Brennan of the Artillery Depot, Lieutenants Brady, O'Neill, Kenny and Brierton of the Anti-aircraft Battalion. Lieutenant Michael J. McLoughlin from Rostrevor, County Down was in charge of the demonstration and laid three mines. One of the mines he was working on exploded and McLoughlin took the full brunt of the blast. He was a very experienced engineer, having graduated from Queen's University, Belfast and had served in the army since 1936. He was an instructor in the Military College, Curragh. Apparently, he jumped on the mine to take the brunt of the blast but the result of the explosion was still devastating. Someone, possibly McLoughlin shouted, 'we have seven seconds' before taking the brunt of the blast. The fifteen killed were:

Corps of Engineers
Lieutenant Michael J. McLoughlin, Rostrevor, County Down
Anti-Aircraft Battalion
Lieutenant John J. Brierton, Summerhill, Cork
Lieutenant John D. Fennessy, Chapelizod, Dublin
Lieutenant Thomas O. O'Neill, Faranferris, County Cork
Sergeant Thomas Stokes, Sandymount, Dublin
Corporal Edward J. Kennedy, Drumcondra, Dublin
Corporal William Shannon, Ballinteer, Dundrum
Gunner James McDonnell, Crumlin, Dublin
Gunner John Murphy, Harold's Cross, Dublin
Gunner Gerald O'Hagan, Donnybrook, Dublin
Gunner James Osborne, Summerhill, Dublin
Artillery Depot and School
Company-Sergeant Patrick McMahon, Usher's Island, Dublin
Sergeant Michael Scullion, Letterbrack, Letterkenny, County Donegal
Corporal Denis Cleary, Ballinamuck, County Waterford
Corporal Colm Heffernan, Kilbeggan, County Westmeath
Corporal John Taylor, Drumcondra, Dublin

Company-Sergeant William Bonar had the terrible task of having to identify eleven of the dead men, Sergeant Richard Lennon identified the others and both attended the coroner's court to confirm their identities. There were thirteen more detained in hospital as follows:

Artillery: Sergeant Morgan, Drumcondra, Dublin; Corporal Crowley, Bandon, County Cork, Corporal Shannon, Ballinteer, Dundrum; Gunner Brannigan, Castleblayney, County Monaghan; Company-Sergeant McNamara, Kildare, Sergeant Delaney, Aughrim, County Wicklow; Corporal J. Corcoran, Highfield Avenue, Cork; Gunner McAllorum, Killarney Street, Dublin; Gunner Ward, Sandymount; Corporal Hayes, Sean McDermott Street, Dublin and Corporal McNamara, New Inn, County Tipperary.

Engineers: A/Corporal Cotton, Dalkey, County Dublin and Private Davern Thurles, County Tipperary.

Corporal Toddy McNamara, one of the injured lost his sight. He attended a school for the blind in England where he learned telephony with British soldiers injured during the Second World War. He got civilian employment in Kildare Barracks where he remained as a telephone operator until the 1980s.

The Magee Gun

The Artillery Corps awarded a shield to the most efficient battery in the Corps during the Emergency years. In 1943, the Artillery Shield was won by 13 Battery, I Field Artillery Brigade. Captain K. O'Brien accepted the shield on behalf of the battery from the Minister for Defence, Oscar Traynor at a ceremony in Kildare Barracks. Commandant Pierce Wall commanded a parade of five artillery batteries and a guard of honour drawn from the Artillery School and Depot under the command of Captain R.N. Cooke was inspected by the Minister.[17] The Magee trophy was won by the III Field Artillery regiment in 1944 which was presented with the trophy at Ballincollig Barracks in December by the Chief of Staff Lieutenant-General McKenna.[18]

The records of competition winners are scarce but those for 1944 and 1945 survive:[19]

1944

Sub-section Commander Trophy: V/200464 Sergeant J. Cloherty, 11 Field Battery VI Field Artillery Regiment

Battery Shield: 11 Battery, VI Field Artillery Regiment

Anti-Tank Battery Trophy: 3 Anti-tank Battery, III Field Artillery Regiment

Regimental Trophy: III Field Artillery Regiment

Coastal Defence Artillery Fort Competition: Fort Carlisle

Anti-Aircraft Artillery Competition: No. 4 Medium Battery AA Section, Clontarf

1945

Sub-section Commander Trophy: V/200469 Sergeant J. O'Brien, 11 Field Battery VI Field Artillery Regiment

Battery Shield: 20 Battery, IV Field Artillery Regiment

Anti-Tank Battery Trophy: I Field Artillery Regiment

Regimental Trophy: III Field Artillery Regiment

Coastal Defence Artillery Fort Competition: Fort Berehaven

Anti-Aircraft Artillery Competition: No. 5 Medium Battery AA Section, Ringsend

Of course, in addition to the artillery competitions, there was still time for annual sports during the Emergency years:

A very successful sports meeting was held at Kildare Barracks on Wednesday of last week. There was keen competition in all events and high standards were attained. Much amusement was provided by the inclusion of novelty items such as a pillow fight on a greasy pole, and an unusual type of obstacle race.

The highlight of the evening was the tug-o-war. The final between the 4 Battery and the Depot and School was a dour struggle. The final pull lasted fully eight minutes and was won by the 4 Battery, which also won the Battery Cup with 37 points. Other placings being Artillery School and Depot 1 points and 3.7 Howitzer Battery 22 points.

The attendance included Col. McNally, Officer Commanding the Command; Majors Tuite and McLoughlin; Commdts Gribben, Kelly and Hally. The prizes were presented by Commdt. J.P. Kelly.

100 yards confined: 1. Gnr. O'Reilly 2. Gnr. McGonigle 3. Gnr. Power

220 yards confined: 1. Gnr. Power 2. Gnr. Stafford 3. Gnr. Murphy Time: 24 secs

High Jump: 1. Gnr. Brabston 5 ft 0 ins 2. Cpl. Roche 4 ft. 11 ins

Three-legged Race: 1. Cpls. Reidy and Fitzgerald 2. Gnrs. Walsh and Daly, 3. Gnrs. Flanagan and Ryan

100 yards open: 1. Cpl. Curran 2. Gnr. McGonigle 3. Cpl. Burke Time: 11 secs

880 yards confined: 1. Gnr. Powell 2. Gnr Stafford 3. Gnr Walsh Time: 3 mins 8 secs

Long jump confined: 1. Gnr Power 17 ft. 3 ins. 2. Lt. Bovenizer 17 ft 2 ins. 3. Cpl. Fitzgerald 17 ft. 0 ins.

Pillow Fight: 1. Gnr. Mulcahy 2. Gnr. Doyle 3. Gnr. Locke

Hop, Step and Jump: 1. Cpl. Neville 2. Sgt. Dowling 3. Lt. Bovenizer

16 lb Shot: 1. Cpl. Reidy 2. Gnr. Aston 3. Sgt. Hughes

56 lbs Shot: 1. Sgt. Hughes 2. Gnr. Whelan 3. Cpl. Reidy

Boys' Race: 1. Joe More 2. John Scanlon

Girls Race: 1. P. Prendergast 2. M. Nolan

One Mile Open: 1. Cpl. Burke 2. Cpl. Lenihan 3. Gnr. Burke

Discus: 1. Sgt. Hughes 2. Cpl. Reidy 3. Cpl. Fitzgerald

Obstacle Race: 1. Gnr. Murphy 2. Gnr. Stafford 3. Gnr. Howard

Band Prize: Bandsman Smith

Veterans' Race: 1. Gnr. Larkin 2. Sgt. Lacey 3. Gnr. Jordan

Best Turn-out: 1. Depot and School 2. H.Q.

Relay Race: 1. Depot (Sgt. Lacey, Cpl. Quinn, Cpl. Cantwell, Gnr. Powell) 2. H.Q. 3. 4 Battery

Tug-o-war: 4 Battery

440 yards open: 1. Pte. Morrin 2. Cpl. Curran 3. Sgt Hayes.

The next sports day at Kildare produced another keenly fought tug-o'-war competition with the *Leinster Leader* reporting that 'The various ties aroused very keen interest and, so enthusiastic were the spectators that it was with difficulty that the stewards prevented them from invading the pitch and giving bodily aid to their respective favourites.' In the end 'A' battery defeated the Potential NCOs in a pull that lasted over four minutes. The day was run by the commanding officer of Kildare Barracks, Captain J.P. Kelly and the sports committee headed by Lieutenant C. Clarke. The results were as follows: 100 yards: 1. Corporal Farrell, 2. Gunner Gorman; 440 yards: 1. Gunner McGonigle, 2. Volunteer Askin; 880 yards: 1. Sergeant Scullion 2. Gunner Harbinson; 1 mile: 1. Gunner Holihan 2. Sergeant Scullion; Relay race: 1. Potential NCOs 2. Depot HQ Company; Obstacle race: 1. Corporal Fitzgerald 2. Volunteer O'Riordan; Sack race: 1. Gunner Mulkearns 2. Gunner Bennett; Wheelbarrow race: 1. Corporal Clarke and Gunner Brabston; 16lb shot: 1. Gunner Bennett 2. Gunner Browne; Long jump: 1. Corporal Farrell 2. Corporal Clarke; High jump: 1. Corporal Fitzgerald 2. Gunner Brabston; Tug-o-war (final): 'A' Battery beat Potential NCOs by 2 pulls to nil.

A concert was held after the sports, the No. 3 Army band contributed to the entertainment and the following took part in the concert: Lieutenants D.O'Connell, C. Mattimoe, D. Reddin and O'Shea; Corporal Cooney, Gunners Coyle, Askin, Mulkearns, Lawlor, Conway, Brown, McDermott, Doyle, Mahony, Murphy and Dunne; Corporal Fitzgerald and Sergeant McCann.

The men were well catered for in the barracks but there was a shop across the road, in the small row of houses that was there at the time, run by Brennans where the soldiers could buy tea, bread and scones to supplement their diet. At the time, there was a civilian barber in the barracks named Charlie Graham. He was ex-British army and spoke with an accent to match. Business was good as there were plenty of men in the barracks during the Emergency. Henry McCracken was in for a haircut one day and in conversation with him.[20]

Graham:	Plenty of new recruits in these days
McCracken:	These ones are very good by all accounts
Graham:	There hasn't been a good recruit in here since the turn of the century!

Further accommodation for military families was also addressed in the construction of the new barracks and houses at Melitta Terrace were occupied in March 1943 with the following tenants:

Melitta Terrace
No 1 58555 Sergeant J Moore (I FAR)
No 2 70871 Sergeant E. Fox (3 Battalion)
No 3 47135 Gunner McGrath (Depot Artillery)
No 4 20066 C/S G. Farrell (CT & MD)
No 5 65947 Gunner W. Lacey (Depot Artillery)
No 6 56246 Sergeant-Major F. Whitty (Depot and Artillery School)

Gunners also found themselves before the courts during the war years. A Private William Egerton who acted as an orderly in the barracks appeared before Kildare District Court for the theft of a wallet belonging to Captain Patrick McCann and a fountain pen and some cigarettes belonging to Mrs Elizabeth Dalton of the barracks. Egerton was given two months imprisonment and Private James Keddy who received the fountain pen was given fourteen days.[21] There were also more sinister crimes, such as a colt revolver being stolen from the barracks in June 1940. Superintendant Flynn of Kildare Garda Station recorded that Captain Joseph Kelly reported a Colt Revolver, No. C537, .45, value £7 missing from No. 4 Battery at the Artillery Barracks, Kildare. The weapon was in the control of 76270 Corporal James Hawkins and was also used by Corporal John Brennan on the occasion of 'stand-to' parades. The revolver was issued without ammunition which would be drawn from the stores when required. Corporal Hawkins slept in a room, No. 4 D Block in the new barrack s and was in control of thirteen members of the Volunteer Reserve force attached to 4 Battery who also slept in the same room. The Superintendant reported that:

Off the dormitory where Cpl. Hawkins slept there is a small apartment used for lumber purposes. This apartment on the first floor is 15 ft. from the ground. There is one window on same. It is connected with the dormitory by an internal door, the key of which was held by Cpl. James Hawkins. Hawkins kept the revolver in this apartment, which he always kept locked, keeping the key on his person.

The Gardai established that the lock was not tampered with although the fire escape was in close proximity to the window which could have been a point of entry to the room. They also established that Corporal J. Fitzgerald, No. 2 Battery was in charge of the particular room in April 1940 and had reported his key missing and this was never recovered, nor was the lock changed. The Gardai made enquiries about the antecedents of all those who slept in the particular dormitory and received reports from their native areas. The revolver was never recovered.[22]

CHAPTER 20

PEACETIME 1947–1959

Be at the bursting doors of doom and in the dark deliver us,
St Barbara of the Gunners

ST BARBARA OF THE GUNNERS, G.K. CHESTERTON

St Barbara of the Gunners, erected at Kildare in 1954. (Courtesy of Martin P. Fleming)

The Chief of Staff's report for 1947–48 summarises the military perspective of the Artillery Corps after the Emergency years:

> The Artillery Corps is organised in a Directorate, Depot and School at Kildare, 3 Field Artillery Regiments, 4 Fixed Anti-Aircraft Regimental Cadre Headquarters and Coast Defence units in each of the Southern and Western Commands.
>
> The Corps establishment provides for a total of 945 all ranks. Total strength as on the 31 March 1948 was 635 all ranks or 33% under establishment.
>
> Field Regiments are equipped with 4.5-inch howitzers and 75 mm guns, both of which types are obsolete, in addition to a small number of 2-pdr A.T. guns, also obsolete, and 40mm light antiaircraft guns which are modern. The Anti-Aircraft artillery are equipped with 3.7-inch guns which require modernisation.
>
> Courses – Depot and School: The following courses were conducted at the Depot and School during the period:
>
> 40mm Bofors AA/AT Course:7 officers from the field artillery
> Conversion course CDA to AA:9 officers from AA cadres
> 1st Standard Artillery Course:15 officers
> 2nd Standard Artillery Course:15 officers
> 24th Potential NCOs course:12 students
> In addition 150 recruits completed training and were posted to units. 11 recruits are still undergoing training.[1]

A profile of post-war Kildare Barracks appeared in the *Irish Press* in January 1947 as part of a series of light profiles of different branches of the Defence

Forces. The profile is worth reprinting in its entirety.

> Even if you don't know a howitzer from a water-pistol, there is something impressive and faintly awe-inspiring about Big Guns. At the Kildare Depot and School they have a fairly representative selection, ranging from 75mm field guns through 18-pounders to 3.7 ack-ack jobs. One of the things which has most entranced them to date is the 40mm Bofors light anti-aircraft weapon which can hurl a lot of high explosive higher than most.
>
> The two biggest guns, however, around the Kildare establishment of the Corps are Messieurs les Commandants Jim Dolan and Ned Shortall, respective i/c Depot and School.
>
> Jim is dry, quiet spoken, with the real artilleryman's devotion to his weapons. Ned Shortall – young for his elevated rank – seldom reached in the early thirties – is one of those born-not-made officers whom any army would love to follow into anything from the jaws of death to a blackboard session on the theory of fuses.
>
> They were obliging, too; they wheeled out rows of howitzers for us in the barrack square. Each howitzer had its regular team of six gunners in attendance. There were a lot of howitzers and a lot of gunners.[2]

A Second World War Veteran!

The veteran of the North African campaign at Kildare was none other than a dog who made an appearance in the *Irish Press*:

> The dog's name is Buckley. At first glance he suggests an Airedale, but is really a canine cocktail, large hairy, and very well trained. On his collar he wears a metal tag that reads:
> Buckley, property of Cpl Ferguson, 35343974. HQ Detail, 37thBatt. APO 874.
>
> Corporal Ferguson was a U.S. soldier attached to Headquarters Detail of the 37th Battalion and his army post office number was 874.
>
> When he went home to the U.S., quarantine would not allow

Buckley to accompany him, so the dog was looked after by many people and finally passed into the hands of an Irish nun in London, sister of the Kildare Corps' Battalion quartermaster – Sergeant J. Nolan.

The BQMS was interested in a dog which had been born in North Africa, had subsequently fought alongside the 8th Army in Italy and France, and been wounded in the leg during the Rhine crossing. So Buckley came to Kildare.

When his new owner decided that barrack life was too cramped for Buckley, and gave him to Sergeant-Major William Downey, who lived three miles distant, all went well until the day when Mr. Downey left the army and put on a civvy suit for the first time. Then Buckley bit him, too. And now the dog is back in camp, veteran mascot of the Corps.[3]

Magee Barracks

The Barracks was renamed *Dun MhigAoidh* or in English Magee Barracks in October 1952 after Sergeant James Magee of the Longford Militia. The choice of name was appropriate linking the modern gunner back to the first recognised Irish gunner – Gunner James Magee. Magee was a pikeman who had originally served with the Longford Militia. With the arrival of the French army under the command of General Joseph Humbert at Killala Bay on 23 August 1798, many Irish rebels linked up with the French as they crossed the Connacht countryside. On 8 September 1798, after a short battle at Ballinamuck, the French surrendered to a numerically superior British force, to be treated as prisoners of war. This was not an option for the Irish who were deemed as rebels committing treason and once the French surrender was negotiated, the British attacked the Irish lines. Magee manned a 6-pounder French gun and fired into the British troops. The Irish lines held largely due to the accurate firing of the field pieces. When the 6-pounder he commanded was damaged by a British round, four gunners lifted the gun and Magee fired it again. The recoil killed the four men and Magee was taken prisoner. Despite being in French uniform, he was executed on the field as a deserter from His Majesty's Army.

The Artillery Corps constructed a bronze model of Magee's six-pounder field gun in 1943 at the workshops of the Depot and School. The Magee

Gun Trophy was wrought in bronze by Company-Sergeant Joseph Scanlon at Kildare, with research and design by Captain Danaher and the base prepared by Captain Lambert. Captain Danaher and C.S. Scanlon also prepared another bronze trophy known as the Dunboy Trophy for coastal artillery. Liverpool-born Scanlon was an early enlistee in the Free State army being with the corps at Kildare since the beginning.

The Magee trophy was inscribed with the following:

MAGEE GUN
LOST WITH HONOUR
AT BALLINAMUCK
8TH SEPTEMBER 1798

On the front is inscribed:

THE REGIMENTAL TROPHY
ARTILLERY CORPS
PRESENTED BY
DEPOT & SCHOOL ARTILLERY CORPS

St Barbara of the Gunners

A statue of St Barbara was erected in the barracks in 1954. The local gunners were asked to contribute one shilling towards the cost.[4] The statue was unveiled in April 1954 and Colonel James McLoughlin, Director of Artillery paid tribute to the spirit of the corps who had contributed towards the work of the erection of the new statue and particularly to Lieut P. McDonald, Cadet School, Military College who, while on the staff of the Artillery Depot, had conceived and initiated the project.

The statue was the work of the Dublin sculptor Arthur Breen and was made of limestone on a base of Wicklow granite. The inscription on the base of the statue from G.K. Chesterton's St Barbara of the Batteries reads:

'Be at the bursting doors of doom and in the dark deliver us,
St Barbara of the Gunners'

The statue was moved following the closure of the barracks and is now situated at the Artillery Depot in Plunkett Barracks, Curragh. St Barbara's Day was celebrated in the barracks on 4 December each year as it is with other artillery units throughout the world. The British, US and Swiss military attachés attended ceremonies in the barracks to celebrate the feast-day.

There were a number of changes in Director of Artillery in the 1950s. D.J. Collins from Blackrock, County Cork took over in November 1955. He was commissioned in August 1922 as a Captain and had taken over Fort Carlisle from the British on 11 July 1938. He was first officer commanding of Coast Defence Artillery until January 1953 when he was appointed officer commanding Artillery Depot and School at Kildare.[5] There was a new Director of Artillery in December 1956 when Colonel Patrick J. Hally took over. He was born in 1908, came from Carrick-on-Suir, County Tipperary and had entered the army as a cadet in 1928, being commissioned as a second-lieutenant in 1929. He served with the Artillery Corps until 1941 when he was appointed officer in command of the 16 Infantry Battalion. After the Emergency he was a staff member of the Command and Staff College at the Curragh before being appointed to army headquarters in 1953.[6] P.J. Hally was appointed as Adjutant-General of the Defence Forces in 1957 and was replaced by Lieutenant-Colonel Patrick Curran. Curran was born in Dublin in 1908 and, like Hally, entered the Cadet School in 1928, being commissioned in 1929 as a graduate of the 1 Cadet Class. He attended the Command and General Staff Course at Fort Leavenworth, USA in 1938–39. He served in artillery until 1941 when he was appointed officer commanding 31 Infantry Battalion at Ballincollig, County Cork. In 1947, he was transferred to the Instructional Staff in the Military College, Curragh.[7]

Curran was replaced by William Donagh, a native of Kells, County Meath. Donagh joined as a cadet in 1930 and was commissioned in 1931. He was cadet master at the Curragh from March 1952 until his appointment as Director of Artillery in 1959. Arthur A. Dalton was born in Dublin in 1909 and joined the army as a cadet in 1929. He was appointed Director of Artillery in January 1959 and died in August 1960. He was the only Director of Artillery to die in service and a firing party from Kildare Barracks under Lieutenant J.H. Murphy attended the funeral. Another Cork native at this time was Joseph Higgins from Ballyhooly who was officer in charge of the VI Field Artillery Regiment in 1968. He had a brother Daithi Higgins who was killed in action while serving with the Spanish Foreign Legion on 8 September 1938 during the Spanish Civil War.

Post-War Training

A visit by the *Irish Press* in 1947 gave a feel for the training regime for new gunners at Kildare.

> In a classroom we found a recruit class, rows and rows of nicely barbered heads – with not a blend among them! – all intent on the fuse diagram. If you don't know the meaning of compo rings, creep springs, and percussion pellets, you ought to be in the artillery. There are in the barracks about 50 of these recruits and something over 100 trained men.

[Training had changed dramatically since the pre-war days of the horse.]

> The Artillery Corps is divided into three main branches: Field Artillery, Anti-Aircraft Artillery, and Coastal Defence Artillery. Highly mechanised today, it nevertheless retains the memory of its colourful origins as a 'Mounted Arm' in the spurs of its officers and the bandoliers of the men.
>
> Mechanisation extends to training as well. On the Newton indoor Anti-Tank Range a full-size 18-pounder field gun is trained on a wire-propelled miniature tank. When the gunner gives the order to fire the room echoes to the explosion – not of the field-piece itself, but of the .22 rifle which is strapped beneath the belly of the giant.
>
> Life in the Kildare Barracks is pleasant, say both officers and men. The place itself is new and comfortable; the job is interesting; the food good.
>
> And they have fun too – a dance every Wednesday, a whist drive every Friday. They have snooker, billiards, and table tennis, a playing-field for outdoor games, and a team of boxers in training. And Ned Shortall and Jim Dolan to look after them. A pleasant place.[8]

With the war over, training courses in England had become available again and two officers attended the Long Gunnery Staff Course at Larkhill with

Commandant C.E. Shortall attending the Fifth Course from September 1947 to September 1948 and Commandant Bill Rea attending the Sixth Course from January to December 1948. Commandant J.H. Byrne and Lieutenant B.J. Greer attended the Long Gunnery Staff Course for coastal defence at Plymouth from October 1947 to October 1948 and the month-long Regimental Officers Survey Course at Larkhill was attended by Lieutenant J.P. Duggan and P. Wickham in July 1947. The Corps prepared a demonstration shoot for the 10 Command and Staff Course in the Glen of Imaal in April 1948, and further shoots for the Infantry School, Cadet School and Cavalry School.[9]

The 25-Pounder Field Gun

1949 was the year that the 25-pounder field gun was introduced to the Irish army. The gun had served well for a number of armies during the Second World War and the decision was made to modernise the Irish weaponry with the purchase of 48 such guns. The weapon's main advantage was in combining the attributes of a field gun such as the 18-pounder with those of a howitzer to allow for higher-angled firing. The first shoot was carried out on 21 June 1949 at Seskin Gun Position in the Glen of Imaal. The Minister for Defence Dr T.F. O'Higgins, The Chief of Staff Major-General Liam Archer and the Director of Artillery Colonel James McLoughlin were in attendance.[10] Three batteries comprising of eight guns each gave seven different demonstrations in attack and defence including the demonstration of a 'stonk' – the linear placing of shells in a given area to make it impassable for troops.

The History Sheet of one of these guns fired in June 1949 survives and outlines all rounds that it fired until its last round in July 2004. The early records show that the gun barrel was first fired at Woolwich on 3 March 1944 and fired 18 rounds at the demonstration held on 21 June 1949. However, the gun was manufactured in June 1942 and had fired the equivalent of over 400 rounds by the time it was purchased by the Irish and was used for training during the Second World War or may have served in action against the enemy with the British army.[11] The 25-pounder would serve the army for sixty years with the final ceremonial shot carried out by the Irish Defence Forces in the Glen of Imaal in July 2009.

The 120mm Mortar

In 1952 the 120mm Thomson-Brandt heavy mortar was introduced into the

Defence Forces following assessment by a military board including Commandant Shortall of the Artillery School at Bourges in France. The mortar arrived at Kildare in June 1952 and was fired in the Glen of Imaal on 19 July. It provided the hardest hitting artillery piece in terms of high explosive and lethal effect on a target with the Artillery School using four mortars for instructional purposes and the 8 Battery in Mullingar having a full battery of twelve mortars. When the Defence Forces were reorganised in 1959, three new artillery regiments were formed and six regiments now included a heavy mortar battery including the 11 Heavy Mortar Battery at Edenderry, County Offaly, part of the VI Field Artillery Regiment at Kildare Barracks. The 120mm mortar proved its worth in action in December 1962 and January 1963 when the 38 Battalion serving with the United Nations forces in the Congo included, for the first time, a mortar troop commanded by Captain Thomas O'Boyle. The mortar troop were the first Irish artillery unit to go into combat overseas in a number of actions and had proved their worth. All further deployments overseas in the Congo, Cyprus and Lebanon would subsequently include heavy mortar troops.

The Gunners in the 1950s

Michael Moriarty was born in Bandon, County Cork and served with the Ennis Battalion of the FCA from 1 December 1949 before entering the Cadet school at the Military College at the Curragh on 21 November 1950. He was commissioned as a second-lieutenant on 23 November 1952 and posted to the Artillery Corps together with six other new officers to complete the four-month young officers' course at the Artillery School.[12]

> Having completed our commissioning leave, seven young Second Lieutenants reported to the Artillery Depot in Magee Barracks, Kildare to commence the basic training course for young officers, known unsurprisingly as the Young Officer's Course. While all the corps and services had their own schools, housed in mainly unsuitable buildings, the 'Tillery', as it was often called in the early years, boasted a new barracks for its depot and school in Kildare town. The new barracks also featured easily the largest barrack square in the Defence Forces, designed to hold large concentrations of horse artillery units for parades and training.

Our principal instructors were Commandant Bill Rea, the School Commandant, and Commandant Ned Shortall, both of whom had received training in Britain in the latest artillery techniques. Another was Captain Tommy Wickham, whose specialty was battery and regimental survey. The chief NCO instructor was Battery Sergeant Louis Carroll, a lovely gent, who was fond of his pipe and who behaved like a kindly grandfather to young officers. The NCO instructors were all very experienced and gave us a great grounding in what was a long course of complicated and detailed training. Safety took a prominent place in everything we did – a mistake could be very dangerous during live practice.[13]

After completing their initial training in the Artillery School at Kildare, the seven second lieutenants were then given their first postings:

0.7544 Second-Lieutenant Noel Bergin to I Field Artillery Regiment

0.7546 Second-Lieutenant Jeremiah Healy to II Field Artillery Regiment

0.7548 Second-Lieutenant Kevin Duffy to I Field Artillery Regiment

0.7552 Second-Lieutenant Padraic O'Farrell to IV Field Artillery Regiment

0.7556 Second-Lieutenant William Phillips to I Field Artillery Regiment

0.7571 Second-Lieutenant Michael Moriarty to IV Field Artillery Regiment

0.7573 Second-Lieutenant Michael McMahon to II Field Artillery Regiment

Here the new officers would continue their training with senior officers and NCOs in the fine arts of Artillery. George Murphy joined the Defence Forces in 1951 and was commissioned as a second lieutenant in 1953. Murphy was from Naas, County Kildare where his father had been a Garda Superintendant. His father, Nicholas Murphy was originally from Blackwater, County Wexford and had served with the Republican movement during the 1916 Rising and War of

Independence with the North Wexford IRA. George Murphy recalled:

> After commissioning in 1953, I was sent to Kildare with Noel
> O'Driscoll, Michael O'Driscoll and Noel Clancy for our conversion
> course to become artillery officers. All newly-commissioned second
> lieutenants were trained as infantry officers but it was up to their
> new corps to train them in the relevant skills such as signallers,
> cavalry or in our case as gunners. We lived in the officers' mess at
> Kildare and it was an impressive place with central heating and
> showers.

Murphy recalled that there was no live firing during initial training. 'It was all
about tactical exercises in the school, map reading, observation and identifying
suitable battery positions and observation posts on the Curragh.' Murphy would
have a long career in the Artillery Corps serving at McKee Barracks, Dublin;
Ballincollig, Cork and at Birr, County Offaly with the FCA. He served overseas
in the Congo, Cyprus, Lebanon, El Salvador and Angola and would finish his
career as Director of Artillery.[14]

One gunner who enlisted in the army in 1950 and was posted to the Artillery
Corps at Kildare in March 1950 was Pat McCarthy. He recalled that:

> We had completed ten weeks in McDonagh Barracks (General
> Training Depot), the place was overcrowded, Commandant W.
> Rea, later Colonel and passed to his reward, arrived one day – and
> interrogated us – the sheep on right, the goats on left – anyway
> we embussed for Kildare and Depot Artillery. About forty of us
> under the baton of the late Lt. P McDonald. It was a great thrill at
> the time to come to a comparatively new barracks. Col. P. Curran
> was Commanding Officer in 1950 and Sgt Major Pat Egan 'Pat
> the Dog' was Barracks Sergeant-Major. Practically every county
> in Ireland was represented. There was only Depot Staff, Recruits
> and attachments like Tiffy Scanlon, Tiffy Johnson, 'Saddler'
> Pete Scanlon, 'Tip Cart' Matt Creevy, Medic Sergeant Christy
> Burke (Doc), Corporals M. Murphy, 'Soldier' Ryan and 'Daisy'
> O'Connor of the MPC.[15]

Another gunner who enlisted in the 1950s was John Ryan. He was from Wexford and had enlisted in 1954. He had an uncle Nicholas Ryan who was wounded during World War One. Ryan served two years in McDonagh Barracks, Curragh before emigrating to England. He returned home every year to carry out two weeks training as an army reservist before re-enlisting in 1961. One older gunner in the barracks in the 1950s was Jim Rankin, another one of the old timers. He was head cook and got an extension of service. He had the distinction of being stationed in Dublin Castle in August 1922 when news came through that General Michael Collins had been shot dead in Cork.[16]

CHAPTER 21

The Anti-Aircraft Regiment

They were solicitously attentive with cups of tea, armchairs, and such things, but when they got on to the techniques of anti-aircraft artillery their enthusiasm ran away with them and I collapsed under an avalanche of esoteric terms that made the sort of anti-aircraft gunners that I used to know something about seem as remote as bows and arrows.

THE IRISH TIMES CORRESPONDENT, 1955

The Air Defence Regiment, Kildare, circa 1985. (Courtesy of Donnie Finn)

The anti-aircraft batteries that had served the nation so well during the Emergency years as a battalion were disbanded in 1945 and reorganised into four AA battery cadres with two in Dublin and two in Cork. In 1949, the Artillery Corps acquired its first radar. Two members of the Royal Artillery; Captain Dan Buckley and Battery Sergeant-Major V. Page came to Kildare to conduct the initial training course in July and August. Students on the course were Commandants M. McCarthy, J. Dolan and E. Shortall, Captains E. de Barra, D. Burke, T. Banahan, P. O'Neill and F. Flanagan, Lieutenants W. Murphy, D. O'Grady and H. McCracken. An anti-aircraft radar set was erected in the barracks under the supervision of a specialist from the British War Office.[1] In 1952 the AA battery cadres were disbanded and the AA Training Regiment was established at Kildare on 16 June 1953 under the command of Lieutenant-Colonel Arthur Dalton. Officers underwent a number of courses in England and subsequently the regiment acquired the L60 and L70 Bofor 40mm anti-aircraft gun that was used by all NATO armies. A batch of new army recruits who trained at McDonagh Barracks, the Curragh in the summer of 1953 were posted to the new anti-aircraft regiment in December 1953 to make up the required strength:[2]

No.	Name	County of origin
99727	Butler, Michael	Kilkenny
99696	Canavan, Patrick	Galway
99745	Cassidy, Desmond	Antrim
99743	Daly, Bernard	Dublin
99237	Daly, John	Dublin
99707	Dempsey, James	Offaly
99729	Doyle, Patrick	Wexford

99736	Flanagan, William	Dublin
99752	Hughes, Patrick	Tyrone
99753	Hughes, Michael	Tyrone
99710	Lawlor, John	Kilkenny
99740	McDonnell, John	Meath
99666	McManus, Peter	Monaghan
99748	O'Brien, Patrick	Kildare
99647	O'Leary, James	Dublin
99695	Rice, Bernard	Dublin
99683	Rock, Anthony	Dublin
99708	Stewart, John	Antrim
99703	Woolhead, David	Dublin

Two of these recruits were brothers. Patrick and Michael Hughes from County Tyrone were two of thirty recruits in No. 10 platoon. Training in the General Training Depot McDonagh Barracks involved constant drilling and exercise. Every Saturday the recruits completed a five-mile march and training also required recruits to swim in full battle dress in the Curragh swimming pool. The corporal in charge, Nick Fahy, was an artillery man and he kept an eye out for potential gunners. When the time came for posting out of the Training Depot, the recruits were interviewed by Lieutenant-Colonel Daly and nineteen recruits were sent to the Artillery Corps to man the Air Defence Regiment.

Patrick and Michael Hughes came from a nationalist family from Tyrone. Their uncle Oscar Heron, served with the Royal Air Force during the First World War, being awarded the Distinguished Flying Cross and Belgian Croix de Guerre. He was credited with thirteen air victories. He served with the Irish Air Corps and was killed, together with his gunner, Private Richard Tobin, in an air accident during a display in the Phoenix Park in August 1933, ironically in an exercise with the anti-aircraft battery. His brother Charles Heron was a Garda Superintendent based in Dublin. Patrick and Michael only intended serving in the army for five years, Patrick left and emigrated to America but Michael remained on and served as a Company Quartermaster Sergeant at Kildare.[3]

After initial training at the Curragh and about ten days leave, the new recruits were posted, in December 1954, to Kildare Barracks or *Dun MhicAoidh* as it was then known. The new men were now one-star gunners and had to undertake a two-month course to gain a second star. Training was on Bofors, 25-pounder field guns and there was also some infantry drill. Gunners were initially not allowed near the guns until they reached an acceptable standard of training. Finally, the three-star gunner course turned the men into proper gunners. Patrick Doyle from Wexford was only 14 years old. At that time, recruits were not asked for proof of birth. Once the attesting officer formed the opinion that the recruit was seventeen, they were allowed to join. This policy would mean that when the army later served in the Congo there were sixteen-year-olds involved in heavy fighting.

Michael Hughes didn't stay a gunner for long. In about October 1954, he was paraded before the commanding officer and told that he had been selected for an NCOs course. In May 1955 he was presented with his corporal's stripe by the Director of Artillery, Colonel McLoughlin. Michael recalled that the director's son, Colm, was also on the course. They were often short of money and Colm would seek his father out on the occasions that he came to Kildare for a loan on behalf of the men to be repaid on payday (The Director of Artillery was primarily based in Dublin from the late 1940s). Patrick Canavan was the son of Thomas Canavan of Headford, County Galway. Following his posting to the Anti-Aircraft Regiment, he spent a period training with the FCA in Limerick. He rose quickly to the rank of Sergeant largely due to his outstanding record for instruction, administration and general military ability. He served overseas on three occasions but died after a short illness in June 1965.[4]

When the FCA and Defence Forces were fully integrated in 1959, the AA regiment became 1 Anti-Aircraft Regiment with its headquarters at Kildare. The new structure meant that the 1 Air Defence Battery at Kildare was joined by 2 Air Defence FCA Battery in Dublin and 3 Air Defence Battery at Limerick with headquarters at Kildare. The 4 Battery of the Air Defence Regiment was added in 1979. The Air Defence Regiment was different to any other unit in the country at the time in that all the anti-aircraft units were directly administered and commanded from Kildare. It was also the only battery of any description at Kildare as the rest of the units in the barracks were for the purposes of training only i.e. School and depot. The senior staff in the Anti-Aircraft Regiment at Kildare in the 1960s were:

Officer in Command:	Lieutenant-Colonel Denis Burke
Battery Commander:	Captain Ciaran O'Halloran
Adjutant:	Captain Tadhg O'Neill

An *Irish Times* correspondent attended an anti-aircraft battery shoot at Gormanston, County Meath in 1955 but did not have the enthusiasm that the military had for the occasion.

Gormier [Gormanston, County Meath] has become a much better place than it was when I was there last. They have cleared away a lot of the old huts, and the place looks neater and more soldierly.

I haven't become any better looking since I was there last – a point which was borne in on me by the almost reverent approach of the young officers (beardless boys most of them), who obviously decided to give the Army Fragile-Old-Gentleman treatment to the aged civilian thrust into their midst. They were solicitously attentive with cups of tea, armchairs, and such things, but when they got on to the techniques of anti-aircraft artillery their enthusiasm ran away with them and I collapsed under an avalanche of esoteric terms that made the sort of anti-aircraft gunners that I used to know something about seem as remote as bows and arrows.

It got a bit easier when Colonel McLoughlin the Director of Artillery and Commandant Burke of the AA Regiment explained it. They had pity on my senility and put the technical terms into elementary English so that I got some notion of what it was all about. Both my mentors emphasised that what I was to see was not a demonstration but merely a test of some shells and fuses coupled with what they described as a blooding of young officers and newish gun-teams.

Gormanston proved an ideal location for anti-aircraft shoots as the gunners fired out to sea. There were however, often complications as shipping had to be kept away from the area and aircraft taking off and landing at Dublin airport had to be delayed during shoots. This was not just a problem for Gormanston as the Glen of Imaal was also close to aviation flight-paths. The batteries carried out a number of shoots at the Glen of Imaal but primarily trained at Gormanston, generally in September of each year. The 1 Battery at Kildare retained responsibility for cash in transit duties and more importantly deployment at airports on the occasion of visits to the country by foreign dignitaries when the full resources of the unit were put into use.

The RBS 70 Missile

There were a number of improvements in the weaponry available to the corps in the 1980s. Prior to the visit of Margaret Thatcher to Ireland, the Artillery Corps recognised the shortcomings in defensive equipment and invested in the RBS 70 anti-aircraft system. Captains Ó Neachtain, Richardson, Donnelly, Fogarty and Brown were sent to Sweden for training on the new equipment in April and May 1980. The missile system was delivered in October 1980 and a simulator was delivered later in the same year. Captain Eoghan Ó Neachtain had the pleasure of demonstrating the system to Ireland's most well-known television presenter Gay Byrne on *The Late Late Show* in November 1980. The publicity served a valuable purpose as it let the Provisional IRA know that the army had the capability of protecting visiting dignitaries from attack by air at a time when the capabilities of the IRA were expanding.

Live firing of the RBS 70 proved difficult. There were no suitable ranges to fire the unit with the Glen of Imaal being too short. A number of potential firing locations were sought as far away as County Kerry and Mayo but the risk to commercial aircraft and shipping made it more practical to travel to Sweden. Colonel George Murphy and Commandant Ray Quinn travelled to Vidsela in Northern Sweden to view live firing and evaluate the possibility of Irish gunners using Swedish ranges for live firing of anti-aircraft missiles. They also evaluated a 'clip-on' night firing device. Paddy Walshe, Eoghan Ó Neachtain, Eamonn Fogarty and Dave Brown travelled to the Arctic Circle to fire the first round on behalf of the Artillery Corps. The Artillery School took one live system and the Air Defence Regiment received six systems.[5] The advantage of this type of equipment was mobility, with the system being capable of being loaded onto a light vehicle very quickly and even carried to a location. The missile had a range of five kilometres and a ceiling height of eight kilometres and was put into use to protect the airspace around Dublin during visits by important visitors to the State.

In 1986 the Corps took delivery of the Giraffe radar system that provided advance warning surveillance and was integrated with the RBS 70 anti-aircraft missile system. Commandant Murray, Captain Ó Neachtain and Captain O'Higgins attended training in Sweden. The Artillery School subsequently commenced radar training courses for the Giraffe in October 1986.

CHAPTER 22

MILITARY AND BARRACK LIFE

Did discharge one round .303 value 7d
Fined 20 shillings. Penal reduction 7d

COURT OF INQUIRY, KILDARE BARRACKS, 1955

Corpus Christi procession, Kildare Barracks. (Martin P. Fleming)

L ike all military units, the Artillery Corps recorded gunners as they arrived and departed from the Depot. For example, the following were attached to the Depot from 13 March 1961 to 4 May 1961 to participate in the 34 Potential NCOs Course:

Name	Regiment	Home
Gunner P. Murphy	I FAR	Kilkenny
Gunner J. Barrett	I FAR	Cork
Gunner P. Quinlan	I FAR	Tipperary
Gunner M. Young	I FAR	Tipperary
Gunner T. Fletcher	II FAR	Armagh
Gunner E. Brennan	II FAR	Kilkenny
Gunner T. McAney	II FAR	Monaghan
Gunner F. Maguire	II FAR	Meath
Gunner J. Moore	II FAR	Wicklow
Gunner J. Mullen	II FAR	Tipperary
Gunner N. Williams	II FAR	Dublin
Gunner B. Brennan	III FAR	Limerick
Gunner J. Kiernan	IV FAR	Westmeath
Gunner R. Wilson	IV FAR	Westmeath
Gunner J. M. Lee	VI FAR	Kildare
Gunner M. Connolly	I ADR	Curragh
Gunner P. Keyes	I ADR	Portlaoise
Gunner D. Finn	I ADR	Kildare
Gunner P. McNamara	I ADR	Kildare

One old soldier in Kildare was Michael Guerons. He was another ex-British army man who had enlisted in 1922. He was well known for entertaining the gunners about his previous army years and had a great knowledge of the Boer War. He retired in 1956 on reaching 60 years of age. After he retired, having no family, he remained in the barracks living in C block and carrying out general duties. When he passed away, a nephew came over from England to collect his personal belongings. It turned out that Guerons was not born in 1895 as presumed but was actually born in 1885 and had seen service in the Boer War as a boy soldier!

Discipline

Military discipline remained strict throughout the 1950s and 1960s. As in previous regimes, absence without leave (AWOL) remained the most common crime. The general punishment for such crimes was a fine and forfeiture of pay normally matching the length of the absence so that a two-day absence would result in a fine and two days loss of pay. Other crimes and an example of punishments included:

Leaving Barracks by an unauthorised route	Fine 5 shillings
Absence from place of employment	Fined 7/6
Dirty on guard duty	Warning
Disobeying a lawful command	Fined £3
Disobeying a lawful command by a s/officer	Fined 2 shillings
Did discharge one round .303 value 7d	Fined 20 shillings
Penal reduction 7d	

The military also had to deal with soldiers causing difficulty outside barracks. For example a soldier was arrested by the Gardaí for fighting and was returned to Kildare Barracks and fined for 'creating a disturbance in a public place'. Another gunner received a fine for negligently driving a military vehicle and damaging it against a kerb.

Other men were found guilty of more serious military crimes. A gunner in the late 1950s was charged with:

I. When a sentry leaving his patrol without being regularly relieved
II. When a sentry being found asleep
III. When in custody escaped

The unfortunate gunner was brought before a court martial and imprisoned for forty days. The location of the sentence could vary between the Curragh Detention Barracks or Arbour Hill in Dublin for longer sentences. There were more serious tragedies. A number of gunners from Cork who were attached to Kildare Barracks were involved in a fight at a local nightclub after which a 17-year-old named Michael Burke was killed when kicked and beaten with chairs at the Derby House close to the barracks.[1]

Sport

Sport played a major part in barrack life in the 1950s and 1960s and hurling was prominent. Many of the gunners at Kildare came from hurling counties such as Limerick and Tipperary. The barrack team won the Todd Burns Cup in 1952 in hurling. The team were:

> Gunners Ryan, Watson, McCarthy, Morgan (Capt), Duggan, Furlong, Halpin, Connolly, Fitzpatrick, Buckley, Sergeants Reidy and Costolloe, Corporals Foley, Fahy, Finlay and McEnerny, BQMS Nolan and Lieutenant P. McDonald.

Boxing continued to play a part in military life. A one-month boxing course was held in the Depot in November 1961. The participants were: W. Smyth, M. Guilfoyle, L. Little, P. Whelan, T. Murphy, T. Gaffney, P. Barcoe, G. O'Brien, J. Geraghty, S. Flaherty and T. Brady.

The barracks also had its own pitch and putt course from the 1950s when there was a strong Kildare league with the artillery team being prominent.

Soccer was also prominent in the barracks through the late twentieth century. A team representing Magee Barracks won the Curragh Command Soccer League in 1997 after a gap of thirteen years. Gunner Simon Donnelly, BQMS Eamon Fitzsimons, Sergeant George Power and Corporal Noel Dowling had also represented the barracks in matches throughout the 1970s, 1980s and 1990s. The 1997 players were Gunner L. Gleeson, Gunner M. Houlihan, Gunner J. Fogarty, Gunner T. Houlihan, Corporal D. O'Connor, Sergeant G. Setright, Gunner S. Donnelly, Sergeant G. Power, Corporal K. O'Neill, Gunner M. Cosgrave, Gunner A. Bowe, Corporal S. Gratten (Capt), Gunner T. Donnelly, Gunner P. Moore, BQMS E. Fitzsimons, Gunner C. Murphy and Corporal E. Loughman. The team was managed by Corporal Kieran O'Neill.

The Film Industry

The Irish Army played an enormous part in the development of the film industry in Ireland from the 1950s onwards. From the *Blue Max* in 1966 when members of the Air Corps flew many of the planes, to *Braveheart* (1995) and *Saving Private Ryan* (1998) when over 1,500 members of the Reserve Defence Forces – (*Forsa Cosanta Áitúil*) were used in the film. The Artillery Corps played another role in the development of the industry. Sixty artillery pieces were removed from the original gun sheds at the rear of the barracks, including two large horse-drawn 60-pounders field guns, twenty-five howitzers and thirty 18-pounder field guns. The Artillery Corps decided to offer them for sale as they had become obsolete and parts were no longer available for the guns. They were sent to Dublin and ultimately transported to America for use in Hollywood.[2]

Entertainment

Kildare barracks was a hub of activity for all who served there. The gunners socialised in the barracks in the evenings, played football, took part in quizzes and even had their own pitch-and-putt course. At Christmas, the children were well catered for with an annual party. Military life meant that soldiers did not have annual leave in the same way as in modern times and many lived in the barracks, meaning that there was a permanent presence on the site with senior NCOs living in until the 1970s.

The Artillery Corps adopted a well-known military tune – *The Limbers*, which dated from the early 1900s and was known to artillery gunners as early as the First World War.

Over hill, over dale – we have hit the dusty trail
And the limbers keep rolling along
'Counter march', 'right about', hear those wagon soldiers shout
And the limbers keep rolling along.

This song could still be heard in the barracks up to the 1980s. The Artillery Corps also participated in a popular radio quiz called 'Question Time' when a team drawn from the barracks took on a team of five townspeople in a programme which was broadcast from the Tower Cinema, Kildare in 1947 compared by the Radio Éireann presenter Jimmy Henry. The barracks was represented by

Commandant Mattimoe, Sergeant J. Phelan, Captain P. McCann, Sergeant-Major Egan and Lieutenant A. Smith. The town was represented by Leo Brennan, Joe Darcy, D.H. Lenihan, Stephen Talbot and V. Foley. The adjudicators were Reverend Father Foynes and Lieutenant-Colonel P. Curran.[3]

> The contest proved a huge success, with an all-round high standard of answering. Final victory went to a popular businessman, Mr. Leo Brennan (of the 'town five') who completed the course without a single fault to take the honours (and the two guineas) from Commdt. Mattimoe, Artillery Barracks team, who was just pipped in the final essay.
>
> Of the total ten competitors, three (Commdt. Mattimoe, Messrs. Brennan and Foley) reached the final with full marks, and the winner was the only one to preserve the unblemished record to the end.

The Troubles

In August 1969 when families were being burnt out of their homes in Belfast, refugees had come across the border to various military bases. On 24 August 1969, Kildare was made available and 127 refugees made the barracks their home, which was only surpassed by Gormanston in Meath with 413 refugees.[4] It was reported that in November 1969, there were fourteen families still in Kildare with the assistance of the Red Cross. Paula and Mary Burke, daughters of Dinny Burke, who lived in the barracks at the time remembers the refugees arriving in the barracks and being billeted in the men's quarters. Paula and Mary recall helping out on a few occasions during this time particularly when the refugees were being fed in the NCOs mess. There was a certain amount of chaos in the barracks with so many Belfast families roaming the area at all hours of the day and night. The rosary was recited every evening at an altar set up outside the doors of the artillery school.[5]

It was not the only involvement that Kildare had with the troubles. Its barracks were the closest barracks to Portlaoise Prison where members of the IRA were detained. When riots broke out in the early 1970s, the artillery hastily mobilised and headed for Portlaoise to quell them. Once the initial disturbances were quelled, a unit was assigned to guard duty at the prison with an additional unit on standby at all times at Kildare. This was not the first time that Kildare was put on alert because of the troubles. After a mass escape from the Curragh internment camp in December 1958, 400 soldiers and eighty Gardaí were mobilised to capture the escapees who had broken down a wire fence in the camp after causing a disturbance. It was reported that:

> In Kildare town there was a particularly large number of troops on street patrol. Soldiers were on duty at Newtown Cross, Tully Stud, the local wallpaper factory, Standhouse road and the Tully road. For two hours after the break the Tully road was closed to traffic and was not reopened until 6 p.m.[6]

A number of other soldiers got involved in these troubled times by stealing gelignite from an explosives manufacturing company at Enfield, County Meath which they were guarding between May and October 1974. Two soldiers of the Depot Artillery, Gunner John Lipsett and Gunner Joseph Gorry would ultimately go to prison for their involvement in the affair. The judge told the men that their crime was a grave breach of trust on the part of two members of the Defence Forces.[7]

The army further resolved some of its problems with accommodation for married soldiers through the construction of St Barbara's Park in 1980. The first tenants to occupy St Barbara's Park in November 1980 were:

No 1	817372	BQMS T. O'Reilly	(1AA Regiment)
No 2	819476	Sergeant S. Sage	(Depot Artillery)
No 3	823106	Corporal P. Hayden	(Depot Artillery)
No 4	820494	Sergeant G. Power	(1 AA Regiment)
No 5	820304	Corporal F. Foran	(Depot Artillery)
No 6	813487	Sergeant J. McHugh	(Depot Artillery)
No 7	823506	Sergeant M. Kavanagh	(1 Arm Squadron)
No 8	819083	Corporal F. Matthews	(Depot Artillery)
No 9	832206	Corporal J. Whelan	(Depot Artillery)
No 10	820302	Sergeant M. Kelly	(Depot Artillery)
No 11	823632	Sergeant L. Hunt	(Depot Artillery)
No 12	823353	Corporal M. Hennessey	(Depot Supply & Transport)

No 13   820331   Corporal J. Anderson   (Depot Artillery)

No 14   820479   Sergeant J. McConnan   (1 AA Regiment)

Civilians and Soldiers

Paula and Mary Burke were daughters of Denis Burke and moved to the barracks in 1964. Denis (1916–94) was from Whiddy Island, County Cork and had joined the army in 1936, being commissioned in 1938, serving initially with the 1 Field Artillery Brigade in McKee Barracks, Dublin. During the Emergency he was with the AA battery serving time in the Phoenix Park and subsequently found himself in Collins Barracks, Cork where he met his future wife, a military nurse named Clara Harmon, and they subsequently married in 1948.

He found himself in Kildare in 1954 living at East Lodge in the town before a spell in Ballincollig, County Cork and moving into the barracks with his family in 1964 where he raised three daughters, Mary, Paula and Katheryn. Mary and Paula Burke recalled growing up in the barracks in the 1960s.[8] There had an orderly named Gunner Ben Daly who was with them for sixteen years who polished boots, shone brass buttons and kept the Sam Browne belts in order. There were two secretaries in the barracks, Monica Moore and Dorothy Doyle who were the only women employed there at the time while Toddy McNamara, who had lost an eye in the tragedy at the Glen of Imaal in 1941 worked at the telephone exchange. On rare occasions when their parents were away, the Burke girls would be brought into the Officers' Mess to get their dinner prepared in a separate room by the cook Joe Hall. Toddy McNamara suffered another unfortunate incident on one occasion in the telephone exchange. During a particularly bad electric storm at Kildare, a lightning strike hit the Ordnance workshop and destroyed the chimney. The electric current from the lightning strike blew McNamara across the room although he was not badly hurt.

There were other differences too for children growing up in a barracks. The children addressed and knew gunners by their ranks such as Sergeant Murphy who repaired the clocks and Sergeant McCann a Northerner. The children were also saluted by the personnel in the barracks at a time when there was great respect for all. One abiding memory for anyone in Kildare from this time was the military parades. On the feast of Corpus Christi every year, six officers would form a guard of honour which marched along the route of the annual procession, and the gunners would line the route as it made its way around the town to the Presentation convent. There was also a mass parade every Sunday morning as the men marched out of the barracks to the local church.

Liam O'Keeffe was employed as the switch operator on the telephone system from December 1985. He replaced Toddy McNamara who was there from the 1940s and Billy Scully who was there for a short period before O'Keeffe. The switchboard at Kildare was known as the 'shocking switch' as it was a plug-in system so that if the operator's hands got sweaty while working the system, it tended to give off an electric shock! This problem was temporarily solved by the operator sitting on a rubber mat wearing a rubber armband! In 1990, the switchboard was replaced by a digital one solving the problem once and for all. Liam got off to an audacious start in the barracks. Not being familiar with military way, after lunch on his first day he took a short cut and drove across the main barrack square to get back to work. 'Sacrilege!' was the view of Sergeant Jim Fortune who was on the barrack square with a parade at the time.

There were plenty of civilians employed in the barracks at the time such as former artillerymen Dick McCarthy and Jim Gillespie who acted as storemen, Dorothy Dempsey was a typist, Jim Magee, foreman with the board of Works; Noel Hennessy, a carpenter; Pat Hennessy, painter; Seamus Maher, Jack Brett, John Reidy and Joe Byrne.[9]

Another Dog Tale
Above the switch-room were the offices of the VI Field Artillery Regiment where Captain Seamus McDermott was Staff Officer in the 1980s. Captain McDermott had a Great Dane dog that he brought around the barracks. McDermott recalled an incident involving his Great Dane and the switch operator, Liam O'Keeffe:

'He was the most placid, docile dog in Ireland but had one awful fetish – he hated the sound of ringing phones. Kildare was a quiet country barracks. No one bothered us much and tea/coffee was always 11.00 to 11.30 – everything shut down for that. So it was always safe to leave the dog in the office, except one fateful day. I must have sloped off to the mess early and the dog was minding the office.

Liam [O'Keeffe] rang looking for me only to be answered by snarls and growls and an awful rumpus. Liam ran out to the hall and listened and sure enough there was a terrible noise coming from Captain McDermott's office so he ran out to the square where he met a Lieutenant on his way to coffee. 'Oh please help, I think Captain McDermott is gone mad and he is growling at me on the phone and now there's a terrible commotion in his office.' The lieutenant, a wise man from County Clare calmed Liam down and assured him that he would find Captain McDermott in the mess – which he did. Well no western brawl would account for as much damage that the dog did in the office – the phone eaten to shreds along with everything else not tied down – all because of one phone-call from Liam O'Keeffe.[10]

The Artillery Club

In 1971 the officers of the Artillery Corps began to discuss establishing an artillery club. Discussions were held during the year and serving officers were consulted about the proposal. A drafting committee at Kildare consisting of Captain M.P. Dunne, Lieutenant Ray Quinn, Lieutenant Paul Allen and Lieutenant Brian Wickham met to draft a constitution. The club was formed in March 1973 on the fiftieth anniversary of the foundation of the Artillery Corps and was recorded in *The Irish Times*:

> Nobody who has ever served in the legal armed forces of John Bull's Other Island needs any additional definition when there is a mention of the Corps. Admittedly, there are unfortunates – almost untouchables – in outfits like Infantry, Cavalry, Air Corps, Engineers, and even S. and T., who become unpurpled at the tacit assumption of the Gunners that their Corps needs no prefix, but members of the Corps ignore this, writing it off as the pardonable envy shown everywhere by lesser breeds towards the elected Ubermensch.[11]

The Irish Times noted on the anniversary of the foundation of the club that: 'Bang-bang men (that is to say men of the Big Bangs) are reminded that the annual general meeting of the Artillery Club will be held tonight in Magee Barracks, Kildare, at 20.00 hrs. Supper will be served and Gunners who require stabling for the night will be accommodated if they stand to attention and make suitable noises before the Hon. Secretary, who should be present with his range-finder.'[12] The Artillery Club also awarded a trophy known as the Jackie Jones Trophy to the best student on each Young Officers Artillery Course.

CHAPTER 23

UNITED NATIONS SERVICE

Distinguished Service Medal
For distinguished service with the United Nations Force
in the Republic of the Congo, in displaying leadership
and devotion to duty to a high degree. Although painfully
wounded during hostilities in December 1961, he refused
to leave his platoon and subsequently, whilst looking after
his men, he received the wound from which he died.

DSM CITATION TO 87410 SERGEANT PATRICK MULCAHY

The 4 Light Anti-Aircraft Battery founded on 27 October 1961 for service in the Congo. Foundered on 15 November 1961, services no longer required. The Officers are Commandant Denis Burke, Captain Des Duff, Captain Kevin Duffy, Lieutenant Patrick Ghent, Lieutenant J.H. Murphy. (Courtesy of J.H. Murphy)

Unlike practice in many other armies, Irish military service on overseas missions with the United Nations has been voluntary. The battalion-strength contingents that served abroad from the 1960s were created specifically for that purpose from personnel, including women from the 1980s, and were drawn from various home units. Each battalion was made up of a headquarters unit, an A Company drawn from the Western Command, a B Company from the Southern Command and a C Company drawn from the Curragh and Eastern Commands. Accordingly, in the Congo, Kildaremen tended to serve overseas with C Company of the relevant battalion.

One of the first gunners to serve overseas was Gunner Donnie Finn of the Air Defence Regiment at Kildare who served with C Company of the 33 Battalion in the Congo from August 1960 to January 1961. Finn was born at Kildare and was the son of John Finn, originally from Kilbeggan, County Westmeath who served with the Engineering Corps at the Curragh. Donnie Finn had originally enlisted in 1959 and was posted to the Air Defence Regiment together with the rest of his platoon. He recalled that two of the gunners with him were only 14 years old. Other gunners to serve with him at the time were Jim Rooney, Paul Keyes and Paddy Ronan. As there were no artillery units serving overseas, the gunners were referred to as privates, which caused some principled confusion in the ranks. Finn recalled that: 'There was often confusion as an officer or NCO might ask is Private Finn present to which I would reply, no sir, but Gunner Finn is here!'

Some of the first gunners from Kildare to serve overseas did so with the C Company 34 Infantry Battalion in the Congo. Corporal R. Connolly and Gunners J. Nolan, A. Synnott, M. Lackey and H. Jeanes were posted to the battalion in December 1960. Corporal A. Flynn was posted to Leopoldville in April 1961. A number of Kildare gunners also served with the Headquarters Company of the 36 Infantry Battalion in the Congo. Gunners R. McCarthy,

W. Watson, C. Baldwin, C. Connolly, T. Coughlan, J.J. Guidera, K. Herron, L. Hunt, H. Jeanes, A. Murphy, M. Phelan, D. Roche and J. Ryan were posted to the Battalion in November 1961. Sergeant P. Hughes followed them out to UN headquarters at Leopoldville in August 1962. Gunner Michael Phelan, who was born in the Curragh, County Kildare was only 17 years old and had only been in the Artillery Corps since May 1960. He may have been the youngest Irish soldier to serve in the Congo. He recalled that 'In November 1961 they were looking for volunteers for the Congo. I had just turned 17 when I volunteered and was looking for adventure.'[1] Phelan shared a villa with the other gunners from Kildare Barracks, but of course, in the Congo they served as infantry and carried Bren guns and the FN rifle. The 37 Infantry Battalion included Corporal J. Furlong, Gunners J. Darby, H. Meehan and J.J. Redmond. C Company, 38 Infantry Battalion included Corporals J. Nolan, R. Connolly, M. Flynn and Gunners J. Nolan, D. Roche, J.P. Rochford, J. Ryan, J. Wilson and so the nominal roll of men serving overseas continued.

Large-scale artillery deployments never occurred overseas, however, in addition to gunners serving as regular soldiers for overseas service, the Artillery Corps did provide a Heavy Mortar Troop starting with the 39 Infantry Battalion to the Congo in November 1962. The Heavy Troop were drawn from a different home-based artillery regiment on each occasion. As a consequence, those who trained them at Kildare did not get an opportunity to serve as a unit abroad until a unit served in Cyprus. Life in the Congo was a shock for Irish soldiers and conditions were very primitive. The food was often of a poor quality. As John Ryan recalled, 'When you got a biscuit you had to give it two taps to get the weevils out before eating it.'[2] Contacting home was very difficult and meant that letters to the troops often caused as many problems as they solved, leaving men concerned about family issues. Accordingly, as one gunner recorded, younger soldiers often had to be watched carefully when they received bad news from home to ensure they didn't do themselves any harm.

Sergeant Joseph P. Flanagan of the VI Field Artillery Regiment received serious leg injuries with two other men at Kamina, Congo on service with A Company of the 34 Infantry Battalion when a grenade accidentally exploded.[3]

Anti-Aircraft Battery for Congo

The Artillery Corps did prepare to send a unit to the Congo in 1961 when 4 Light Anti-Aircraft Battery was formed at Kildare on 27 October 1961. This followed an event at Jadotville in the Congo the previous month when A Company of the 36 Irish Battalion were attacked by Katangan and mercenary forces. The Irish forces held out for five days inflicting heavy casualties on the Katangans before being forced to surrender. One of the biggest difficulties faced by the Irish was a Fouga jet that was able to attack their positions unhindered as they were lightly armed with no air defence. Accordingly a decision was made to prepare an anti-aircraft battery for the Congo. Commandant Denis Burke who was Officer commanding the anti-aircraft training cadre at Kildare was appointed commander of the battery with Captains Des Duff, Kevin Duffy, and Lieutenants P. Ghent and J.H. Murphy. The company sergeant was Sergeant Christy Walsh. Preparations were made at Kildare for the 60 officers and men to travel to the Congo.

> Several gun crews were in training in the barracks yesterday with 40mm Bofors anti-aircraft guns. The battery will take eight of these guns with it to the Congo. Made in Sweden, they are very manoeuvreable and effective defensive weapons. They fire 2lb shells at the rate of 120 a minute, and have a range of 6,000 feet.
>
> The men of the Congo-bound battery – it will be known as the 4 Anti-Aircraft Battery – include a number who have seen service in the Congo. Those who have not been there received some of their 'shots' against tropical diseases yesterday.[4]

The men had their blue berets issued for United Nations service and the forward element got as far as Dublin airport; but at the last minute the trip was cancelled and the army never sent an artillery unit overseas. The 4 Light Anti-Aircraft Battery was disbanded on 15 November 1961. There was never any explanation as to the reason for not going overseas with suggestions about the cost or that the British had objected to the deployment.

Elizabethville – Battle of the Tunnel

A number of gunners were awarded the Distinguished Service Medal in the Congo. Sergeant Patrick Mulcahy, a Tipperary man who was born in 1925, paid the ultimate price. He had enlisted in the army in 1943, served with the I Field Artillery Regiment at Kildare for the duration of the Emergency, re-enlisted in November 1946 and served with VI Field Artillery Regiment at Kildare and with 6 Battery at Naas. He fought at the Battle of the Tunnel on 16 December 1961 in Elizabethville, Congo and with A Company, 36 Infantry Battalion when Irish soldiers seized the tunnel from Katanganese and mercenary forces. He was killed, together with Private Anthony Wickham while repulsing in a counter attack. Mulcahy was manning a mortar and died later that day of his wounds.

His Distinguished Service Medal (DSM) citation reads:

> 87410 Sergeant Patrick Mulcahy
> For distinguished service with the United Nations Force in the Republic of the Congo, in displaying leadership and devotion to duty to a high degree. Although painfully wounded during hostilities in December 1961, he refused to leave his platoon and subsequently, whilst looking after his men, he received the wound from which he died.

Another gunner who fought in the tunnel was Patrick Canavan from Headford, County Galway. He enlisted in the army in 1953 and was posted to the anti-aircraft regiment at Kildare. He participated in a number of actions including 'The Roundabout' and 'King Leopold Farm' and was part of the unit trapped at 'The Tunnel'. Canavan would go on to serve with 39 Infantry Battalion in the Congo and in Cyprus with the 41 Infantry Battalion.

Three other gunners were also awarded the DSM with distinction in December 1962 at Katangan in the Congo; Sergeant John Quirke, Corporal William Allen and Captain Thomas O'Boyle. Another gunner who was in action with the mortar troop in the Congo was Lieutenant Bill O'Dwyer who would later become commanding officer of Kildare Barracks. The citations for the awards, which were for service with the

Heavy Mortar troop, were as follows:

76595 Sergeant John Quirke
For distinguished service with the United Nations Force in the Republic of Congo, for leadership and courage. The heavy mortar troop with the Irish unit in Katanga in December 1962 and January 1963, took part in numerous engagements supporting Indian and Ethiopian troops as well as their own. On all occasions the troop performed in a most efficient manner. Sergeant Quirke, as a non-commissioned officer in charge of ammunition, by his initiative and disregard for his own safety, succeeded in maintaining the supply of ammunition to the guns, despite tremendous difficulties. His actions contributed largely to the success of the unit.

81154 Corporal William Allen
For distinguished service with the United Nations Force in the Republic of Congo, for leadership and courage. The heavy mortar troop with the Irish unit in Katanga in December 1962 and January 1963, took part in numerous engagements supporting Indian and Ethiopian troops as well as their own. On all occasions the troop performed in a most efficient manner and Corporal Allen was, by his personal example, leadership and courage, largely responsible for the action of his detachment.

Captain Thomas O'Boyle
For distinguished service with the United Nations Force in the Republic of Congo, for leadership. The Heavy Mortar Troop commanded by Captain O'Boyle took part in numerous engagements in Katanga in December 1962 and in January 1963, supporting Indian and Ethiopian troops as well as their own. On all occasions the troop performed in a most efficient and praiseworthy manner, due to the example, leadership and devotion to duty of Captain O'Boyle.

Captain O'Boyle's son Lieutenant-General Conor O'Boyle became Chief of Staff of the Defence Forces in August 2013. Lieutenant-General O'Boyle was also an artillery officer and like his father he served his time at Kildare.

Cyprus

The gunners also saw service in Cyprus throughout the late 1960s and 1970s. Normally, gunners who served overseas received a certain amount of training at Kildare and the Mortar Troops selected from amongst the units of the Artillery Corps to head overseas would rotate between the various artillery regiments. However, at a time, when soldiers were poorly paid, there were very few perks in military life so the Depot and School at Kildare managed to convince the Director of Artillery to allow a unit comprising of gunners stationed at Kildare Barracks to serve in Cyprus as one unit and so it was that the Heavy Mortar Troop, 19 Infantry Group that served in Cyprus during 1970–71 was made up almost exclusively of Kildare barracks gunners. There was plenty of free time in Cyprus and a lot of sports were organised between the Irish and British forces serving overseas. The Irish managed to beat the British Army in virtually every event in the early 1970s including rugby, basketball and shooting competition. The British began to bring in troops from Malta to bolster their teams for these events.

John Ryan recalled that during a tour to Cyprus in 1966–67, an issue emerged over the ceasefire line. Prior to the arrival of the Irish contingent, the Swedish army had marked the ceasefire line by painting boundary stones grey. When the Irish took over, they painted the stones white for ease of viewing from the Irish observation posts. However, as each Irish contingent rotated, the Turks moved the markers resulting in a significant shift of the line over the terms of three Irish contingents and causing considerable concern to the locals. Ryan, a corporal at the time, was delegated to survey the ceasefire line with Sergeant John Moore, II Field Artillery Regiment. Detailed maps were obtained from British army engineers and it soon transpired that the Turks had removed markers from the landscape to make the job more difficult. Once the work was completed and the line was to be moved, the Irish arrived in three Panhard armoured cars to discuss moving the boundary markers with a Turkish general. Sergeant Moore explained the situation to the general who said that it was difficult to keep track of where the line should be in the landscape to which Moore replied: 'Yes sir, but the mountains don't move.'

Lebanon

Michael Hughes recalled his service with the United Nations in Lebanon when he was part of the initial units that headed across the border into Lebanon in May 1978. It was his first time overseas and he recalled the trepidation and excitement amongst the men as they travelled from Israel into Lebanon. 'There were over 800 men in that unit. We had to set up camp from scratch at Haris, including pitching tents and preparing defences before moving to a new camp at Tibnin.' There were also dangers. 'On one occasion while travelling across the Irish zone delivering a container as a favour, we were shelled with eight mortar rounds landing around us. The driver wanted to turn around but I reckoned it was better to keep going. After that, when we got to our destination, no one even helped us unload the container.'[5]

One gunner was awarded the Military Medal for Gallantry with Distinction in April 1980 at At Tiri, Lebanon on United Nations service. The Defence Forces were involved in action against the South Lebanese army who attempted to set up a checkpoint in the border village of At Tiri in contravention of the United Nations mandate. On the morning of 7 April personnel of the Irish Battalion Reserve came under heavy continuous fire from the De Facto forces which had taken up positions around the village. Private Stephen Griffin was seriously injured and Captain Adrian Ainsworth who was a forward observation officer at the Irish checkpoint went to assist him. Griffin lay beside a stone wall a few hundred metres from the checkpoint. Ainsworth and a medical orderly, Private Michael Daly, crawled across open ground under constant heavy close-range fire. In assisting Griffin, Ainsworth and Daly had to walk upright on the return journey. Griffin subsequently died on 16 April in hospital. The Military Medal for gallantry is the highest military award in the State. Ainsworth, the son of an Assistant Garda Commissioner, Joe Ainsworth, joined the Defence Forces as a cadet in 1973 and was commissioned in 1974. He was stationed with the VI Field Artillery Regiment at Kildare before going overseas. His citation read as follows:

> 0.8639 Captain Adrian Ainsworth
> For displaying exceptional bravery and compassion of a high order when at At Tiri, South Lebanon on the 7th of April 1980, at grave danger to his own life from direct and sustained hostile fire, he

without hesitation crawled a distance of two hundred metres to aid a grievously wounded comrade, and still under fire on the return journey, brought him to a place of safety.

Daly was also awarded the Military Medal for gallantry, which was awarded at a separate ceremony held in Dublin.

Syria

Commandant Thomas P. Wickham went to Syria on 3 May 1967 to serve with the United Nations Truce Supervision Organisation, a body set up to observe and maintain the ceasefire in the Middle East. On 5 June 1967, Syria launched an attack on Israel and the six-day war began when the Israelis inflicted a rapid defeat on Syrian forces. Commandant Wickham, who was unarmed, was travelling with a number of American UN observers during a change of observation posts when they came to a Syrian checkpoint at Rafid. At a time of heightened tension, a Syrian guard saw the American uniform flashes and opened fire, shooting Wickham in the back and killing him instantly. Wickham was born in Dublin and joined the Defence Forces in 1940. He served with the Artillery Corps and in the Congo in 1962 with the 38 Infantry Battalion. Prior to service in Syria, he was the artillery instructor in the Command and Staff School, Military College, Curragh and prior to that had served as an instructor in the Survey and Counter Bombardment section of the artillery school. In honour of Commandant Wickham, the Artillery School renamed one of their lecture halls as Wickham Hall. His son, Brian followed him into the army and was a cadet at the Military College, Curragh at the time of his father's death. The Syrian soldier was charged with the murder of Wickham and went on to serve a prison sentence for the crime.[6]

CHAPTER 24

The Reserves – *An Fórsa Cosanta Áitiúil*

The greatest resource of an FCA unit is the endless supply of recruits. The 5th Battery area is well endowed with schools which provide recruits of a very high standard. By instilling discipline into the youth of the area, the 5th Battery is providing a useful and indeed an essential service to the community. It prepares them for leadership by exposing them to responsibility, which in turn leads to maturity.[1]

COMMANDANT LARRY BRADLEY

Inspection of VI Field Artillery Regiment at Kildare Barracks by Brigadier General Pat Grennan, GOC Curragh Command, 2 April 1982. Batteries, left to right are: 11 Battery under Commandant Maurice Scanlon, 5 Battery under Commandant John Miley and 6 Battery under Commandant Oliver Murphy. (Courtesy of John Gibson)

Writing on the twenty-fifth anniversary of the foundation of the VI Field Artillery Regiment, Commandant Larry Bradley, Officer in Command of the 5 Battery wrote:

> What is it that causes men to abandon their jobs or holidays, to forsake temporary and permanent relationships and the normal run of the mill worries of life for a full two weeks Annual Training? What madness urges a lad out of his bed at 8 a.m. on a winters morning to attend a Sunday field day, or worse still, to remove himself from a cosy chair in front of a blazing fire and television entertainment, to change into a cold uniform and step out into the darkness heading for the pick-up point on his way to Kildare Barracks on Thursday nights. Madness! Some one will say, absolute bloody madness![2]

This was the Reserve Defence Forces known from 1946 to 2005 as *An Fórsa Cosanta Áitiúil* (FCA). The FCA was a replacement for the Local Defence Force (LDF) that had served the country so well during the Emergency years and its predecessor the Volunteer Force that served during the 1930s. The LDF units in the Kildare–Offaly area were the Edenderry Battalion, the North Kildare Battalion based in Naas and the South Kildare Battalion based at Kildare. With the integration of the Permanent Defence Forces and FCA in 1959, the three local reserve infantry battalions were reformed as the VI Field Artillery Regiment in October 1959 consisting of the 5 Field Artillery Battery (Kildare), 6 Field Artillery Battery (Naas) and the 11 Heavy Mortar Battery (Edenderry), with the regimental headquarters at Kildare. Many infantrymen of the Local Defence Force transferred to the new unit on its establishment. However, prior to 1959, the FCA had worked closely with the Permanent Defence Forces as previous reserve forces had done in the 1930s and 1940s. An example is the 1950 shoot in the Glen of Imaal:

> The Glen of Imaal will be silent this week-end when gunners from Regular and FCA units return to their bases in Dublin, Cork and Mullingar, after two weeks of intensive battle training in Coolmoney Camp.
>
> Radio telephony was the means of communication. All day long the air of the various 'nets' was thick with requests to neutralise enemy machine guns, enemy mortars and for blobs of shells known as 'mike targets', 'concs' and 'stonks' accordingly as the tactical situation developed. A feature of these tactics was the stress laid on infantry-artillery co-operation. Very often it was the infantry company commander who called down the fire when the forward observation officer became a 'casualty'. The situations became really exciting when gunners fired muzzle bursts to protect their gun positions against infiltrating 'enemy'.
>
> At the conclusion of the last day's shoot, the Director of Artillery, Colonel J. McLoughlin, expressed his satisfaction at the way the camp was run, and at the lessons learned from the exercises, especially from the last 'Exercise Frolics'. He expressed the hope that next year the FCA batteries would go on to bigger and better things, and said that he was impressed by the whole-hearted co-operation that existed between FCA and Regular units. The FCA was a vital and integral part of the field artillery in this country, he said.

At this particular 1950 shoot, Lieutenant-Colonel Donnelly was officer in command of II Field Artillery Regiment; Lieutenant-Colonel Denis J. Cody was officer in command of IV Field Artillery Regiment and Lieutenant-Colonel J.O. Kelly was officer in command of I Field Artillery Regiment. The Dublin FCA Battery Commanders were Captains John Curtain and Patrick Loran; the Mullingar FCA were commanded by Captain Fred Loane, and the Cork Battery Commander was Second Lieutenant Jack O'Connell. Commandant Edward Shortall was Camp Commandant and

Commandant William Rea was Instructor of Gunnery.[3]

Some of the original LDF infantry who became gunners in the VI FAR were as follows:

> North Kildare Battalion: Peter Brennan, Ger Kinchella, Charlie Geoghegan, Paddy Winders, George Keogh, Seamie Moore. Edenderry Battalion: P. Buckley, J.P. Keane, M. Collins, Des Farrell, T. Judge, Bob O'Connor. South Kildare Battalion: Mattie Nolan, Jack Murphy, S. Brennan, Dinny Collins, Roland Garrett, Tony Smith, Connie Byrne, Jim Mahoney, Fred McGowan, Paddy Dooley.

The new unit witnessed a shoot at Gormanston, County Meath in 1959 and carried out their first shoot in the Glen of Imaal in August 1960 under the instruction of Commandant Tom McDunphy. 5 Field Battery and 6 Field Battery, consisting of eight guns each, fired 18-pounder field guns and 11 Heavy Mortar Battery fired the 120mm heavy mortar. The *Leinster Leader* reported that Corporal Willie Gibson was very proud that his gun crew fired sixty-two shells from their 18-field guns during the two days practice. The battery commander of the 5 Battery was Matt Nolan a professor who taught at Newbridge College. It was a great tribute to the early reserve gunners that after less than a year in existence, they were capable of carrying out such a shoot.

There was little difficulty in keeping the VI FAR up to full strength with plenty of willing recruits in County Kildare. The VI Field Artillery Regiment had an enormous advantage over other FCA units. As an artillery unit they learned infantry drill and attended range practice to learn to shoot as other units did, however, as artillerymen, they got to fire the guns and being co-located with the Artillery School at Kildare meant that the unit practised on the most modern weapons and used the most modern equipment that was available such as the various simulators in the artillery school and the anti-aircraft regiment. The 5 and 6 batteries at Kildare aimed to keep two six-gun batteries of 25-pounders in operation with two full gun crews trained per gun. In 1982, the regiment trained on the recently-acquired 105mm Light Guns and had the privilege of carrying out a shoot with them at camp in August 1982. They also had easy access to transport, a vital element in keeping a reserve unit going. There was a payback for the Artillery School: young officers and NCOs got invaluable instructional experience training the FCA units. The FCA were intrinsically linked to the town of Kildare. With so many military families in the area, it became a rite of passage for young men to serve as gunners, and for many, their first annual shoot in the Glen of Imaal was their first time away from home.

The Artillery Corps made a concerted effort to bring the reserve forces up to the highest standards of training so that both permanent and reserve artillery units could work together. Each year the FCA battery commanders met their regular counterparts and discussed the training schedule, recruiting and rosters for the year, equipment and budgets. The training schedule for early 1983 survives:[4]

January
a. Recruitment and commencement of recruit training
b. Annual range practices. Range date: 30 January 1983 – 6 and 11 Batteries
c. Potential NCO courses commence – 6 Battery
d. Artillery training: commence specialist training i.e. mortar board, Morcas, director, signals and No's 1 course.

February
a. Recruit training
b. Annual range practices: Range dates: 6 February: 5 Battery; 20 February: All Batteries
c. Potential NCO courses continued
d. Artillery specialist training continues
e. Arges 69 Grenade

March
a. Recruit training
b. Throwing grenade – grenade range: 6 March 1983
c. ONE shooting competition: 27 March 1983
d. Artillery specialist training continues
e. Potential NCO courses: 6 Battery

Birth certificates for recruits will be submitted to regimental headquarters. Recruitment should cease by end of February.

Annual range practices should be closely observed with a view to picking battery teams for ONE competition in March.

Ceremonial drill should be practiced by all batteries in preparation for Easter parades and guard of honour.

Like their regular counterparts, the reserves held annual training camps with instruction at Kildare followed by practice in the Wicklow mountains, which were the highlight of their year and a quartermaster's logistical nightmare as headquarters and equipment had to be put in place for the annual shoot. Kildare Barracks was full to capacity during the summer months as FCA artillery batteries from the entire country converged there for annual training which included a spell in barracks in addition to the shoot at the Glen of Imaal. A surviving copy of routine orders from 1967 gives an indication of the orders that were issued to the FCA batteries in reporting to Kildare:[5]

> The annual camp for elements of the 6 FAR will take place during the period July-August 1967.
>
> To fulfill the commitments of the requirements for Annual Camp the following will take place:
>
> 22/7/67 – 11/8/67 About 12 O/Ranks per Bty will report for 3 weeks training, the first week being devoted to a course for signallers, Acks and No. 1s.
>
> 29/7/67 – 11/8/67 Remainder of the regiment will report for annual training to Kildare.

A special ceremonial medal parade was held at Magee Barracks on 7 August 1967 to award service medals to members of the VI Field Artillery Regiment. The following FCA officers were presented with medals:

Officers: Medal and Bar

Commandants P. Buckley, M. Nolan, J. Frost, P. Brennan

Captains P. Bradley, M. Collins, P. Dooley, D. Farrell, F. McGowan, S. Brennan

Officers: Medal
Lieutenants O. Murphy, J. Moore
NCOs: Medal and Bar
Sergeants C. Byrne, G. Coll, D. Collins, R. Garrett, A. Smyth,
J. Wright, T. Cooke, P. Winder,
RSM J Kinshella
B/S: J. Mahoney, C. Geoghegan, J. Murphy
NCOs: Medal
Sergeants C. Kelly, F. Lawler, J. Miley

There was one tragedy in the barracks on 22 July 1969 when a young FCA gunner from Cork was killed on the barrack square. Gunner Gerard Sullivan, aged 16 and his brother-in-law, 28-year-old Sergeant David Doherty returned to barracks just before midnight and were running across the barrack square when Gunner Sullivan tripped over a low wall. He was dead on admission to the Curragh Military Hospital. [6]

Another example of an FCA shoot in the Glen of Imaal survives for 1981. The following orders were issued to the three batteries of the VI FAR for that particular camp:

Annual Camp for 6 Field Artillery Regiment will be held in Coolmoney Camp from 1 August 1981 to 14 August 1981. OiC Training Troops Commandant G.C. Murphy.

Attachments
Cooks as detailed by Quartermaster, Magee Bks, Kildare
Drivers as detailed by CTO, Curragh Command

Mission
6 Field Artillery Regiment will mobilise at 1000 hrs on Saturday 1 August 1981 at Magee Barracks, Kildare to move to Coolmoney Camp for Annual Training.

Execution
6 Field Artillery Regiment will carry out the operation in two phases:
Advance party – move at 1000 hrs on the 31st July 1981. Gun group to follow at 1300 hrs same day.

5 Field Artillery Battery, 6 Field Artillery Battery and 11 Heavy Mortar Battery will mobilise at 1000 hrs on Saturday 1 August 1981 at Magee Bks and move to Coolmoney Camp.

Tasks

1. Advance party move at 1000 hrs 31 July to Coolmoney Camp
   Take over accommodation
   Allocate accommodation to batteries
   Provide security in Coolmoney Camp on Friday night
   Prepare for reception of main party on 1 August
   Move gun group to Coolmoney Camp at 1330 hrs on 31 July 1981
   Prepare meal for main party 1700 hrs 1 August 1981

2. 5, 6, & 11 batteries will mobilise FCA personnel at 1000 hrs 1 August 1981 at Magee Barracks.
   PDF staff will report with their respective batteries
   Medical inspection at Magee Barracks at 1130 hrs
   Tea/Sandwiches Magee Barracks, 1230 hrs
   Move by army transport at 1330 hrs to Coolmoney Camp.
   Take over battery accommodation from advance party.
   Dinner Coolmoney Camp at 1700 hrs.[7]

The advance party sent to the Glen of Imaal were under Captain McDermott with BQMS Hughes second in command and Second-Lieutenant M. Dooley in command of the gun group. During the 1981 training, the camp staff were:

Camp Commandant:	Commandant George C. Murphy
Camp Adjutant:	Captain Seamus McDermott
Camp Sergeant Major:	BQMS Michael Hughes
Camp Orderly Room:	Corporal Hayden
Camp Rations:	Sergeant Connelly

An example of the training carried out in 1981 included a shoot from 1400 hrs on Monday 10 August, 1000 to 0400 hrs on Tuesday 11 August. The batteries were positioned at Leitrim, Seskin and Camara, three well-known gun positions in the Glen of Imaal, with the observation post also at the Leitrim position.

The 5 and 6 Batteries fired 25 pounder high-explosive shells in a battery neutralisation shoot. The 120mm mortars were manned by the 11 Battery and they carried out quick actions and the 81mm mortars carried out a coordinated illumination shoot. The senior officer was Commandant George Murphy. The gunnery instructors were Commandants Paddy Walshe, Brian O'Connor, Ray Quinn and D. Scully under the commandant of Lieutenant Colonel Michael Moriarty.

The range officers were Lieutenants Guing and Gibson. Safety officers were Lieutenants P. Graham and L. Hogan. The 1981 shoot was marked by the retirement of a number of stalwarts of the FCA who had given many years' service. Captain Fred McGowan, Sergeants H. McGuigan, R. Garrett and A. Smith retired from the 5 Battery with a stand-down parade held at Coolmoney Camp in the Glen.

Training camps were also held on occasion at Duncannon, County Waterford, such as in 1982, and the FCA also carried out winter training exercises in addition to annual camps. In 1984, the VI FAR carried out a winter exercise and overnight camp in the Glen of Imaal. The aim was to conduct infantry tactics by day and night, map reading and signal exercises with an advance party of one officer, one BQMS and thirteen other ranks ordered to set up camp at Stranahely wood with the necessary tents, sleeping bags and safari beds.

A shoot carried out by the VI FAR in July 1991 from Leitrim position used the 120mm mortar and the 25-pounder guns. The senior officer at the shoot was Commandant Peter O'Grady with Commandant Tom Carter Senior Instructor of Gunnery at the observation post and Captain O'Sullivan Senior Instructor of Gunnery at the gun positions. Safety officers were Captain T. Ging, 6 Battery and Captain M. Hogan 11 Heavy Mortar Battery. The range officer was Captain L. Hogan.

Due to the voluntary nature of the FCA, the number in each battery fluctuated over the years. Each year a decision had to be made about the number of gunners allowed to attend annual training. The training camp, with live-firing exercises and money in the part-time soldiers' pockets, was the highlight of the year and a reward for the hours of training on cold Thursday nights at Kildare. The military were keen to keep costs down and some years were more difficult than others. Oliver Murphy, commanding 5 Battery recalled one particular year when preparations were being made in April for the annual camp.

I had a meeting with the regimental commander in April one year to discuss plans for the annual camp. The CO asked me: 'How many men have you on parade.' I told him there were eighty men. The CO told me that due to cutbacks, only fifty could go that year. We had a short discussion on who would tell them and how to decide who would have to miss the camp so I got the register to have a look. I gave the CO the list of gunners who would miss out on camp. There were the sons of two very senior army officers on the list that would miss the camp. Whatever happened in the meantime, the money was found and everyone got to attend summer camp that year! They were the lucky ones because there were a few years when no one got to attend annual camp.[8]

The FCA also participated in shooting competitions with the FN rifle, light machine gun, the Gustaf sub-machine gun and falling plates competitions. An interesting aspect of these competitions was the mandatory instruction that: 'All words of command during the competition, will be given in Irish.'

Of course the glory of participating in firing competition did not come without a price. There were duties to be performed by the units in support of the shooting teams which included, cleaning the butts, firing points and trenches; provision of filled sandbags for the firing points to be emptied at the end of the shoot; ensuring that red warning flags were erected on the appropriate locations on the Curragh, including the Water Tower and sentries posted for the duration of the shoot. One of the hazards of the Curragh, of course, was the sheep, who had to be herded off the ranges and kept away during shoots. There were also shoots held under canvas in winter as recalled by Larry Bradley:[9]

Arrival in the woody glades of the Glen was as smooth as *Southern Comfort*. Tents were erected in no time at all and eventually the whole camp area took on the appearance of a Sioux Camp – minus the women, children and horses of course. Then came the issue of the sleeping bags. Now I can only speak for myself when I say that very definitely somebody had died in my sleeping bag and nobody ever discovered it.

The night firepower demonstration was par excellence, exceptionally detailed and expertly demonstrated. The use of flares and tracer was in a league of its own and the frightening crescendo of machine guns with their deadly rate of fire left one wondering about protective cover. As far as I was concerned the sand bags were for rabbits. Being near the merry time of Christmas, Commandant Maurice Scanlon fired one flare that ended up in a tree and directly over the silhouetted 'enemy' targets. It was the first time any of us had seen a 'Kerryman's Christmas tree'. Smithy was heard screeching! The highly effective accuracy from the 84 A/Tank under flares consoled us with the thoughts that we were not in the Cavalry Corps. Direct hits were scored two out of three, very good considering this was our first time. Our PDF instructor Captain Dave Brown and Captain Mick Smith were chuffed. It was to their credit and certainly to the credit of our NCO regular instructors. The CO Commandant Ray Quinn was to be congratulated on undertaking this extensive and ambitious exercise.

In 1984 the officer commanding the 5 Battery, Commandant Oliver Murphy together with Seamie Moore organised a trip to Larkhill on the Salisbury Plains in the United Kingdom to see how the British artillery operated. The visit was very successful and instructive to those who participated, and a follow-up piece appeared in a local newspaper. However, there were some grumblings from the military in Dublin when they found out about the visit as to who sanctioned the overseas trip and an article prepared for the army magazine *An Cosantóir* was not submitted for publication!

At that time the officers of the VI Field Artillery Regiment were as follows:

<u>Regimental Headquarters</u>
Officer commanding: Commandant Raymond Quinn
Staff Officer: Captain Adrian Ainsworth
Training Officer: Captain David Brown
<u>5-Field Battery</u>
Battery Commander: Commandant Larry Bradley

Troop Commandant A Troop:	Captain M. Mangan
Troop Commandant B Troop:	Captain G. Coll
GPO B Troop:	Lieutenant C. Cox

6 Field Battery

Battery Commander:	Commandant Seamus Moore
Troop Leader C Troop:	Captain John Miley
Troop Leader D Troop:	Lieutenant A. Burke
GPO D Troop:	Lieutenant A. Guing
Asst GPO D Troop:	Lieutenant P. Graham
GPO C Troop:	Lieutenant G. Gibson

11 Heavy Mortar Battery

Battery Commander:	Commandant M. O'Scanlon
Troop Commandant F Troop:	Captain D. O'Connor
Asst GPO F Troop:	Lieutenant P. O'Brien
Troop Leader E Troop:	Lieutenant L. Hogan
Troop Leader F Troop:	Lieutenant S. Whelan
GPO:	Second-Lieutenant M. Hogan
GPO F Troop:	Second-Lieutenant P. Daly

Commandant Larry Bradley, commander of the 5 Battery which recruited in the Kildare area, noted on the twenty-fifth anniversary of regiment's foundation that:

> The greatest resource of an FCA unit is the endless supply of recruits. The 5th Battery area is well endowed with schools, which provide recruits of a very high standard. By instilling discipline into the youth of the area, the 5th Battery is providing a useful and indeed an essential service to the community. It prepares them for leadership by exposing them to responsibility, which in turn leads to maturity.[10]

Former Battery Commander Oliver Murphy estimated that more than 10,000 young men passed through the ranks of the VI Field Artillery Regiment at Kildare during the years 1959–98. The strength of each battery tended to be about 120 gunners with about fifty new gunners trained every year. The VI FAR had a remarkable level of consistency over the years. In the mid 1980s, the three battery commanders had served for more than twenty years each and their other officers were not far behind with service.[11] Many of their NCOs similarly had long-service including RSM Murphy, BQMS Joe Meade, BQMS Frank Lawlor, B/S Tom Morrissey, B/S Charlie Byrne, Sergeant Podger Dunne, Sergeant Larry O'Reilly and Sergeant 'Kipper' Herron.

However, despite the professionalism of the FCA during these years, the integration of the PDF and FCA could only go so far as the FCA were volunteers who returned to their families, college or day jobs once the shooting ceased:

Headquarters
6th FA Regiment
Magee Barracks
Kildare

Eastern Command OCs Inspection
4th April 1976

You are hereby detailed to parade at Magee Barracks, Kildare at 09.45 hrs on Sunday 4th April 1976 for a unit inspection by the Officer Commanding Eastern Command. The parade will consist of an inspection, march past and drill. Dress for the inspection will be your best uniform, neatly pressed, (with white lanyard) complete with Unit and Command flashes and rank markings. If you are not in possession of any of these items you may obtain them at your Battery HQ. You will be expected to have your hair in a neat fashion, and be clean shaven.

A large turnout is expected. Your presence will be considered as a worthwhile contribution to the success of the inspection. Your absence will be noted for future reference.

Captain R. Quinn
Training Officer 6th FA Regiment[12]

There were other limitations too. The PDF wore the 1958 pattern web equipment while the FCA wore 1937 pattern webbing. The FCA were armed with the .303 rifle and Bren machine-gun while the regular soldiers were armed with the more modern FN rifle and general purpose machine-gun (GPMG) and in later times, the Steyr. The Steyr was apparently acquired in a barter agreement in exchange for butter, a practical way of dealing with the infamous butter mountain of the 1980s.

The ceremonial role of the regiment was a vital element of its activities, e.g. participating in St Patrick's Day parades and other public ceremonial occasions often acting as the public face of the Defence Forces. In June 1992 the regiment fired an eleven-gun salute for President Mary Robinson at Kilkenny. There were also a number of military tattoos and charity events as gunners hauled 25-pounders throughout the country. Ultimately the departure of VI FAR from Kildare was the beginning of the end for the regiment. In 2005, after forty-six years VI FAR amalgamated with VII FAR to become 62 Reserve Artillery Regiment as a combat support unit for the II Eastern Reserve Brigade.

The last battery commanders of the VI Field Artillery Regiment at Kildare in 1998 were:

VI Field Artillery Regiment
Commanding Officer: Commandant James Murray
Regimental Sergeant-Major: RSM Tom Murphy
Regimental Quartermaster-Sergeant: RQMS Frank Lawlor

5 Battery
Battery Commander: Commandant Ger Coll
Battery Sergeant-Major: BSM Paddy O'Shea

6 Battery
Battery Commander: Commandant John Miley
Battery Sergeant-Major: BSM Charlie Byrne

11 Battery
Battery Commander: Commandant Michael Scanlon
Battery Sergeant-Major: BSM Larry Reilly

CHAPTER 25

THE ARTILLERY SCHOOL: THE LATE TWENTIETH CENTURY

Amongst all the arts that adorne the life of man on earth....
Yet none comparable to the art and practice of artillery.

'THE ARTE OF SHOOTING GREAT ORDNANCE', LONDON 1587

Demonstration of the 25-pounder field gun, Glen of Imaal. (Courtesy of Paddy Walshe)

The traditions of professionalism and expertise which had been built up by the pioneers of the Artillery Corps in the 1920s with the establishment of the Artillery School at Kildare in 1931 and an artillery presence at the Military College, Curragh from the early 1930s continued throughout the rapid expansion of the corps during the Emergency years, post-war Ireland and adaption for sending troops overseas with United Nations missions from the 1960s onwards.

The Depot and School continued to keep artillery as advanced as was possible during these years both through their own initiative and through links to other armies. The first fire-control simulator was purchased by the School in 1974 when the Saab Scania BT-33 was brought into service. Lieutenant-Colonel Torsten Jeppson of the Swedish army came to Kildare to demonstrate the equipment. The links with the British continued with Captain J.H. Murphy attending the Long gunnery course at Larkhill in 1964 and Captain Raymond Quinn attending the same course from September 1976. Quinn recalled that the British were somewhat taken aback to discover that the Irish had invested in some of the most advanced systems available at the time. The then Chief of Staff of the Defence Forces Lieutenant-General Carl O'Sullivan (1919–2008) and the Director of Artillery Colonel McDunphy were keen on ensuring that the corps was kept up-to-date with the most modern equipment. Following his return from the UK, Quinn briefed the senior staff on modern developments in artillery. A demonstration of a field artillery computer system was organised for the Glen of Imaal, and following that it was agreed to invest in fire control systems and laser range finding equipment.[1] In 1979, the corps began to receive many new items of electronic fire control equipment such as laser range finders used by observation officers to determine the map location of a target. The field artillery computer system calculated the correct elevation, bearing and meteorological corrections for an identified target and was an enormous change from the calculations that had been required up to then. Sergeant-Major John

Ryan who was an instructor in the school at the time and a trained surveyor, was able to manually check the target and range calculations made by the computer system with pencil and paper to ensure that the corps was getting good equipment! Of course the time factor and greater accuracy meant that the computerised systems had major advantages.[2]

In 1980 the following were the senior officers of the Corps at Kildare:

Director of Artillery:	Colonel T.M. McDunphy
Staff Officer:	Commandant N.S. O'Connor
OC Depot and School, Kildare:	Lieutenant Colonel T.A. Ryan
Artillery School Commandant:	Lieutenant Colonel S.B. Condon
Regimental Sergeant-Major:	RSM John Ryan
Field Section:	Commandant K. Doyle
	Commandant B.J. O'Connor
Missile Section:	Commandant P. Walshe
Battery Commander 3 Field Battery:	Commandant P.F. Nowlan
Artillery Instructor Military College:	Commandant J.H. Murphy

The following is a list of all artillery units, both regular and reserve in the Defence Forces at the time which Kildare was ultimately responsible for training and supporting:

I FAR (1 Field Battery, 17 Field Battery) Murphy Barracks, Cork.

II FAR (10 Field Battery, 18 Field Battery) McKee Barracks, Dublin.

III FAR (9 Field Battery, 12 Field Battery, 16 Heavy Mortar Battery) McCann Barracks, Templemore.

IV FAR (8 Heavy Mortar Battery, 22 Field Battery) Columb Barracks, Mullingar.

V FAR (4 Field Battery, 7 Field Battery, 13 Heavy Mortar Battery) Mellows Barracks, Galway.

VI FAR (5 Field Battery, 6 Field Battery, 11 Heavy Mortar Battery), Magee Barracks, Kildare.

VII FAR (14 Field Battery, 19 Heavy Mortar Battery) McKee Barracks, Dublin.

VIII FAR (2 Field Battery, 21 Heavy Mortar Battery) Murphy Barracks, Cork.

IX FAR (15 Field Battery, 20 Field Battery) Columb Barracks, Mullingar.

I ADR (1, 2, 3, 4 Air Defence Batteries) Magee Barracks, Kildare.

Coastal Defence Artillery Fort Mitchell, Cork, Fort Dunree, Donegal.

The Milan anti-tank system

The Corps also took delivery of and fired the first missile system employed in Ireland with the purchase of the Milan anti-tank weapon. Two instructors from France were sent to Kildare for two months to train the artillery school staff in the operation of the system. The Milan missile was not an artillery weapon but the task of testing it was given to the Artillery School. The range at the Glen of Imaal had been closed following an accident in 1977 when five soldiers of the 4 Infantry Battalion, Southern Command were killed when a bomb from an 81mm mortar exploded in its barrel. The firing of the Milan was the first time the range was opened since the accident. Lieutenant Dave Brown of the Artillery School had the honour of being the first to fire a weapon that could 'hit a card-table at a mile' on 19 December 1979. The Artillery School subsequently carried out the initial training for the Defence Forces in the system after which it was passed on to the Infantry Weapons School.

Missile aiming course commenced in January 1982. This also required the establishment of a new branch of the Artillery School at Kildare with Commandant Paddy Walshe taking command of the Guided Weapons and Air Defence Wing (GWAD) in 1980. The RBS 70 system that was introduced in 1980 to the anti-aircraft regiment was upgraded in 1996 when night training facilities were added. Two officers and four NCOs of the Air Defence Regiment were sent to Karlskoga, Sweden in October 1996 for an intensive two-week training course on the use of the Bofors clip-on Night Device. Lieutenant Mairead Ledwidge, Lieutenant Jim Deery, Corporals Eddie Doyle, Ger Mulhall, Padraig Murray and Seamus Grattan first had to spend two weeks at the Guided Weapon and Air Defence section of the Artillery School at Kildare to fine-tune their skills before travelling to Sweden for training on the infra-red night sights system.[3]

In 1995, the BT-33 simulator was replaced by the Phoenix Simulator with Commandant Peter O'Grady, Captain Connors and B/S Morris the first to be trained on the new system.

Replacing the 25 pounder – the 105mm gun

The replacement of the 25 pounder field guns which had served the Corps so well since their introduction in the 1940s was the next most significant development. A board was set up to consider a replacement and three weapons were short-listed, a US-manufactured 105mm gun, the Russian 122mm and 130mm guns and the British 105mm light gun. Ray Quinn who was on the board was very familiar with the British gun having trained with it at Larkhill. US guns were being offered at a very cheap rate but came with the condition that over 200,000 rounds of ammunition would have to be bought with each gun purchased – an astronomical amount of ammunition for a small army. On the Russian guns, one of the assessment board remarked: 'This is Catholic Ireland, we can't be using communist guns!' The 105mm was mobile and could be carried by helicopter. There was also the option of a shorter barrelled version which could fire cheaper ammunition for training purposes. The decision was made: eighteen guns for three batteries were ordered and duly arrived from the British Aerospace Royal Ordnance Factory in 1980 with six of them being the shorter-barrel version. The first firing of the 105mm light gun occurred on 12 March 1981. Lieutenants Dermot Scully and Barry O'Sullivan together with Sergeants Martin 'Lags' Page and Tom Ryan were sent to Larkhill in England for training on the guns in preparation for training the rest of the Corps with the II Field Artillery Regiment at McKee Barracks, Dublin receiving their guns in 1982. Two further batteries of 105mm light guns and a sizeable quantity of ammunition were delivered in April 1998 when the IV Field Artillery Regiment in Mullingar received its guns.[4]

With reductions in the size of the Defence Forces in the 1980s and 1990s, training was reduced. Commandant George Murphy took command during the 1980s with Captains Ray Quinn, David Brown and Seamus McDermott as the main instructors in the Artillery School. The School was responsible for training newly commissioned officers as artillery officers and gunners who had come from general training at the Curragh. In addition, various courses were run for NCOs on a constant basis.

3 Field Battery

A very important innovation introduced at Kildare in June 1977 was the 3 Field Battery to act as a demonstration unit for the Artillery School for all the various courses in the barracks and in particular for demonstration shoots in the Glen of Imaal. This system operated well in the British Army where an entire artillery regiment was posted to Larkhill on a two-year rotation to act as a depot battery. The School would have liked to get a regiment at Kildare but the Director of Artillery Tom McDunphy knew how the Department of Defence operated and did not believe this would be sanctioned. He decided that by requesting a battery, they would succeed and they did. Prior to this, many live shoots in the Glen of Imaal were carried out by other units or by composite groups from the School and Depot or in conjunction with the reserve unit, the VI Field Artillery Regiment manned by FCA personnel. The first battery commander was Commandant Paddy Nowlan with Lieutenants Eoghan Ó Neachtáin and Adrian Ainsworth. Donnie Finn was appointed the first Battery Sergeant-Major and Michael Hughes as the Battery Quartermaster Sergeant-Major. The battery was originally under the command of Lieutenant-Colonel Michael McMahon, VI Field Artillery Regiment but moved at a later stage to the Depot and School.[5] Donnie Finn stayed with the battery until 1995 when he became the Regimental Sergeant-Major with the anti-aircraft battery. The 3 battery had the pick of the best available gunners in the barracks and was an excellent training ground for officers and men as they carried out far more shoots than any other battery in the corps. They also managed to put together the most experienced Sergeants and No.1s. These included Paddy Confrey, 'Butch' Halpin, Liam Hunt, Judge Kenny, Mick Monaghan, Martin Page and Peter Webb. On the tenth anniversary of the foundation of the battery, in June 1987, 'an impressive parade was inspected by Brigadier-General Maguire GOC Curragh Command who also took the salute as the battery proceeded in a drive past of ACMATS[6] (four wheel drive vehicles) and 105mm Light Guns under the command of Captain Ryan'.[7]

An example of a training shoot carried out by the 3 Field Battery with the 105mm gun survives for 1991.[8] The surviving records indicate that the safety distance for the 25-pounder guns was 800 metres. The heavy mortars were deemed more dangerous with a safety distance of 1,000 metres.

Range Detail for Mon/Tues 23/24 September 1991

Senior Officer I/C Practices:	Lieutenant Colonel W. Dwyer
Senior IG at Observation Post:	Commandant T. Carter
IG at Gun Position:	Captain E. Fogarty
Safety Officer:	As detailed by Battery Commander 3rd Battery
Range Officer:	Lieutenant T. Clonan (at Leitrim Observation Post)

1. Senior officer in command practices will ensure that the safety officer(s) are capable of performing the duties on the equipment being fired.
2. The attention of senior officers in command practices, range officer, safety officer and all officers involved in the firing practices is directed to:
   Standing Orders, Curragh Command
   Artillery Training, Volume III Pamphlet No. 9, Planning, Control and Safety for Live Firing Practices
   IT/3/1971, Safety Precautions to be observed during live mortar firing practices
3. The gun position officer will ensure that an accurate record is kept of the surplus charges handed back by each unit on the conclusion of a mission, and supervise their destruction after end of practice.
4. Authority from Operations Officer, Curragh Command for permission to use ranges checked – Serial Number 94091
5. Ordnance Officer, Medical Officer and ambulance located as per orders of senior officer I/C Practices.
6. Lasers will be regarded as weapons and used in accordance with IT 5/1980 and will not be used until range officer reports range is clear.
7. Ranges to be cleared two hours before practices commence.
   Lieutenant Colonel J.G. Prendergast
   Commandant, Artillery School

When the 3 Battery left Kildare in 1998 Commandant Martin Molloy was the

Battery Commander. Other commanders of the Battery were:

Commandant Paddy Nowlan:	1977–78, 1980–81
Lieutenant-Colonel Kevin Doyle:	1979–80
Commandant Leo Hughes:	1981–82
Commandant J. Burke:	1982–86
Commandant Peter O'Grady:	1987

The Artillery School transferred to the Curragh in 1998 together with the Air Defence Regiment and VI Field Artillery Regiment but the Artillery Depot was no longer. The School became part of the Military College Combat Support Unit at the Curragh where it continues to train gunners through various artillery courses, organise live firing exercises and provide technical assistance on matters relating to the guns.

CHAPTER 26

NOT JUST BRICKS AND MORTAR

The loss of both Magee Barracks and Murphy Barracks
will sadden gunners of all ages who were stationed
therein. It is a reminder to us all that tradition cannot
be built on bricks and mortar alone. Military traditions
are built on achievements and professionalism and are
fostered by the unit no matter where it finds itself.

LT. COL. J. G. PRENDERGAST, DIRECTOR OF ARTILLERY, NOVEMBER 1998[1]

The last day of Kildare Barracks – 24 September 1998

The closure of Kildare Barracks was an unexpected shock to those whose lives revolved around the barracks. On 16 July 1998, the commanding officer got word to muster the men together as there was an important visitor arriving. A number of members of the media also arrived outside the gate. The Minister for Defence, Michael Smyth TD arrived by helicopter with a number of journalists and was greeted by a guard of honour as he proceeded to Trodden Hall to meet the assembled men. There were approximately 150 personal in the barracks on that day. He advised all of those present that the barracks had to close and that they had to be gone within a month. The Minister explained that the money saved in transferring to the Curragh would be reinvested in suitable accommodation for the Artillery Corps. Liam O'Keeffe, the switch operator in the barracks remembered the occasion very well:

I sat beside Dorothy Dempsey and the minister addressed the gathering. He said that Kildare cost £10 million a year to maintain and that this could be saved if they moved to the Curragh and that the barracks had to close. I could not contain myself and I began to ask some questions. I stood up and told the minister 'We're a family here in Kildare and you're breaking us up. If Clonmel Barracks [which was in his constituency] was being closed you would not stand idly by.' The minister stared at me with glass eyes. I told him that I hoped there would be a tribunal in ten years' time about this decision, to which there was cheering and applause.

One officer present questioned the suitability of accommodation for the VI Regiment as by all accounts they would be moving into horse stables. In the meantime, the Parliamentary Secretary wrote 'finish up' on an A4 sheet and handed it to the minister and that was the end of the meeting.[2]

There was some heckling of the Minister as the shock dawned on those assembled that the barracks that they had built their lives around was about to close. Another gunner present recalled that the Minister stared out the window instead of addressing the men directly. He said to the Minister 'Minister, we are down here, not outside the window.' Just weeks previously, the commanding officer Lieutenant-Colonel Gerry Swan received assurances that the barracks would not close and he sanctioned works to be carried out on a men's club. There had also recently been work carried out on repairing the anti-aircraft simulator – the dome trainer. This circular building was often the source of bewilderment and the wags in the barracks often told unsuspecting visitors that the commanding officer had converted to Islam and that the building was his own private mosque! The telephone system was also upgraded around this time. However, there was little acknowledgement that the institution that was the barracks was not just a place of work. Those involved in the barracks either serving or retired, socialised in the evenings there, were involved in sports clubs and other organisations from the barracks and the closure of the barracks destroyed a community at the stroke of a pen.

With the reorganisation of the Defence Forces in the 1990s and a review carried out by Price Waterhouse, a Defence Forces Review Implementation Plan was prepared which looked at the role of a number of barracks including Kildare. Consideration was given to the transfer of the Artillery School and Air Defence regiment to Connolly Barracks, Curragh. The military raised concerns about the transfer of the Artillery School to the Curragh particularly as Kildare was purpose built for artillery and there was an interdependency between the Air Defence Regiment and the Artillery School. In a relatively small army where the Artillery School used air defence expertise and equipment such as the Giraffe Radar, the Dome simulator and their guns, while the Air Defence Regiment used the RBS 70 simulator and night simulation devices, it was practical to have both units situated in close proximity to each other. Similarly, the Ordnance Corps artificers provided technical support to both units. There were concerns about the capability of getting appropriate accommodation in the Curragh and the expense of converting suitable accommodation. There was also the practical issue of having to invest in additional equipment, which was being shared at the time.

There were a number of discussions held on a replacement unit to transfer to Kildare Barracks and the possibility of a Depot staff remaining in place to manage the barracks. Ultimately, however, a Government decision was made to close a number of barracks. In 1998, Kildare and Naas in County Kildare, Ballincollig, County Cork and Castleblaney, County Monaghan became surplus to requirements and the barracks closed on 24 September 1998 as the Artillery Corps returned to the Curragh. Following the minister's visit to Kildare, the gunners were given a few weeks to pack up an entire barracks and transfer to the Curragh. It was suggested at the time that some business people saw the potential for the redevelopment of the site for housing and other facilities and saw this as preferential to having a barracks in the town. The town was also promised a percentage of the site for community facilities. Unlike the 1930s, there were no deputations concerned about the closure of the barracks and an institution that had helped develop the town over the previous century was closed down with little complaint from the town. In the end, the Artillery Corps marched out and moved on to inferior and unsuitable accommodation at Plunkett Barracks, Curragh. The position in Kildare was in marked contrast to that in Kilkenny where in 1996, there was concern about the closure of the barracks and the potential transfer of troops to Kildare Barracks. Ironically, it was the 3 Battalion which had been suggested as a unit to transfer to Kildare that was transferred to Kilkenny, thus saving it and leaving Kildare surplus to requirements. It was estimated locally that the barracks at Kilkenny was worth 8 million per annum to the local economy.[3] Kildare Barracks closed on Thursday 24 September 1998.

The local media recorded the occasion of the closure of Kildare:[4]

A few silent tears were shed as the national flag was lowered and soldiers left Magee Barracks in Kildare town for the last time.

The official marching out took place on Thursday last and the staff attached to Depot Artillery Regiment, the Air Defence Regiment and the 6 Field Artillery Regiment, which includes FCA staff, left for the last time.

The men were followed by two anti-aircraft guns, as well as field guns and 25 pounders to be redeployed at Connolly Barracks and Plunkett Barracks on the Curragh Camp.

The formalities got underway with the arrival of Brig. Gen. Frank Colclough, GOC Curragh Command. He was welcomed by Lt. Col. Gerry Swan, O.C. Magee Barracks, and he inspected a Guard of Honour drawn from soldiers attached to the barracks, which also has a small number of civilian staff.

The ceremonial marching out was preceded by the lowering of the colours, performed by Sgt. Joe Foley and Captain Pat Graham before an attendance made up mainly of relatives of those who had served at the barracks.

The ceremony was conducted with typical military precision and soldiers from the three units marched around the square, followed by their vehicles, for the last time before departing for the Curragh Camp.

Kildare closed just as the Artillery Corps were preparing to mark its seventy-fifth year with a number of special events. The Director of Artillery Colonel J.G. Prendergast wrote in November 1998:

A special Corps Day to commemorate the 75th Anniversary was planned for Glen Imaal on Sunday 6 September. Unfortunately due to the imminent sale of Magee Barracks, Kildare and Murphy Barracks, Ballincollig and the requirement to have them vacated before the end of September 1998 we were obliged to defer these celebrations. The loss of both Magee Barracks and Murphy Barracks will sadden gunners of all ages who were stationed therein. It is a reminder to us all that tradition cannot be built on bricks and mortar alone. Military traditions are built on achievements and professionalism and are fostered by the unit no matter where it finds itself. [5]

The barracks became a temporary centre for refugees from the conflict in Kosova in the former Yugoslavia as it had in 1969 during the troubles, and then a centre for the housing of the increased number of refugees arriving in Ireland in the early 2000s. In 2007 the last remaining refugees left the barracks and it was finally deserted. Proposals to convert the barracks into houses were shelved as the boom years of the Celtic tiger disappeared while the tramp of smaller feet will march through the barracks in one small corner as a Gaelscoil opens in 2014. It is hoped that whatever fate awaits the barracks, that the place it served in Kildare for almost 100 years will not be forgotten. The Artillery Depot disappeared in 1998 and the Artillery School that had served the country so well became part of the Combat Support College at the Defence Forces Training Centre in the Curragh.

St Barbara of the Gunners

In the commotion of getting the barracks vacated, one gunner was left behind. St Barbara remained defiant inside the barracks gate to the closure of the barracks. The former commanding officer Gerry Swan was anxious to bring Barbara with them to the Curragh.[6] However, there was a concern that the statue, that had been paid for by the voluntary subscription of the members of the Artillery Corps in 1954, might get damaged in the move to the Curragh. Eventually a specialist was located and a budget allocated to get the statue moved. St Barbara was transferred to the Curragh where she now stands in a prominent location facing west towards the spiritual home of artillery in Ireland that is Kildare Barracks.

Notes

Notes – Chapter 1

1 Bradley, J., 'The Cathedral and Town of Kildare' in *Journal of the County Kildare Archaeological Society,* Vol. XIX p.35.

2 An Tostal Souvenir Booklet 1953, (Kildare, 1953).

3 Corrigan, M., *All that Delirium of the Brave,* (Kildare County Council, Naas, 1998).

4 An Tostal Souvenir Booklet 1953, (Kildare, 1953).

5 WO 121/38/204 Peter Kelly, National Archives, United Kingdom.

6 *Nottingham Evening Post,* 17 February 1892.

7 House of Lords Debates, 3 August 1899.

8 Papers of Percy Whitehouse, 04/37/1 Imperial War Museum p.6.

9 *Kildare Observer,* 7 July 1900.

10 Mr Courtenay Warner, House of Commons, 14 August 1901.

11 'The Kildare Hutments' in *The Irish Builder,* 15 August 1900.

12 *Kildare Observer,* 14 December 1901.

13 *Leinster Leader,* 12 January 1901.

14 *Kildare Observer,* 26 January 1901.

15 *Kildare Observer,* 17 August 1901.

16 *Leinster Leader,* 26 April 1901.

17 *Kildare Observer,* 26 January 1901.

18 *Kildare Observer,* 13 October 1900.

19 *Yorkshire Gazette,* 1 September 1888.

20 *Kildare Observer,* 13 October 1900.

21 *Kildare Observer,* 15 December 1900.

22 *Kildare Observer,* 8 June 1901.

23 *Kildare Observer,* 11 January 1902.

24 Costello, C.A., *Most Delightful Station The British Army on the Curragh 1855–1922* (Cork Collins Press, 1996), p.254.

25 AD/119426/006 'Maps and Plans Collection', Military Archives, Dublin.

Notes – Chapter 2

1 *Western Daily Press,* Bristol, 10 April 1902.

2 *The Irish Times,* 5 March 1902.

3 *London Gazette,* 2 February 1900 and Doherty, Richard & Truesdale, David *'Irish Winners of the Victoria Cross'* (Four Courts Press, Dublin, 2000).

4 WO363 Personnel File of George Edward Nurse, National Archives, United Kingdom.

5 *Kildare Observer,* 5 May 1906.

6 Author's collection.

Notes – Chapter 3

Page 7–*Kildare Observer*, 1 March 1902.

Page 8 – *Derby Daily Telegraph*, 13 October 1906.

Page 10 –Census of Ireland, 1911, pp.80–81.

1 *Kildare Observer*, 10 September 1904.

2 *Kildare Observer*, 12 April 1902.

3 *Kildare Observer*, 8 November 1902.

4 *Kildare Observer*, 8 November 1902.

5 *The Irish Times*, 7 April 1903.

6 *The Irish Builder*, 8 April 1903

7 *Kildare Observer*, 13 July 1901.

8 *Kildare Observer*, 4 October 1904.

9 *Kildare Observer*, 5 November 1904.

10 *Kildare Observer*, 16 July 1910.

11 *Kildare Observer*, 4 April 1914.

12 *Kildare Observer*, 4 December 1909.

13 *Kildare Observer*, 9 March 1901.

14 *Kildare Observer*, 10 September 1904.

15 Bergin, F., 'Kildare and Other Sewerage Works' in Transactions of the Institution of Civil Engineers of Ireland, Vol. XXXIV 1908, pp. 71–92.

16 *Kildare Observer*, 13 August 1904.

17 Bergin, F., 'Kildare and Other Sewerage Works' in Transactions of the Institution of Civil Engineers of Ireland Vol. XXXIV 1908 pp.71–92.

18 *Kildare Observer*, 10 October 1914.

19 *Kildare Observer*, 5 January 1901.

20 *Kildare Observer*, 17 August 1901.

21 *Kildare Observer*, 2 November 1902

22 *Leinster Leader*, 11 July 1903.

23 *Leinster Leader*, July 1903.

24 Interview with Frank Goodwin, October 2012.

25 *Kildare Observer*, 20 June 1903.

26 *Leinster Leader*, 3 November 1906.

27 *The Mercury*, 26 June 1908.

28 *The Irish Times*, 24 October 1914.

29 *Kildare Observer*, 13 June 1914.

30 *Kildare Observer*, 15 December 1917.

31 *Leinster Leader*, 30 March 1907.

32 *Kildare Observer*, 18 January 1902.

33 *Kildare Observer*, 31 January 1903.

34 Kildare Roman Catholic Baptismal Register.

35 *Kildare Observer*, 5 May 1906.

36 *Kildare Observer*, 5 May 1906.

Notes – Chapter 4

1 Whitehouse, Percy 'Recollections of service in the army, from 1913 to 1919' 04/37/1 Imperial War Museum, p.7.

2 Whitehouse, p. 6.

3 *Kildare Observer*, 19 May 1906.

4 British army service record, Joseph Michael Mealyer, No. 71525 Royal Artillery WO/97.

5 British army service record, Alfred Passfield Service Record, No. 1826 Royal Artillery WO/97.

6 British army service record, Augustus William Skingsley, No. 85686 Royal Artillery WO/97.

7 Extracted from *The Times* various dates.

8 *Kildare Observer*, 7 July 1906.

9 *Kildare Observer*, 26 May 1906.

10 *Kildare Observer*, 19 July 1913.

11 *Freeman's Journal*, 14 October 1905.

12 *The Times*, 7 October 1907.

13 *The Times*, 19 February 1908.

14 Killed at Le Cateau with the same battery on 26 August 1914.

15 *The Times*, 16 January 1912.

16 Whitehouse, Percy 'Recollections of service in the army, from 1913 to 1919' 04/37/1 Imperial War Museum, p. 5.

17 *Leinster Leader*, 10 June 2009.

18 *The Times*, 23 October 1911.

19 Whitehouse, p. 7.

20 *Kildare Observer*, 17 September, 1904.

21 Whitehouse p. 9.

22 Whitehouse, p. 10.

23 Whitehouse, p. 10.

24 *Kildare Observer*, 19 April 1902.

25 *The Times*, 6 May 1904

Notes – Chapter 5

1 Irish Prison Registers, National Archives of Ireland.

2 Irish Prison Registers, National Archives of Ireland.

3 *Kildare Observer*, 25 October 1902.

4 *Lichfield Mercury*, 25 September 1903.

5 *Shields Daily Gazette*, 28 September 1903.

6 *Leinster Leader*, 25 May 1907.

7 *Kildare Observer*, 7 March 1903.

8 PRO British Army Service Records 1760-1915 Coram, Frederick, No. 17328 Royal Field Artillery.

9 *Derby Daily Telegraph*, 8 December 1903.

10 *Kildare Observer*, 7 June 1902.

11 *Kildare Observer*, 21 February 1903.

12 *Leinster Leader*, 20 April 1907.

13 *The Irish Times*, 9 May 1906.

14 *Kildare Observer*, 1 August 1908.

15 Irish Prison Registers, National Archives of Ireland.

16 *Kildare Observer*, 1 July 1911.

17 *Kildare Observer*, 3 September 1910.

18 *Freeman's Journal*, 1 December 1909.

19 *Kildare Observer*, 17 August 1906.

20 Irish Prison Registers, National Archives of Ireland.

21 Irish Prison Registers, National Archives of Ireland.

22 Irish Prison Registers, National Archives of Ireland.

23 *Kildare Observer*, 16 July 1910.

24 *Leinster Leader*,10 January 1914.

Notes – Chapter 6

1 *Kildare Observer*, 12 March 1904.

2 *Kildare Observer*, 6 April 1912.

3 *Kildare Observer*, 11 November 1905.

4 *Kildare Observer*, 19 November 1910.

5 *Kildare Observer*, 24 February 1912.

6 *Kildare Observer*, 28 January 1911.

7 *Kildare Observer*, 11 November 1905.

8 *Kildare Observer*, 11 August 1906.

9 *Kildare Observer*, 16 June 1906.

10 *Kildare Observer*, 23 June 1906.

11 *Kildare Observer*, 20 June 1906.

12 *Kildare Observer*, 11 August 1906.

13 *Kildare Observer*, 31 August 1907.

14 *Kildare Observer*, 20 July 1907.

15 *The Irish Times*, 23 September 1912.

16 *The Irish Times*, 28 September 1912.

17 *Kildare Observer* 3 July 1909.

18 Sandes, E., 'Enlisted ; or, My Story' (Curragh, 1915) p. 205.

19 *The Irish Times*, 15 February 1910.

20 *Kildare Observer*, 19 January 1903.

21 *Kildare Observer*, 21 December 1907.

22 *Leinster Leader*, 4 April 1914.

23 *Kildare Observer*, 14 March 1914.

Notes – Chapter 7

1 Ferguson, Sir James, *The Curragh Incident*, (London, 1964) p.61.

2 Beckett, Ian, *The Army and the Curragh Incident*, (Army Records Society, 1986) pp.107–8.

3 Beckett pp.83–4.

4 Beckett, Ian, *The Army and the Curragh Incident*, (Army Records Society, 1986) p.160.

5 Whitehouse, Percy, 'Recollections of service in the army, from 1913 to 1919' 04/37/1 Imperial War Museum, p.11.

Notes – Chapter 8

1 *Leinster Leader*, 16 August 1914.

2 *The Irish Times*, 15 August 1914.

3 Whitehouse, Percy, 'Recollections of service in the army, from 1913 to 1919' 04/37/1 Imperial War Museum, p.12.

4 Public Records Office Kew.

5 *Kildare Observer*, 22 August 1914.

6 *Kildare Observer*, 29 August 1914.

7 Irish Prison Registers, National Archives of Ireland.

8 Irish Prison Registers, National Archives of Ireland.

9 Whitehouse, Percy, 'Recollections of service in the army, from 1913 to 1919' 04/37/1 Imperial War Museum, p.13.

10 *Aberdeen Journal*, 17 December 1914.

11 *The Times*, 16 September 1914.

12 *Hull Daily Mail*, 20 October 1914.

13 *Dundee Courier*, 27 August 1915.

14 *Dundee Courier*, 18 November 1914.

15 *The Times*, 24 September 1914.

16 *Kildare Observer*, 31 October 1914.

17 *Liverpool Echo*, 18 September 1914.

18 *Kildare Observer*, 22 August 1914.

19 *Kildare Observer*, 22 August 1914.

20 *Leinster Leader*, 24 August 1914.

21 Irish Prison Registers, National Archives of Ireland.

22 *Kildare Observer*, 1 May 1915.

23 *Kildare Observer*, 7 November 1914.

24 *Kildare Observer*, 21 August 1915.

25 *Leinster Leader*, 17 July 1915.

26 *Kildare Observer*, 14 August 1915.

27 *Kildare Observer*, 25 March 1916.

28 Postcard, author's collection.

29 Postcard dated January 1918, author's collection.

30 Costello, 'A Most Delightful Station', p. 291

31 *The Irish Times*, 8 January 1916.

32 *Kildare Observer*, 10 June 1916.

33 *The Irish Times*, 21 May 1918.

34 *Kildare Observer*, 29 May 1915.

35 Michael Dillon 3968, Irish Guards, Pension Record.

36 John Forde No. 9014 16th Lancers, Pension Record.

37 Patrick McDonnell No 9016 16th Lancers Pension Record.

38 Joseph Fyland No 75252, RFA .

39 James Byrne 287454 Royal Engineers.

40 Jack Geoghegan, Private 127824 RAMC.

41 J. Davies to Zoar Church, November 1918, People's Collection Wales.

Notes – Chapter 9

1 Postcard, author's collection.

2 *Kildare Observer*, 5 June 1920.

3 Durney, J. *Kildare and the War of Independence*, (Mercier Press, Cork, 2013) p.120.

4 Papers of Eamonn O Modhrain.

5 *Police Gazette*, Vol XXXVII No. 3507 March 14, 1921.

6 Sheehan, W. *Hearts and Mines*, p.117.

7 Dáil Éireann Debates, Volume 2, No. 41 Question: Married Quarters, 20 March 1923.

8 *Kildare Observer*, 20 January 1920.

9 *Kildare Observer*, 3 September 1921.

Notes – Chapter 10

1 *London Gazette*, 14 January 1879.

2 *London Gazette*, 6 January 1880.

3 *London Gazette*, 8 January 1901.

4 'Things heard, seen and remembered'. Unpublished memoir of Lt. Col. Justin Hooper pp.16–17, The Great War Archive, Oxford.

5 *Irish Independent*, 28 June 1920.

6 *The Times*, 25 January 1922.

7 Cabinet Papers CP3641. Situation in Ireland week ending 14 January 1921, National Archives, United Kingdom.

8 *Kildare Observer*, 18 February 1922.

9 WO 35/34287 Correspondence from Lieutenant-General Jeudwine, 'Evacuation Files', National Archives, United Kingdom.

10 WO 339/43238 Court of Inquiry assembled at Kildare, Wogan-Browne, J.H., National Archives, United Kingdom.

11 WO 339/43238, Wogan-Browne, J.H., National Archives, United Kingdom.

12 *Kildare Observer*, Letter to the Editor, 18 February 1922.

13 LE/4/14 'Liaison and Evacuation Correspondence – Kildare', Military Archives, Dublin.

14 *Kildare Observer*, Letter to the Editor, 18 February 1922.

15 William Graham, Grey Abbey, Kildare was a 2nd Lieutenant with 'F' Company, Carlow Brigade IRA.

16 LE/4/14 'Liaison and Evacuation correspondence – Kildare', Military Archives, Dublin.

17 LE/4/14 'Liaison and Evacuation correspondence – Kildare', Military Archives, Dublin.

18 LE/4/14 'Liaison and Evacuation correspondence – Kildare', Military Archives, Dublin.

19 *The Times*, 14 February 1922.

20 *The Times*, 15 February 1922.

21 Cabinet Papers CP 3747 'Weekly Survey of the State of Ireland', page 235, National Archives, United Kingdom.

22 Cabinet Papers CP 3769 'Report by the General Officer commanding-in-chief on the Situation in Ireland', 21 February 1922, National Archives, United Kingdom.

23 Cabinet Papers CP 3747 'Survey of the

State of Ireland', page 235, National Archives, United Kingdom.

24 Sheehan, William *Hearts and Mines. The British Fifth Division Ireland 1920–22*, (Cork, 2009) page 122.

25 *Kildare Observer*, 18 February 1922.

26 *Kildare Observer*, Kildare District Nursing Association, 18 February 1922.

27 Lt. Col. J.C. Milton, MBE, Liaison Officer, HQ, 5th Division; Lt. Col. P.L. Hanbury, CMG, DSO, 2nd Btn King's Shropshire Light Infantry; Lt. Col. W.T. Hodgson, DSO, MC, The Royal Dragoons.

28 WO 339/43238 Wogan-Browne, Lt. J.H., National Archives, United Kingdom.

29 Sheehan, *Hearts and Mines*, page 85.

30 WO 339/43238 Wogan-Browne, Lt. J.H., National Archives, United Kingdom.

31 WO 339/43238 Wogan-Browne, Lt. J.H., National Archives, United Kingdom.

32 WO 339/43238 Wogan-Browne, Lt. J.H., National Archives, United Kingdom.

33 LE/4/14 'Liaison and Evacuation correspondence – Kildare', Military Archives, Dublin.

34 LE/4/14 'Liaison and Evacuation correspondence – Kildare', 17 February 1922.

35 Interview with Billy Graham, September 2011.

36 Papers of Eamonn Ó Modhráin (Private Collection).

37 LE/4/14 Liaison and Evacuation correspondence, Military Archives, Dublin.

38 Correspondence with author, September 2011.

39 1911 Census of Ireland, National Archives of Ireland.

40 Papers of Eamonn Ó Modhráin (Private Collection).

41 Mountjoy Prison, General Register of Males 1921–26, National Archives of Ireland.

42 Durney, James *Civil War in Kildare* (Cork, 2011), page 40.

43 Mountjoy Prison, General Register of Males 1921–26, National Archives of Ireland.

44 WO 339/43238 'Court of Inquiry', Wogan-Browne, J.H., National Archives, United Kingdom.

45 Mountjoy Prison, General Register of Males 1921–26, National Archives of Ireland.

46 British Cabinet Paper CP 3769 'Report by the General Officer commanding-in-chief on the situation in Ireland for week ending 18/2/22'.

47 WO 339/43238 Wogan-Browne, Lt. J.H., National Archives, United Kingdom.

48 *The Times*, 18 April 1927.

49 *The Clongowian*, 1927 pp.103–104.

Notes – Chapter 11

1 WO35/182 34287, National Archives, United Kingdom.

2 *The Irish Times*, 14 January 1922.

3 WO 35/34287, National Archives, United Kingdom.

4 Dáil Debate, 9 May 1923.

5 *Freeman's Journal*, 10 May 1923.

6 Dáil Debate, 15 November 1923.

7 *Western Daily Press*, 12 July 1923.

8　Liaison and Evacuation Correspondence LE/4/14 Military Archives.

9　WO35/182 34287, National Archives, United Kingdom.

10　*Kildare Observer*, 15 April 1922.

11　*Kildare Observer*, 8 April 1922.

12　*Kildare Observer*, 29 July 1922 and Durney, page 187.

13　*Kildare Observer*, 8 April 1922.

14　WO 35/34287 National Archives, United Kingdom.

Notes – Chapter 12

1　*Leinster Leader*, 25 August 1973.

2　Dáil Debates, Volume 5, 16 November 1923.

3　Dáil Debates, Written Answers, 6 May 1924.

4　*Garda Review*, February 2007.

5　*Kildare Observer*, 26 August 1922.

6　*Kildare Observer*, 30 September 1922.

7　Papers of Eamonn Ó Modhráin.

8　*An-t-Oglach*, 1 September 1923, p. 20.

9　Dáil Debates, 15 November 1923.

10　Dáil Eireann, Volume 7, Questions, 29 May 1924.

11　Ballyfair, National Army Census 12–13 November 1922, Military Archives Dublin.

12　*An-t-Oglach*, 1 December 1923, p. 8.

13　*An-t-Oglach*, 1 December 1923, p. 8.

14　*An-t-Oglach*, 9 February 1924, p.13.

15　*An-t-Oglach*, 2 August 1924, p.13.

16　*An-t-Oglach*, 2 August 1924, p.13.

17　*An-t-Oglach*, 2 August 1924. p. 13.

18　Dáil Éireann Debate Volume 6, No. 34 Kildare Barracks Regulations.

19　*Kildare Observer*, 11 October 1924.

20　Dáil Éireann Debate Volume 2, No. 41 Questions: Married Quarters.

Notes – Chapter 13

1　*Irish Independent*, 27 April 1923.

2　See National Army Census at Military Archives, Dublin.

3　British Service Record, Gunner Hugh Bryan, Regimental number 100888.

4　Obituary of Lieutenant General Patrick Mulcahy, *The Irish Times*, 18 May 1987.

5　Obituary of Colonel Patrick Maher, *The Irish Times*, 7 July 1986.

6　*Irish Independent*, 29 July 1923.

7　*An-t-Oglach*,1 December 1923, p. 16.

8　Personal File, James McLoughlin, Military Archives, Dublin.

9　*Kildare Observer*, 28 February 1925.

10　Artillery Corps 1923–1998.

11　Whitmore-Brennan, W.J., *Army List & Directory 1926*, (Department of Defence, Dublin 1926).

12　Captain William Tierney resigned his commission in September 1926. *An-t-Oglach*, 11 September 1926, p. 17.

13　Medal Index Card, Major Garrett Brenan, UK National Archives.

14　*An-t-Oglach*, 1 December 1923, p. 16.

15　*An-t-Oglach*, 22 November 1924, p. 8.

16　*Irish Press*, 15 June 1959.

17　Dáil Debate, Written answers, 16 May 1928.

18　Artillery Corps 1923-1998.

19　*An-t-Oglach*, 28 March 1925, p. 6.

20 *An-t-Oglach*, 11 July 1925, p 8.

21 *An-t-Oglach*, 22 August, 1925, p. 10.

22 Dáil Debate, 14 May 1925.

23 Dáil Debate, 14 May 1925.

24 Mulcahy, Lieutenant-General P.A. 'At the Beginning' in *An Cosantóir*, November 1973, p. 379.

25 *An Cosantóir*, January, 1974.

26 *The Irish Times*, 'Review in the Phoenix Park 2,500 Troops on Display', 25 September 1925.

27 *An-t-Oglach*, 19 September 1925, p. 19.

28 *An-t-Oglach*, 19 September, 1925.

29 *An-t-Oglach*, 3 October 1925, p. 7.

30 *An-t-Oglach*, 5 June 1926, p. 7.

31 *An-t-Oglach*, 14 August 1926, p 19.

32 *An-t-Oglach*, 7 August 1926.

33 *An-t-Oglach*, 19 September 1926, p. 19.

34 Interview with Billy Graham.

35 *An-t-Oglach*, 14 August 1926, p. 19.

36 *An-t-Oglach*, 9 October 1926, p. 12.

37 *An-t-Oglach*, 26 June 1926, pp. 12–13.

38 *An-t-Oglach*, 7 August 1926, p. 11.

39 Unpublished memoir of Lawrence Newman courtesy of Paddy Newman.

40 Unpublished memoir of Lawrence Newman courtesy of Paddy Newman.

41 Interview with Paddy Newman.

42 Attestation Paper, Bertie Stuart Campbell Thomson, Royal Canadian Field Artillery.

43 Interview with Ciaran O'Halloran.

44 Maher, Tom 'Walk/March' in Artillery Corps 1923–98.

45 Bureau of Military History Witness Statement 410 Thomas McNally, Military Archives.

46 Interview with Crisp Culleton.

47 *Irish Independent*, 11 February 1957.

48 Interview with David Scott junior.

Notes – Chapter 14

1 Camp Diary, Coolmoney Camp, 18 May 1936 to 17 July 1936, Artillery School, Curragh.

2 Interview with Colonel Cyril Mattimoe, 1998.

Notes – Chapter 15

1 Dáil Debates, 26 March 1931.

2 'The Original Anti-Aircraft Battery' in Artillery Corps 1923–1998.

3 Artillery Corps 1923–1998.

4 Unpublished memoirs of Lawrence Newman.

5 *Irish Independent*, 21 September 1936.

6 Coolmoney Camp Diary, Artillery School, Curragh.

7 Irish Defence Forces Handbook, (Dublin, 1968).

8 *An Cosantóir*, November 1973.

9 *An Cosantóir*, November 1973.

10 Artillery Corps 1923–1998 'Early Days' Pal Byrne.

11 *An Cosantóir*, June 1988.

12 Maher, Tom, *'Walk/March'* in Artillery Corps 1923–98.

13 Mulcahy, P. *'At the Beginning'* in Artillery Corps 1923–1998.

14 Unpublished memoirs of Lawrence Newman.

15 Maher, Tom, *'Walk/March'* in Artillery Corps 1923–1998.

16 Correspondence Michael Beary Dept of

Defence to P. Walshe, Dept. of Foreign Affairs NAI DFA Secretary's Files S77.

Notes – Chapter 16

1   *The Irish Times*, 16 August 1927.

2   *Irish Independent*, 5 May 1932.

3   *Kildare Observer*, 18 June 1932 and 25 June 1932.

4   Dáil Éireann, Volume 55, 12 June 1934.

5   *Kildare Observer*, 24 Feb 1934.

6   *An-t-Oglach*, 28 November, 1925, p. 4.

7   *Kildare Observer*, 6 October 1928.

8   *Kildare Observer*, 30 December 1933.

9   *Kildare Observer*, 8 October 1932.

10 *An-t-Oglach*, 16 January 1926, p. 18.

11 G/4/A/5/F/1114 Barrack Inspections – Kildare, Military Archives.

12 G/4/A/5/F/1114 Barrack Inspections – Kildare, Military Archives.

Notes – Chapter 17

1   *An-t-Oglach*, 14 November 1925, p. 8.

2   *The Irish Times*, 28 July 1927.

3   *Kildare Observer*, 4 August 1928.

4   *Irish Press*, 10 July 1933.

5   *Kildare Observer*, 22 July 1933.

6   *Irish Press*, 6 September 1937.

Notes – Chapter 18

1   Dáil Éireann debates, Volume 55, 12 April 1935.

2   See Dáil Éireann debates, Volume 60, 12 February 1936, Volume 69, 6 October 1937, Volume 70, 2 February 1938.

3   Dáil Éireann debates, Volume 55, 12 April 1935.

4   Dáil Éireann Questions, Volume 69, 6 October 1937.

5   *Leinster Leader*, 21 November 1936.

6   Reconstruction of Kildare Barracks, Military Archives, Dublin.

7   *Leinster Leader*, 21 November 1936.

8   Reconstruction of Kildare Barracks, Military Archives, Dublin.

9   77/1/463 'Kildare Artillery Barracks', Irish Architectural Archive, Dublin.

10 *The Irish Times*, 2 September 1938.

11 77/1/463 'Kildare Artillery Barracks', Irish Architectural Archive, Dublin.

12 Irish Architectural Archive, PKS 0463, 11 November 1939.

13 Irish Architectural Archive, Dictionary of Irish Architects 1720–1940.

14 Interview with James H. Murphy.

15 Interview with Ciaran O'Halloran.

16 The Irish Defence Forces, 1940–1949 (Irish Manuscripts Commission, 2011) pp. 602–3

Notes – Chapter 19

1   General report on the Defence Forces for the Year 1 April 1943 to 31 March 1944 in *The Irish Defence Forces 1940–1949* (Irish Manuscripts Commission, 2011) p.319.

2   *The Irish Army Handbook*, 1940.

3   Interview Ciaran O'Halloran.

4   General report on the Defence Forces for the Year 1 April 1943 to 31 March 1944 in *The Irish Defence Forces 1940–1949* (Irish Manuscripts Commission, 2011) p.xxi.

5   Ibid, p. 83.

6   Ibid, p. 140.

7 Ibid, p.188.

8 Ibid, p. 228.

9 Ibid, p. 319.

10 Ibid, p. 397.

11 Ibid, p.448.

12 Ibid, p. 529.

13 Ibid, p. 560.

14 Ibid, p. 587.

15 *Irish Press*, 24 April 1944.

16 Artillery Corps Field Day Programme 1989 [not published].

17 *Irish Independent*, 20 November 1942.

18 *Irish Independent*, 15 December 1944.

19 Ibid, p. 417

20 Interview with Ciaran O'Halloran.

21 *Leinster Leader*.

22 2011/25/187 'Garda Report: alleged larceny of a colt revolver from Military Barracks Kildare' National Archives.

Notes – Chapter 20

1 *The Irish Defence Forces* 1940–1949 (Irish Manuscripts Commission, 2011) p. 661.

2 *Irish Press*, 22 January 1947.

3 *Irish Press*, 22 January 1947.

4 Interview with Billy Graham.

5 *The Irish Times*, 11 July 1955.

6 *The Irish Times*, 10 December 1956.

7 *The Irish Times*, 25 April 1957.

8 *Irish Press*, 22 January 1947.

9 *Irish Defence Forces 1940–1949* p. 662.

10 *Irish Independent*, 22 June 1949.

11 History Sheet QF 25 Pdr Mark II in possession of Kildare County Council.

12 Moriarty, Michael, *An Irish Soldier's Diaries* (Mercier Press, Cork, 2010).

13 *Irish Press*, 22 January 1947.

14 Interview with George Murphy.

15 Magee Barracks 1939–1989.

16 Interview with John Ryan.

Notes – Chapter 21

1 Kennedy, M. and Laing. V., *The Irish Defence Forces 1940–1949* (Irish Manuscripts Commission, 2011), p. 763.

2 Artillery School, Curragh.

3 Interview with CQMS Michael Hughes (Retd).

4 *Connaught Tribune*, 3 July 1965.

5 Cpl E. Loughman 'The RBS 70', *An Cosantóir*, April 1995.

Notes – Chapter 22

1 *Irish Independent*, 22 April 1977.

2 *Irish Independent*, 2 February 1959.

3 *Leinster Leader*, February 1947.

4 *Irish Independent*, 26 August 1969.

5 Interview with Mary Quinn and Paula Lalor.

6 *Irish Independent*, 3 December 1958.

7 *Irish Independent*, 5 February 1975.

8 Interview with Mary Quinn and Paula Lalor.

9 Interview with Liam O'Keeffe.

10 Captain Seamus McDermott via Liam O'Keeffe.

11 *The Irish Times*, 21 March 1973.

12 *The Irish Times*, 29 March 1974.

Notes – Chapter 23

1 O'Donoghue, David *The Irish Army in the Congo 1960–1964.*

2 Interview with John Ryan.

3 *The Irish Times*, 2 March 1961.

4 *The Irish Times*, 31 October 1961.

5 Interview with Michael Hughes.

6 Interview with Ray Quinn.

Notes – Chapter 24

1 Bradley, L. (Ed.) 6th Field Artillery Regiment 25th Anniversary, (Newbridge, 1984)

2 Bradley, L. (Ed.) 6th Field Artillery Regiment 25th Anniversary, (Newbridge, 1984)

3 *Irish Independent*, 2 July 1950

4 Papers of Seamus Moore.

5 Papers of Seamus Moore

6 *The Irish Times*, 24 July 1969, p. 13.

7 Papers of Seamus Moore

8 Interview with Oliver Murphy.

9 Bradley, L. (Ed.) 6th Field Artillery Regiment 25th Anniversary (Newbridge, 1984)

10 Bradley, L. (Ed.) 6th Field Artillery Regiment 25th Anniversary, (Newbridge, 1984)

11 Interview with Oliver Murphy.

12 Papers of Seamus Moore.

Notes – Chapter 25

1 Interview with Colonel Ray Quinn (Retd).

2 Interview with RSM John Ryan (Retd).

3 Lt J. Deery, 'Advance into Darkness', *An Cosantóir*, February 1997.

4 Interview with Ray Quinn.

5 *An Cosantóir*, July 1987.

6 *Ateliers de Construction Mécanique de L'Atlantique*, also known as ALM-ACMAT are French manufactured military vehicles.

7 *An Cosantóir*, July 1987.

8 Papers of Seamus Moore.

Notes – Chapter 26

1 Clonan, Tom (Ed.) Artillery Corps, 1923-1998

2 Interview with Liam O'Keeffe.

3 *Kilkenny People*, 6 December 1996.

4 *Leinster Leader*, 28 September 1998.

5 Artillery Corps 1923–1998

6 Interview with Gerry Swan.

Appendix I
List of Units Stationed at Kildare

BRITISH ARMY AT KILDARE 1900–1922

Unit	Date Arrive	Date Departed
XXXI Brigade RFA (131, 132 133 Batteries) from Aldershot to Fermoy	April 1902	August 1905
XXXIII Brigade RFA (137, 138, 139 Batteries) from Aldershot to Bulford	April 1902	May 1906
XXXVI Brigade RFA (15, 48, 71 Batteries) from Fethard to Dundalk	August 1905	October 1908
XXXII Brigade RFA (134, 135, 136 Battery) from Dundee to Sheffield	May 1906	January 1909
XXVI Brigade RFA (116, 117, 118 Batteries) To Dundalk from Dundalk to Aldershot	Nov 1907 April 1910	Oct 1908 July 1910
XXVIII Brigade RFA (122, 123, 124 Batteries) from Aldershot to Dundalk	Jun 1910	May 1912
XXXXVII Brigade RFA (140, 141 142 Batteries) from Cahir to Borden	Nov 1908	June 1911
VIII (Howitzer) Brigade (37, 61, 65) from Bulford to France BEF	October 1912	August 1914

XXXXV Brigade RFA (11, 52, 80 Batteries)　　　　　June 1911　　　　August 1914
Redesignated XV Brigade RFA in 1913
from Jubulpore to France BEF

The barracks was virtually deserted from August 1914 until the beginning of 1915 when units
of the newly formed 10th (Irish) Division were temporarily accommodated there.

     179 Bty
     69 Bty I brigade RFA
     5 Service Battalion, Royal Inniskilling Fusiliers
     Feb 1915　　　　　　　　　　　　　　April 1915
     from Dublin　　　　　　　　　　　　to Basingstoke

     5 Royal Irish Lancers　　　　　　　　July 1915
     12 Royal Lancers
     3 Cheshire Yeomanry
     A Squadron, IX Cavalry Reserve Brigade　　1916
     398, 542, 882, 884, 885 Batteries　　　　Nov 1918

     CCCXXVI Brigade RFA (882, 884)　　　　January 1917
     c.July 1919
     from Scotland demobilised
     CCCXXV Brigade (A, B, C, D)

     XXX Brigade RFA (128, 129, 130 Batteries)　　1919
     5 Dragoon Guards
     May 1919　　　　　　　　　　　　　December 1919
     From Aldershot
     XXX Brigade RFA (9, 16, 17 Batteries)　　1920
     XXXVI Brigade RFA (15, 48 Batteries)
     XXX Brigade RFA (9 and 17 Bty)　　　　July 1920
     (Also 16 Battery at Leitrim and 47 (H) Battery at Newbridge)
     XXXVI Brigade RFA (71 Bty Kildare)
     (Also 15 Battery at Coolmoney, 48 Battery at Newbridge)

II ÓGLAIGH NA hÉIREANN AT KILDARE 1925–1998

February 1925: Headquarters, Artillery Corps
1 Field Battery (4 x 18-pounder guns) *established on 10 July 1923*
2 Field Battery (4 x 18-pounder guns) *established on 2 January 1925*
The Artillery Corps was formed on 23 March 1923 at Islandbridge
Barracks, moved shortly afterward to McKee Barracks, Dublin before
moving to Kildare in February 1925.

1927: Headquarters, Artillery Corps
1 Field Battery (4 x 18-pounder guns)
2 Field Battery (4 x 18-pounder guns)
3 Field Battery (4 x 4.5-inch howitzers)

1931: Headquarters, Artillery Corps
I Field Artillery Brigade (1, 2, 3 Field Batteries)
Artillery Depot and School
1 Anti-Aircraft Battery

1959: Depot and Artillery School
I Air Defence Regiment
VI Field Artillery Regiment

1977–98 Artillery Depot
Artillery School:
   Field Artillery Section
   Survey and Counter Bombardment Section
   Guided Weapons and Air Defence Section
3 Field Battery
I Air Defence Regiment (HQ and 1 Anti-Aircraft Battery)
VI Field Artillery Regiment (HQ and 5 Field Battery)

Appendix II

Commanding Officer: Kildare / Magee Barracks 1939–1998

Captain D.S. Farrell	1939
Commandant Joseph P. Kelly	1940
Commandant Patrick J. Hally	1940
Major Arthur Dalton	1942
Major William Donagh	1946
Lieutenant-Colonel Patrick Curran	1947
Lieutenant-Colonel Daniel.S. Collins	1953
Lieutenant-Colonel Maurice P. McCarthy	1955
Lieutenant-Colonel Michael Sugrue	1961
Lieutenant-Colonel Ivor P. Noone	1965
Lieutenant-Colonel John S. Nolan	1966
Lieutenant-Colonel Denis Burke	1973
Lieutenant-Colonel John White	1974
Lieutenant-Colonel Michael O. Fitzsimons	1974
Lieutenant-Colonel Thomas McDunphy	1977
Lieutenant-Colonel Thomas O'Boyle	1978
Lieutenant-Colonel Thomas A. Ryan	1980
Lieutenant-Colonel Michael Moriarty	1982
Lieutenant-Colonel Michael McMahon	1984
Lieutenant-Colonel Kevin Doyle	1988
Lieutenant-Colonel William Dwyer	1990
Lieutenant-Colonel James G. Prendergast	1991
Lieutenant-Colonel Michael Moriarty	1993
Lieutenant-Colonel Desmond G. Johnston	1994
Lieutenant-Colonel Leo Hughes	1995
Lieutenant-Colonel Gerard W. Swan	1996

Lieutenant-Colonel Swan was the last Commanding Officer of Magee Barracks which closed in September 1998.

Regimental Sergeant-Majors at Kildare / Magee Barracks 1939–1998

RSM Frank Whitty	1939
RSM William Downey	1943
RSM H. Maxwell	1946
RSM Patrick Egan	1947
RSM David Scott	1957
RSM Patrick Dwyer	1958
RSM Nicolas Fahy	1975
RSM John Ryan	1980
RSM Liam Cosgrove	1996

(*last Regimental Sergeant-Major*)

Commanding Officer: I Anti-Aircraft Regiment 1931–2012

Commandant Maurice P. McCarthy	1931–45

The regiment was disbanded in 1945 and reestablished in 1952 as an AA Training Regiment

Lieutenant-Colonel Arthur Dalton	1952
Lieutenant-Colonel John S. Nolan	1959
Lieutenant-Colonel J. Herlihy	1960
Lieutenant-Colonel Denis Burke	1963
Lieutenant-Colonel Thomas Walsh	1969
Lieutenant-Colonel S. Timmons	1975
Lieutenant-Colonel A. Donnelly	1977
Lieutenant-Colonel D. O'Keefe	1978
Lieutenant-Colonel Ciaran O'Halloran	1979
Lieutenant-Colonel J. Bunyan	1981
Lieutenant-Colonel Michael McMahon	1983
Lieutenant-Colonel Kevin Doyle	1984
Lieutenant-Colonel Patrick F. Nowlan	1988
Lieutenant-Colonel William Dwyer	1990
Lieutenant-Colonel P. L. Hughes	1990
Lieutenant-Colonel Desmond G. Johnston	1992
Lieutenant-Colonel Gerard W. Swan	1995
Commandant Raymond Quinn	1996
Lieutenant-Colonel Nick O'Connor	1997
Commandant Michael Molloy	1997
Lieutenant-Colonel Fergus Bushell	1998

The Air Defence Regiment transferred to the Curragh in September 1998.

Commandant Eamonn Fogarty	1999
Lieutenant-Colonel Thomas Carter	1999
Lieutenant-Colonel Paul A. Allen	2000
Lieutenant-Colonel Seamus McDermott	2004
Lieutenant-Colonel Eamonn Fogarty	2005

| Commandant Michael Moore | 2008 |
| Lieutenant-Colonel Michael Dolan | 2008 |

The I Air Defence Regiment was disbanded in November 2012.

Regimental Sergeant-Major: I Anti-Aircraft Regiment

RSM Patrick Dwyer	1953–57
RSM Charlie White	1958–76
RSM William (Tex) Keating	1976–91
RSM Jim Fortune	1991–95
RSM Donnie Finn	1995–98
RSM Patrick Mullen	2005–12

The Air Defence Regiment was disbanded in November 2012.

Commanding Officer: VI Field Artillery Regiment (*6u Reisimin Airtleire Machaire*)

The VI FAR was formed in 1959 and disbanded in 2005.

Commandant Ivor P. Noone	1959
Commandant Thomas Walsh	1962
Commandant Joseph Higgins	1968
Commandant Thomas McDunphy	1969
Commandant Jim Croke	1972
Commandant Michael McMahon	1976
Commandant Joseph Murray	1980
Commandant George Murphy	1980
Commandant Gabriel Boyle	1982
Commandant Raymond Quinn	1983
Commandant Paul Allen	1986
Commandant Peter O'Grady	1988
Commandant Paul Allen	1989
Commandant Peter O'Grady	1990
Commandant James Murray	1993
Commandant Michael Dolan	1999
Commandant Michael Smith	2000
Commandant David Brown	2003

Unit disbanded in 2005 and replaced by 62 Reserve Artillery Regiment under Commandant David Campion.

Director of Artillery

Colonel Patrick A. Mulcahy	September	1931
Colonel Patrick Maher	June	1935
Colonel Patrick A. Mulcahy	December	1942
Colonel James McLoughlin	January	1949
Colonel Daniel J. Collins	November	1955
Colonel Patrick J. Hally	December	1956

Colonel Patrick Curran	May	1957
Colonel Arthur Dalton	January	1959
Colonel James H. Byrne	October	1960
Colonel Joseph Murray	October	1961
Colonel Mark Harrington	July	1969
Colonel Cyril M. Mattimoe	September	1970
Colonel Mark Harrington	June	1973
Colonel John S. Nolan	June	1974
Colonel Thomas Walsh	September	1976
Colonel Tom McDunphy	September	1978
Colonel Charles J. McGuinn	April	1982
Colonel Patrick F. Monahan	July	1983
Colonel Seamus B. Condon	August	1986
Lieutenant-Colonel P.J. O'Farrell	September	1988
Colonel Michael Moriarty	January	1989
Colonel Michael McMahon	April	1989
Colonel George Murphy	December	1989
Colonel Michael Shannon	December	1991
Colonel Michael P. Dunne	March	1994
Colonel James G. Prendergast	January	1996
Lieutenant-Colonel Brian O'Connor	January	1999

Colonel O'Connor was the last Director of Artillery as the post was replaced by Director of Combat Support which covered artillery and cavalry from October 1998.

Artillery Officers of the General Staff
Chief of Staff

Major-General Patrick A. Mulcahy	1955–1959
Lieutenant-General Tadhg O'Neill	1986–1989
Lieutenant-General Noel Bergin	1992–1994
Lieutenant-General Conor O'Boyle	2013–

Adjutant General

Colonel Patrick J. Hally	1957–1962
Major-General Charles McGuinn	1987–1989
Major-General Tommy Wall	1992–1996
Major-General William Dwyer	1996–1998

Quartermaster-General

Colonel Patrick Curran	1962–1969
Colonel William Donagh	1968–1971
Major-General Kevin Duffy	1991–1993
Major-General Patrick F. Nowlan	1997–1999

Assistant Chief of Staff

Colonel Richard Callanan	1961–1962
Brigadier-General Patrick F. Nowlan	1994–1997

Bibliography

Published Sources

Andrews, J.H., *Kildare: An Early-Christian foundation retaining traces of its ecclesiastical origins* (Irish Historic Towns Atlas Series, 1986).

'Col. Francis W.N. Wogan-Browne' in *The Clongowian* 1927, pp. 103–104.

Beckett, Ian F.W. (ed.), *The Army and the Curragh Incident* (London: Army Records Society, 1986).

Brennan-Whitmore, Commandant W.J. (Ed.), *Defence Forces Saorstat Eireann 1926 Army List and Directory* (Dublin: *An-t-Oglach*, 1926).

Clonan, Captain Tom, (editor) *Artillery Corps 1923–1998* (Curragh, 1998).

Condon, Lieutenant-Colonel S.B. '105mm Light Gun', *An Cosantóir,* May 1981 p.124.

Corrigan, Mario, *All that Delirium of the Brave – Kildare in 1798* (Kildare County Council, 1998).

Corrigan, Mario (editor) *A Contribution to the History of Kildare Town: Druim Criaig, The Ridge of Clay* (Cill Dara Historical Society, 2009).

Corrigan, Mario & Kelly, Ger (editors) *Church of the Oak - Kildare Town* (Kildare: Grey Abbey Conservation Project, 2006).

Corrigan, Mario and Connelly, Joseph (editors) *Kildare Town: Snapshots in Time* (Cill Dara Historical Society, 2013).

Costello, Con, *A Most Delightful Station: The British Army on the Curragh of Kildare, Ireland, 1855–1922* (Cork: The Collins Press, 1996).

Costello, Con, *A Class Apart: The Gentry families of County Kildare* (Dublin: Nonsuch Publishing, 2009).

Crawford, Hugh 'The Kildare Lock Hospital', *Journal of the County Kildare Archaeological Society,* Volume XIX, pp. 369–383.

Crooks, J.J. (Major), *History of the Royal Irish Regiment of Artillery,* (Dublin 1914).

Daly, Jim and Durney, James, *When we were Kings: A history of Gaelic Football in Kildare Town 1887–2011* (Kildare: Round Towers G.F.C., 2011).

Duggan, John P., *A History of the Irish Army* (Dublin: Gill and Macmillan, 1991).

Durney, James, *The Civil War in Kildare* (Cork: Mercier Press, 2011).

Durney, James, *The War of Independence in Kildare* (Cork: Mercier Press, 2013).

Durney, James, *On the One Road: Political Unrest in Kildare 1913–1994* (Naas, Gaul House, 2001).

Artillery Corps Field Day Magee Barracks, Kildare 1939–1989 (Kildare: 1989).

Farndale, General Sir Martin, *History of the Royal Regiment of Artillery: The Western Front 1914–18* (Woolwich: Royal Artillery Institution, 1986).

Fergusson, Sir James, *The Curragh Incident* (London: Faber and Faber, 1964).

Kelly, Joe, *Origins and History of Coolmoney House, Glen of Imaal 1832-1999* (Curragh: Defence Forces, 2013).

Kennedy, Michael and Laing, Victor (editors), *The Irish Defence Forces 1940-1949: The Chief of Staff's Reports* (Dublin: Irish Manuscripts Commission, 2011).

McCarthy, Brian, *The Civic Guard Mutiny* (Cork: Mercier Press, 2012).

McDonald, Henry, *Irishbatt: The story of Ireland's Blue Berets in the Lebanon* (Dublin: Gill and Macmillan, 1993).

McLoughlin, Mark, (editor) *The Curragh: A Lifetime of Memories* (Newbridge: Curragh Local History Group, 1997).

McLoughlin, Mark, (editor) *The Curragh Revisited* (Newbridge: Curragh Local History Group, 2002).

McLoughlin, Mark, 'The killing of Lieutenant John Hubert Wogan-Browne at Kildare, 10 February 1922: A test of Anglo-Irish Relations', *Journal of the County Kildare Archaeological Society Volume* XX 2013, pp. 9-25.

McLoughlin, Mark, 'The killing of Lieutenant J.H. Wogan-Browne at Kildare, 10 February 1922: A test of Anglo-Irish Relations', *Irish Sword*, Volume XIX, Summer 2013, pp.79–95.

McNiffe, Liam, *A History of the Garda Síochána* (Dublin: Wolfhound Press, 1997).

Moriarty, Michael *An Irish Soldier's Diaries* (Cork: Mercier Press, 2010.

Moriarty, Lieutenant-Colonel Michael 'AM 50 (120mm Mortar) – Artillery Workhorse', *An Cosantóir*, September 1981 pp. 257–263.

Nowlan, P.F. 'Guns and Gunners' in *An Cosantóir*, 1991.

O'Donoghue, David, *The Irish Army in the Congo 1960–1964: The Far Battalions* (Dublin: Irish Academic Press, 2006).

Riccio, Ralph A., *The Irish Artillery Corps since 1922* (Poland: MMP Books, 2012)

Sandes, Elise, *Enlisted; Or, My Story. Incidents of life and work among soldiers* (Curragh: 1915).

Sheehan, William, *Hearts and Mines: The British 5ᵗʰ Division, Ireland 1920–1922* (Cork: The Collins Press, 2009).

Talbot, Stephen and Cantwell, Bro. Canice, (editors) *De La Salle Cill Dara 1884–1984* (Naas: 1984).

INTERVIEWS

Lieutenant-General Noel Bergin (retd), RSM Donnie Finn (retd), Mr Billy Graham, Mr Paddy Newman, BQMS Michael Hughes (retd), Mrs Paula Lalor, Colonel Cyril Mattimoe,(deceased), Colonel James H. Murphy (retd), RSM John Ryan (retd), Colonel George Murphy (retd), Major-General Paddy Nowlan, Lieutenant-Colonel Ciaran O'Halloran (retd),Mr Liam O'Keeffe, Lieutenant-Colonel Raymond Quinn (retd), BSM David Scott (retd),Lieutenant-Colonel Gerry Swan (retd).

NEWSPAPERS
Kildare Observer
Leinster Leader
The Times
The Irish Press
The Irish Times
Irish Independent
Irish Press

Periodicals
An-t-Oglach: The Official Organ of the Irish Volunteers
An Cosantóir, Magazine of the Irish Defence Forces
Journal of the County Kildare Archaeological Society
The Irish Builder
The Irish Sword, Journal of the Military History Society of Ireland
The London Gazette

Archival Sources
Ireland
Military Archives, CathalBrugha Barracks, Dublin
LE/4/14 'Liaison and Evacuation Correspondence – Kildare'
G/4/A/5/F/1114 Barrack Inspections – Kildare

National Archives of Ireland
2011/25/187 'Garda Report: Alleged larceny of colt revolver from military barracks, Kildare' Jun–Jul 1940
Mountjoy Prison, General Register Male 1921–1926,
Petty Sessions Order books

Irish Architectural Archive, Dublin
IAA/PKS/0463 Co. Kildare, Kildare, Artillery Barracks, 1937–39

Artillery School, Curragh, County Kildare
Coolmoney Camp Diary 1936 (Artillery School, Curragh, County Kildare)
Nominal Roll, Artillery Corps

Private Collection
Papers of Seamus Moore
Papers of Eamonn O Modhráin

United Kingdom
National Archives, United Kingdom
WO 339/43238 'Wogan-Browne, Lt. J.H.'
WO 35/34287 'Evacuation Files'
CAB/24/133 'British Cabinet Papers'

National Army Museum
1985-04-48 Compiled and Photographed by Captain Roderick MacLeod
Imperial War Museum
04/37/1 Private Papers of Percy Whitehouse: Recollections of service in the army, from 1913 to 1919
The Great War Archive, Oxford
'Things heard, seen and remembered': Memoirs of Lt. Col. Justin Hooper

Index